utation as a social dramatist w~~~~~~  thered by the appearance of his next two plays, *Ghosts* and *An Enemy of the People.* But Professor Holtan's study of the plays which came after these identifies in the later plays values which transcend the social problems of their time, penetrating questions of the human spirit itself.

The eight last plays which Professor Holtan examines in this study are *The Wild Duck, Rosmersholm, The Lady from the Sea, Hedda Gabler, The Master Builder, Little Eyolf, John Gabriel Borkman,* and *When We Dead Awaken.* In these plays he identifies a mythic pattern and unity based in elements of symbolism and mysticism which have puzzled or annoyed readers and critics for years. In his mythic vision Ibsen's lasting contribution far exceeds that of his invention of the social-problem drama, Professor Holtan concludes.

Orley I. Holtan is an associate professor of theatre at Slippery Rock State College in Pennsylvania.

Mythic Patterns in Ibsen's Last Plays

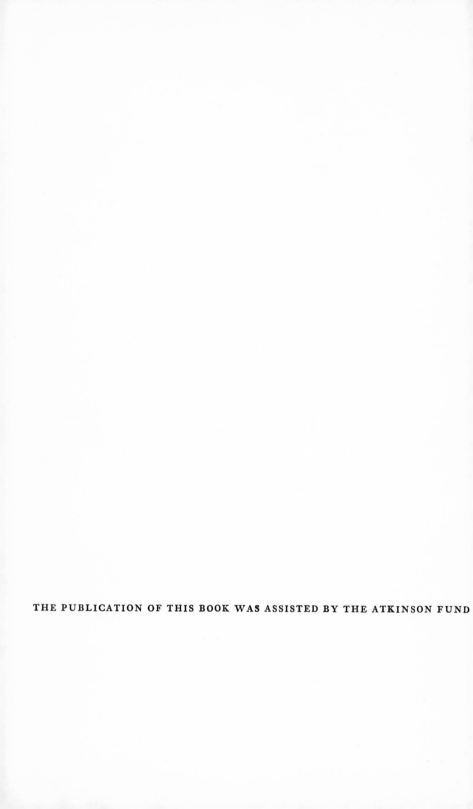

THE PUBLICATION OF THIS BOOK WAS ASSISTED BY THE ATKINSON FUND

MYTHIC PATTERNS
in IBSEN'S LAST PLAYS

Orley I. Holtan

THE UNIVERSITY OF MINNESOTA PRESS *Minneapolis*

ISBN 0-8166-0582-3

FOR JUDITH

ACKNOWLEDGMENTS

⊄ WHEN one prepares a book of this kind one incurs a debt of gratitude to a great many people, far too many to specify. The writing of the book was made much easier because of the previous work of many scholars and critics and would, of course, have been impossible without the work of Henrik Ibsen. Specifically, my greatest thanks go to Professor Alrik Gustafson of the University of Minnesota, who guided the study through its initial phases as a dissertation, and to Professors David W. Thompson and Arthur Ballet, from whom I have learned a great deal. I would like also to thank Professors Daniel Haakonsen and Else Höst of the University of Oslo for their encouragement to attempt publication, and the University of Minnesota Press for valuable editorial suggestions and assistance. Two others deserve my thanks as well; my father, for inspiring in me a love of Norwegian language and culture, and my wife, Judith, for her inspiration and encouragement.

O. I. H.

March, 1970

TABLE OF CONTENTS

Mythic Patterns in Ibsen's Last Plays

INTRODUCTION · AN APPROACH TO IBSEN

❧ HENRIK IBSEN's greatest initial impact on the drama, both inside and out of Scandinavia, came with the publication of *A Doll's House* in 1879. Within months he had achieved a kind of *succes de scandale* by ostensibly advocating the right of a woman to walk out on her husband and children, undermining thereby the traditional bases of marriage. His two following plays, *Ghosts* and *An Enemy of the People*, only furthered his reputation as a social problem dramatist, a propagandist who attacked the social ills of his time without caring whom or what he offended. Ibsen was regarded as the champion of the new and radical ideas, social, moral, and political: he was hailed as hero by the avant-garde of his day and castigated as a scoundrel by the conservative faction. In a sense he can be said to have founded a school and a movement which Bernard Shaw aptly labeled Ibsenism. Eric Bentley points out that in, "Calling attention to the rotten bottoms of ships, the subjection of Victorian wives, the ravages of syphilis, and the corruption of municipal journalism and politics, he made himself the father of the reformist drama of the end of the century." [1]

Until very recently it has been in these terms, reformer, realist, problem dramatist, that Ibsen's reputation was presented to the world, and it is this very fact that has made him seem to many an

3

outdated and slightly musty Victorian curiosity. Yet there have been a few critics who have recognized that there is more beneath the surface of Ibsen's drama than is immediately apparent. As in the portrait busts sculpted by Rubek there is a great deal hidden that reveals itself sporadically and mysteriously, of which we catch occasional glimpses and that moves us strangely without our being able to say why. It is in his later plays especially that this is most apparent, when symbolism and mysticism begin to appear in fairly obvious ways. These later plays—for example, *The Lady from the Sea*, *The Master Builder*, and *When We Dead Awaken*—have puzzled some readers and annoyed others, and many have concluded that in the last few plays of his career Ibsen was turning to intense self-examination, analyzing and seeking to atone for private guilts and obsessions. A few of the more perceptive critics have noted, however, along with the autobiographical, certain elements of myth. George Steiner goes so far as to say that in his last eight plays, beginning with *The Wild Duck*, Ibsen created a new mythology and set of theatrical conventions to express it.[2] Rolf Fjelde points out that throughout his career Ibsen conducted a search for truth in three ways, artistically, historically, and mythically, and that it is the third method that may yet prove to be his most important contribution to the drama.[3]

This third approach to Ibsen's work has been least thoroughly explored, and it is the one which may yield insights that will once again restore the relevance of Ibsen not only to his own time but to ours.[4] The late nineteenth and early twentieth centuries have been painfully aware of a lack of a unifying mythic vision, and the playwright who attempts to discover or provide one must be regarded at least as a heroic searcher for a core of meaning in modern existence.

In this study I propose to examine the mythic sources, patterns, and values of Ibsen's last eight plays individually and as they add up, if they do, to a unified mythic vision. In so doing I make no claim to exclusiveness. The mythic approach is not the only critical tool that can be applied to Ibsen nor is my interpretation of his mythology the only possible one. My study, I hope, will result in opening the plays and providing new insights and avenues of exploration rather than closing them in and providing a definitive interpretation of the plays. That my ideas will overlap with those of other critics I must freely admit; that they differ significantly enough on various points of interpretation so as to provide a worthwhile addition to Ibsen scholarship is my hope. We shall see, I think, as time goes on, that Ibsen stands at the pivotal point in the development of modern drama and that his contribution far exceeds the invention of the social problem drama.

MYTH AND LITERATURE · A DEFINITION
AND A RELATIONSHIP

❡ THE term *myth* almost immediately calls to mind a fantastic tale involving gods, heroes, or supernatural beings, a tale closely related to the ritual and to the religious and social order of a people or a culture. Myth is thus distinguished from folk or fairy tales and from other narratives that serve chiefly for entertainment, and from history, which is a true account of a national or a cultural past. This is essentially the distinction discovered by Malinowski in his research among the Trobriand islanders.[1] Myth, he says, functions "to establish a belief, to serve as a precedent in ceremony or ritual, or to rank as a pattern of moral or religious conduct." [2] Men perform rituals, as Mircea Eliade points out, because the acts those rituals represent were earlier performed by the gods. Through their repetition man brings himself closer to the gods — indeed, occupies the same mythical time as they do. He reactualizes the myth, which serves him as a kind of paradigmatic model for his contemporary action.[3] Thus, myth provides a matrix within which primitive man exists. (A better term here would be *mythical man*; it is devoid of the negative connotations attached to primitive.) Myths humanize the outside world. They provide a means for man to relate himself to his universe and to his destiny by suggesting the workings of providence in the world.[4]

Already these comments have passed beyond the simple definition of myth with which I began. The deeper sense of the remarks of both Malinowski and Eliade is that myth is more than a traditional story which explains natural phenomena; it is an existential posture, a means of relating to the universe and of being in the world. As such it differs in a number of important respects from the scientific or empirical view of nature and existence.

The empirical mode of dealing with nature is to break it up into parts in order to discern the relations among them. Its ultimate aim is to discover general rules or laws and cause-effect sequences that are applicable to natural phenomena. The scientific view of the world aims at synthesis, but it reaches that synthesis through analysis. Science is interested in discovering the mechanical "how" explanation of phenomena, in discerning behind them a natural law which governs their occurrence.

The mythic view does not treat reality in this fashion. This is not to say that mythical man is unable to perceive objective forms and to discern differences among them. For myth, however, those differences are unimportant. It does not differentiate between levels of reality or between reality and appearance; for this reason, dream experience, for example, plays an important part in mythical cultures. Similarly, myth does not distinguish sharply between names and things. To know the name of something is, in a sense, to have power over it. A man's name is not simply a label that is attached to him; it is a part of him and contains within it his inmost essence.

Viewing causality and the relation between reality and appearance in this fashion, myth tends to reduce complex realities and relationships to pre-existing material substances. It tends toward a hypostatization of properties and processes. Disease, for example, is not a condition of the body but something which inhabits it and which can, therefore, be exorcized or transferred from it to another body. The same observation holds true for other qualities such as virtue, courage, or guilt. Since these qualities are viewed

7

as material substances, they may be embodied in such things as amulets, talismans, or badges of office.[5]

Throughout this discussion I have referred occasionally to mythical thought, but Ernst Cassirer would argue that to refer to mythical "thought" at all is a semantic error, at least insofar as we equate it with discursive thought. Rather, myth signifies "an *intuitive* unity preceding and underlying all the explanations contributed by *discursive* thought."[6] Primitive man (who views the world mythically) does not, as has been noted, lack the more civilized man's ability to perceive empirical differences in things. All these differences are, however, rendered at last insignificant by a stronger sense of the essential unity and solidarity of all life.[7]

Clearly, then, myth takes a radically different stance toward the world outside of man than does science. Rather than seeing the world as an impersonal "it" — a subject of contemplation — myth regards it as a "thou" or a "he" which possesses a life similar in kind to the "I" which confronts it.[8] The mythic view of life can be described as active and personal rather than passive and impersonal. As Eliade points out, for the sacred mode of being (which can be regarded as nearly synonymous with the mythical) the world has a structure, it is an ordered cosmos which manifests itself almost as an organism, a living thing, because it was made by and is inhabited by the gods.[9] Cassirer comments much to the same point:

> The world of myth is a dramatic world — a world of actions and of forces, of conflicting powers. In every phenomenon of nature it sees the collision of these powers. Mythical perception is always impregnated with these emotional qualities. Whatever is seen or felt is surrounded by a special atmosphere — an atmosphere of joy or grief, of anguish, of excitement, of exultation or depression. Here we cannot speak of "things" as dead and indifferent stuff. All objects are benignant or malignant, friendly or inimical, familiar or uncanny, alluring and fascinating or repellant and threatening.[10]

Thus, mythically oriented man interrelates with the world in an active sense as he would with other living beings. Indeed, the world is living; it is inhabited by forces that impinge upon and affect human conduct. These forces are neither random nor capricious. They constitute evidence of purpose in the world even though that purpose may not be discernible by man. The myth offers an inclusive teleological explanation of man's daily affairs, his history, and his destiny.

As Malinowski has observed, myth provides for primitive man a means of locating himself in the world and of ordering not only his personal but also his societal behavior. More profoundly, Cassirer argues that man can understand himself only insofar as he can project his own being and make it visible. He learns to understand the physical structure of his own body by himself becoming a creator. Similarly, he learns to understand his spiritual nature by projecting, through myth, language, and art, the standards against which he can measure himself.[11] Cassirer, however, seems intent on proving that man passes beyond the mythical stage to more sophisticated levels of perception and symbolization. The mythical organization of society is superseded by a rational one.[12] Yet myth is never fully suppressed.

> In all critical moments of man's social life, the rational forces that resist the rise of the old mythical conceptions are no longer sure of themselves. In these moments the time for myth has come again. For myth has not really been vanquished and subjugated. It is always there, lurking in the dark and waiting for its hour and opportunity. This hour comes as soon as the other binding forces of man's social life, for one reason or another, lose their strength and are no longer able to combat the demonic mythical powers.[13]

There is clearly contained within this statement a negative value judgment apropos myth and the mythic view. Reason which supersedes it is a morally superior form; only under stress and to man's harm does myth break out once again. There is another argument, however — one that has been advanced by many scholars, particularly those with a psychological orientation. Myth may not after all be the malignant power which Cassirer seems to believe that it is. It may not be deleterious to man's well-being but actually the reverse. Thus C. Kerenyi, who collaborated with C.

G. Jung on a number of projects, feels that myth is one of many modes of expression open to man and that which it expresses is that which could not be expressed in any other way. Consequently, the meaning of mythology is almost impossible to translate into scientific terms.[14]

Like Kerenyi, Jung would argue that at the deepest levels of the subconscious a man never grows beyond his need for myth. Myths, he argues, are experienced rather than invented by primitive man; they are not allegories about physical processes but preconscious psychic revelations. Rather than "standing for" the psychic life of the tribe, these myths *are* that life, its living religion, the loss of which brings catastrophe. Nor is this true only of primitive man. Modern man still experiences fantasies and dreams which well up from the subconscious. Although some of these fantasies may be personal, many others coincide with traditional mythic figures. It was this observation among his patients that was at least partly responsible for leading Jung to the theory of the collective unconscious.[15]

It is true that rational thinking has to a considerable degree superseded mythical thought. Culture and education over the past several centuries have, according to Jung, produced a readjustment of the human mind, turning it from the subjective individual sphere to the objective social. This has not, however, banished what Jung calls fantasy thinking. On the contrary, man seems to have an inner compulsion to create myths and religious beliefs in the very face of demonstrations of their absurdity.[16] Jung goes so far as to say: "One would almost say that if all the world's traditions were cut off at a single blow, the whole of mythology, and the whole history of religion would start all over again with the next generation."[17]

If Jung and Kerenyi are correct and the mythic view of the world is somehow inherent in man, what function does it serve? Why does scientific, rational man still feel in the depths of his being a need for myth? Joseph Campbell, who is strongly influenced by Freud and Jung, sees myth as a mode of spiritual progress.

It has always been the prime function of mythology and rite to supply the symbols that carry the human spirit forward, in counteraction to those other constant human fantasies that tend to tie it back. In fact it may well be that the very high incidence of neuroticism among ourselves follows from the decline among us of such effective spiritual aids. We remain fixated to the unexorcised images of our infancy, and hence disinclined to the necessary passages of our adulthood.[18]

Much of what I have thus far said about myth is capsulized in Steiner's *The Death of Tragedy*. Until the advent of empiricism, he says, the controlling habits of the Western mind were symbolic and allegorical. Man objectified information about his world, his destiny, and the course of his history into imaginative designs or "architectures of the imagination" which ordered the whole cosmos. Two such designs are Greek mythology and medieval Christianity. As time progressed, however, these unified world views lost their hold on the Western mind. The notions of the intervention of the supernatural in human affairs, of the world as purposeful and moral, lost their viability, becoming either abstractions or mere slogans. Thus, the "death" of tragedy of which Steiner writes was preceded by a death of mythology.[19]

As Steiner's observations would suggest, there is an intimate link between myth and literature, a beginning clue to which can be found in the sources from which both arise. Cassirer's argument that all cultural forms ultimately arise out of myth has already been noted. More specifically, he comments that myth and poetry are closely akin and quotes Prescott to the effect that myth is the "mass" from which poetry arises.[20] In fact, myth and poetry both arise from the same psychic source, the substratum of emotion. Yet Cassirer would insist that there is a fundamental difference between the two. The possessors of a myth take it to be literally true, whereas the truth or falsehood of an artistic creation is of little importance to its creator.[21]

Allowing the above observation to be generally true, it may still be possible to make a distinction between kinds of "truth" that once again will bring myth and imaginative literature into close proximity. Those who literally believe that the world was created in seven days as recounted in Genesis would be possessors of a myth in Cassirer's sense. Yet it is safe to assert that there are others who would accept the scientific evolutionary theories as the *literal* truth of the origin of the world and man and still find in the story of the creation and fall a kind of *emotional* truth. They would feel that it tells them something deep and profound about man that is not included in the scientific explanations. For such readers is the book of Genesis myth or is it literature?

Perhaps a partial answer lies in the ideas of Richard Chase and Richmond Hathorne, both of whom have written on the relation between myth and literature. Chase asserts that "Myth is an aesthetic device for bringing the imaginary but powerful world of preternatural forces into a manageable collaboration with the objective facts of life, in such a way as to excite a sense of reality amenable to both the unconscious passions and the conscious mind." [22] It may not be drastically distorting Chase's meaning to say, then, that myth provides an alternate mode of belief, even for the scientific man — one which, though not *literally* true, is emotionally satisfying. Hathorne speaks to much the same point when he defines myth as "literature that directly symbolizes man's position of mystery." [23] For both men myth is a special kind of literature, literature that performs a unique function.

Similarly Harold Watts distinguishes between a "sacred" and a "secular" assertion. The former is a total statement about existence that cannot be proved or disproved but must simply be accepted or rejected. Such an assertion can be codified in dogma, couched in myth, or enacted in drama. The secular assertion, on the other hand, deals with a more restricted aspect of human experience.[24] Hence, although myth and literature are not necessarily synonymous, they occupy, as Northrop Frye asserts, the same verbal universe and in most cultures tend to blend with each other.[25]

Actually, according to Frye, literature ranges along a continuum from pure myth at one end to naturalism at the other. Pure myth consists of stories of gods and heroes who possess powers far beyond those of the ordinary mortal. Thus they are freed from all restrictions of plausibility. Naturalism is an almost totally unidealized representation of everyday reality in which the content is more important than the form or shape of the story. Between these two extremes, however, lies a vast body of literature in which myth is to varying degrees "displaced" — concealed behind ordinary events and only suggested to the reader. In a pure myth we may have a sun god or a tree god; in displaced myths we have an ostensibly real character who is significantly associated with the sun or with trees.[26] It is in this sense of displacement that much modern literature may be said to be mythic.

But myth or mythic literature has both a content and a basic pattern. First of all, myth presents two worlds, usually corresponding to the heaven and hell of the religion contemporary with the myth. The apocalyptic is a desirable world containing fields, gardens, cities, domestic animals, a world clearly beneficent to man. The demonic is the undesirable world hostile to man and abounding in images of wilderness, ruins, and wild beasts.[27] It should be pointed out also that these worlds are frequently in conflict and that man tends to be caught between them, as is clearly the case in the Christian cosmogeny.

The basic pattern of myth Frye calls the "quest myth." This is the cyclical death-rebirth movement which originates in the subconscious and which is very close to the cycle of nature, summer-winter, day-night, light-darkness.[28] Frye divides the pattern into four phases and parallels each with a major type of literature. The dawn, spring, or rebirth phase corresponds to romance, the summer or triumph phase to comedy, the autumn or death phase to tragedy, and the winter or dissolution phase to irony.[29]

Frye's basic pattern is, however, not the only possible one. Joseph Campbell suggests the *monomyth*, a term he borrows from Joyce. The monomyth involves the hero's venturing forth from the ordinary world into a mysterious world of strange powers and forces, some of which are dangerous and others helpful. Ultimately he wins a victory over the destructive powers and returns from his mysterious adventures with the power to do great deeds for his fellow men. Each stage of the unitary myth may be elaborated and

13

presented in detail, but it is always part of the total structure.[30] Since the hero's journey often takes him through the realm of death and back to life there is not a basic contradiction between Campbell's pattern and Frye's. Together they furnish the critic with a highly valuable tool for the examination of literature.

In approaching Ibsen's drama as myth, then, we must be alert for a number of things. First of all, we can seek in the individual plays and in the group of plays for the emergence of a world view or a total statement about the nature of existence. Such a statement will involve a teleological, as opposed to a mechanical, explanation of existence and man's nature and destiny. Secondly, we can seek for the mythic superstructure on which the individual plays or the entire cycle may be built. Third, we can attempt to identify specific mythological and folkloristic symbols and references within the individual plays.

IBSEN'S EARLIER CAREER · FROM MYTH
TO SOCIAL REALISM

❡ CRITICS have traditionally divided the body of Ibsen's work in two ways, into two parts and into three. Some of those who employ the two-part division take their cue from his famous letter to Björnson, in which, angered by Clemens Petersen's reaction to *Peer Gynt*, he says, "If I am no poet, then I have nothing to lose. I shall try my luck as a photographer." [1] Thus, they classify the plays through *Peer Gynt* as "poetry" and those which follow, beginning with *The League of Youth*, as "photography" or realism. [2] Certainly, there is a clear break in both form and content at roughly the point following *Peer Gynt*, but to attribute that break to mere pique at an unfavorable review is to be guilty, as Fjelde indicates, of considerable oversimplification. [3]

Fjelde, who also employs the two-part division, attributes the break to quite a different cause. During the first twenty-five years of the playwright's career, he argues, Ibsen was searching for a form and a theme suitable for modern drama. Beginning approximately with *Pillars of Society* in 1877, Ibsen found his form and continued to develop it. [4] The form, at least outwardly, was the set of conventions of the realistic stage; he concentrated thematically

15

on "plays of the still small voice, tracing the destinies of rebels and outcasts, radical protestants, defenders and martyrs of conscience, probers for truth, broken pioneers of a new faith evolving out of the unfinished life of the spirit." [5]

Yet even within the second half of the dramatist's career there is a rather distinct break between that group of plays which is predominantly realistic and a later group which has been variously labeled mystical, symbolic, and autobiographical. This apparently clear change of focus has prompted other critics to divide the work into three parts. That division follows roughly the lines laid down by Solness in *The Master Builder*; dramas of high idealism ("churches"), dramas of social and psychological realism ("homes for human beings"), and dramas of symbolism, autobiography, and confession ("castles in the air"). [6] The first group obviously includes the plays leading up to and through *Peer Gynt*. The second begins with *The League of Youth* and continues to a dividing point that is not firmly agreed upon. Some critics would place the line between *Hedda Gabler* and *The Master Builder*, others just after *An Enemy of the People*, and still others after *Rosmersholm*.

Actually, both methods of division have a good deal to be said for them, and, paradoxically, there is a sense in which both must be questioned. It is quite easy to see Ibsen's early plays as a search for an appropriate dramatic form. In the group of ten plays from *Catiline* (1848–49) to *Peer Gynt* (1867), Ibsen writes verse drama reminiscent of Shakespeare and Schiller, lyrical, romantic drama, historical drama of Scribean intrigue, a spare kind of prose drama emulating the style of the sagas, and moralistic or philosophical verse drama. He draws for subject matter on ancient history, on ballad, fairy tale, and folklore, on the sagas and Norwegian history, and on his own imagination. Many of these early plays are clearly influenced by the national romanticism which was such an important part of the Norwegian literary climate of the time. In 1841, a mere seven years before Ibsen's first play, Asbjörnson and Moe had published their first collection of folk tales. Their work had been preceded in 1833 by Andreas Faye's *Norske Sagn* and was followed in 1853 by a collection by Landstad and in 1858 by another by Bugge.[7] Indeed, in the fall of 1850, Ibsen had deliberately set out to write a four-act "national play," the title of which was to be *The Partridge of Justedal.* That unfinished play later became, in a revised version, *Olaf Liljekrans.*[8] Further, the first play he wrote after his appointment as "assistant in dramatic composition" at Ole Bull's National Theatre in Bergen drew directly on Norwegian fairy stories.[9]

This element of national romanticism seems to have reached its peak in his work sometime before the writing of *Peer Gynt,* for it is precisely that romanticism, among other things, that he satirizes in the play. After the publication of *Peer Gynt* Ibsen for some reason shifted his focus and wrote a series of realistic plays which ostensibly dealt with contemporary problems and castigated the narrow social conventions of his time and society. (There is, however, the extremely important exception, *Emperor and Galilean,* coming between *The League of Youth* and *Pillars of Society.*) It may be that he was so angered by the criticism of *Peer Gynt* that he resolved to give up "poetry" in favor of "photography." It may be, as Fjelde suggests, that he had here found his theme and his form, and was beginning to explore contemporary life at its most immediate level. Whatever the reason, he seems not to have persisted long in this course, for beginning with *The Wild Duck* another change takes place. The mysterious, the active world of nature, the sense of nonhuman forces affecting human destiny begins to reappear, with the difference that now it operates not in the ancient times of the ballad and saga but in the recognizable present, in the world of the late nineteenth century.

As has been indicated, one may perceive apparent distinctions in form and theme, particularly between the group of plays ending with *Peer Gynt* and that beginning with *The League of Youth.* Yet, unfortunately for those who wish to find dividing lines in his work, Ibsen made a statement in the preface to the 1898 Danish edition of his plays which demands to be taken seriously: "Only by grasping and comprehending my entire production as a coherent and continuous whole will one receive the desired, appropriate impression of the individual parts. My friendly advice to the reader is therefore, short and sweet, that he not temporarily set anything aside, not temporarily skip anything, but that he absorb the plays — read through them and live through them — in the same order in which I have written them." [10]

Implicit in this statement is the conclusion that Ibsen's work constitutes a complete canon through which he was attempting to create a unified and total world view, in his early plays as well as his later ones. If this is so, it suggests, further, that the differences among groups of plays are more apparent than real. Though he turns from verse to prose, from past history to contemporary life, there must be a fundamental unity or underlying theme. If, then, the development of a mythology may be discovered in his later plays, that mythology may very well be implicit in the earlier ones. Such is, indeed, the case. One can see from the very first play elements that reach their full dramatic maturity in the later ones, and the basic outlines of the Ibsenian myth begin to appear quite clearly in three early plays and two lyric poems. The chief accomplishment of the later drama was to put that myth into a contemporary framework and to apply it to modern man.

In speaking of his very first play, *Catiline*, Ibsen asserted that there was much in it that he would still claim as his own and that much that appears in the later plays is already intimated in the first one. Specifically, he refers to "the conflict between one's aims and one's possibilities, between what man proposes and what is actually possible which is at once both mankind's and the individual's comedy and tragedy." [11] It is, in fact, easy to discern in *Catiline* many of the problems and configurations which animate the later plays. In the opening speech Catiline makes it clear that he considers himself one especially set apart, sensing a call, and endowed with the strength and courage to attain to something greater than this life. He senses that he is destined to play the hero's role but holds himself in contempt because he has as yet no goal to which to devote his life. Yet at the end of the same scene Catiline himself calls attention to the miseries of Rome, supposedly a republic but actually suffering under the dictatorship of the Senate. Like the typical mythic hero, Catiline twice receives the "call" to lead a rebellion, to come to the aid of Rome, and twice he refuses. It is only under the urging of the vestal virgin, Furia, that he changes his mind and resolves to lead the conspiracy. Thus, Catiline is clearly the first of a long line of exceptional men in Ibsen whose task takes them beyond the concerns of ordinary mortals and frequently rewards them, as it does Catiline, with death or defeat. The theme is so consistent in Ibsen that one Norwegian critic has termed it his *kravsmystikk*, which can be somewhat inadequately rendered as "mysticism of the call." [12]

But it is not only in the call and the hero's task that *Catiline* prefigures the succeeding drama. Catiline is placed between two women, each of whom tries to exercise an influence upon him, and between whom he must choose. Aurelia, his wife, is gentle, pure, devoted to the "mild gods," and consistently associated with light. Furia, the temple priestess is fiery and demanding and is consistently associated with the darkness and the underground. Both, on separate occasions, try to induce Catiline to go away with them, Furia to some strange land where they will found and rule over their own kingdom, Aurelia to the country where they can live in peace and happiness. Catiline nearly follows Aurelia's call, but Furia, having given up the dream of a new kingdom, induces him to stay and lead the conspiracy to free Rome. At last Furia kills him, but he dies in the arms of Aurelia and as he does so the dawn breaks. One may readily perceive here a typical mythic configuration, the dark and the light lady, an opposition which, as Frye points out, was a convention in the Victorian novel.[13] One finds many such pairs in examining Ibsen's later work. In the sense that each woman represents an opposing force working on the soul of the hero, one sees also the dialectical pattern which informs *Emperor and Galilean* and many of the subsequent plays.[14] G. Wilson Knight's comment admirably sums up both the mythical nature of the play and its connection with the dramatist's later work:

> Much of Ibsen's life work is here turbulently contained: the dark powers impregnated by a mystical Dionysian. . . . authority; the sense of Nemesis as a compelling force; the entwining of crime, fire and death through Furia with great action.

. . . the two women, mild and fierce, the contrast of love and ambition, or again of sex license and great deeds; the impingement of occult powers, the lurid fire impressions, and the concluding intuition of death as dawn.[15]

During the next four years, between 1849 and 1853, Ibsen's literary activity consisted of an unimportant one-act play set in Viking times (*The Warrior's Barrow*), a brief political satire, and some verses and journalistic pieces. His next three plays were all based on fairy tales or ballads and in all of them the supernatural plays an important part (*St. John's Eve, Olaf Liljekrans*, and *The Feast at Solhaug*). He then made a brief excursion into Norwegian history with *Lady Inger of Östraat*, but with *The Vikings at Helgeland* he returned directly to the materials of myth. In the preface to the second edition of *The Feast at Solhaug* he indicates that the initial inspiration for *The Vikings* had come from the Icelandic family sagas which he was then reading in the translation of N. M. Petersen.[16] He reiterates this idea in the preface to the first German edition of his collected works, admitting the play's relation to the *Nibelungenlied* but arguing that the real sources were the *Volsunga Saga* and the Icelandic family sagas. His further comments provide an interesting insight into his thinking at that time concerning the relation between myth and drama.

> The main foundation of my work rests much more on the surviving Icelandic family sagas in which the colossal circumstances and events of the Nibelungenlied and the Volsungasaga seem very often to be reduced to more human dimensions. I believe, on that basis, that I may conclude that the situations and incidents depicted in the two works were typical of our common Germanic life in the earliest historical times. If one accepts this conclusion it disposes of the criticism that this play reduces our national saga-world to a level where it does not belong. For representation on the stage, these idealized and somewhat impersonal saga figures are less suited today than they have ever been before; but apart from that I had only the intention of portraying our life in the old times, not our saga-world.[17]

If this concluding statement is to be taken literally, it would seem to undermine the whole foundation of the argument thus far advanced. One must, however, consider two significant facts. The statement quoted above appeared eighteen years after the play, and it contains a defense against a "criticism" either made or anticipated. Professor McFarlane has convincingly argued that Ibsen did not wish, in this play, to bring the saga world close to reality, that he had nothing but contempt for the realism of his day, and that his aim in *The Vikings at Helgeland* was not only unrealistic but "positively anti-realistic." [18]

An examination of the play itself reveals a number of obvious mythical elements. Throughout the play there are strong suggestions of the active participation of nature in the struggles and storms of men. As with *Catiline*, darkness and storm precede the deaths of the central characters, and after both are dead the storm passes over and "the moon shines peacefully on the scene." Just before the killing of Sigurd, Hjördis sees her *fylgje*, a mythical guardian spirit that when seen in the form of an animal signifies death. [19] After the deaths of the principals, the *Aasgaardsreien* (the ride of fallen warriors to Valhalla) passes over the scene. Ibsen could hardly have believed that such events were "typical of our common Germanic life in the earliest historical times." His principal change, it seems, in the events of the *Volsunga Saga* was the substitution of a bear for the dragon killed by Sigurd. [20] On a still deeper level, the conflict between Christianity and paganism which forms the core of *Emperor and Galilean* is here present in germ. As Professor McFarlane again points out, Sigurd is revealed to have become a Christian; thus his self-sacrifice and self-control are manifestations of Christian virtues, whereas Hjördis remains the "embodiment of the Viking philosophy of life." [21]

It would seem, then, that rather than disavowing myth and arguing for realism in the drama, Ibsen was, in the German preface, arguing for the necessity of "displacing" myth behind superficially ordinary actions (to use Frye's terminology). To render that argument all the more convincing, one needs only to remember that the preface was written in 1876, shortly after Ibsen had completed

Emperor and Galilean and while he was probably at work on *Pillars of Society*.

The pattern of *The Vikings at Helgeland* repeats the basic configuration of *Catiline*. Sigurd, the warrior hero, is placed between two women, the gentle and motherly Dagny and the warlike Hjördis. Hjördis is married to the stable, devoted, and colorless Gunnar, and her dissatisfaction with her marriage and her longing for freedom ultimately result in the destruction of Sigurd and herself. Thus, the play not only repeats the pattern of a past work (and contains the germ of the pattern of *Emperor and Galilean*) but anticipates a number of future plays. Implicit here are the problems of *Rosmersholm*, *Hedda Gabler*, and *The Master Builder*. The device of one man sacrificing the woman he loves so that another may have her is repeated again and again in the later drama (though in the later plays the motive is almost always selfish). *The Vikings at Helgeland* contains, no less than *Catiline*, much that will appear later in the dramatist's work.

After this play, which can justly be termed an experiment in combining myth and realism into a viable form for the modern stage, Ibsen turned to a comedy of contemporary times, written in verse. *Love's Comedy* centers around the love affair between Falk, the idealistic poet, and Svanhild, the passionate and free-spirited young lady who loves him for his strength. The match would seem to be an ideal one, yet the two decide to part, reasoning that their love can survive only if they do *not* marry. Marriage would shackle Falk with the petty demands and irritations of bourgeois existence; a wife would tame his wild free spirit and turn him into the very object of his earlier scorn, a husband. The figures around Falk and Svanhild are archetypes of this bourgeois conventionality. The Pastor; Strawman, with his twelve "little wonders" and another on the way; the petty, regulation-shy law clerk, Stiver; even Falk's former confidant, Lind, who gives up his dream of becoming a missionary in favor of a secure teaching post — all are caricatures of the respectable citizenry of Ibsen's day, but they are also something more. They are the very forces that restrict the hero in his search for the ideal. Falk rejects their smallness as Brand, Solness,

Rubek, and other later characters reject similar situations. The idealist cannot be shackled by the bonds of conventional respectability or practicality. Svanhild, who understands his needs, sends him off into the mountains boldly singing with a students' choir. Thus, Falk is the hero figure once again, sensing the same call to transcend this life that was heard by Catiline. The play is far more than the satire of the bourgeois establishment that it was taken to be in Ibsen's day. That element, which was certainly present, links it to such plays as *The League of Youth* and *Pillars of Society*, but in its deeper concerns with the theme of idealism versus everyday life *Love's Comedy* looks backward to *Catiline* and forward to such plays as *The Master Builder*.

This same concept of the call or the ordained lifework forms the core of his next play, *The Pretenders*. With *Love's Comedy* Ibsen seems to have attempted to place his myth of the call in a contemporary setting, though still clinging to the convention of verse. With *The Pretenders* he returns to Norwegian history and dramatizes a rivalry between Haakon Haakonsen and Skule Bardson for the throne of Norway. The play begins with the establishment through trial of Haakon's legitimate claim to the throne. The machiavellian Bishop Nicholas plants doubts in Skule's mind, and Skule, eaten up by jealousy and ambition, declares himself king and succeeds in temporarily defeating Haakon's party. What ultimately keeps Skule from triumphing, though, is his recognition that, unlike Haakon, he does not have a "king's thought," a goal or governing idea that gives direction to everything that he does. Haakon's "king's thought" is a simple one — "Norway has been a kingdom. It shall become a people." In other words, Haakon has the dream of uniting all of the warring factions into a cohesive whole, even in the face of the discouraging evidence of the sagas and historical precedent. Like Catiline and Falk, he feels himself especially called to fulfill a dream. The lack of such an ideal dooms Skule to failure: he cannot legitimately be a king because his ideal is one of personal power. Therefore Haakon triumphs, and this play, like its immediate predecessor, takes an optimistic viewpoint toward the possibility of the call's being achieved.

The hero's task or call is symbolically, but nonetheless clearly, articulated in two of Ibsen's early poems, "The Miner" (*Bergmanden*, 1851) and "On the Heights" (*Paa Vidderne*, 1859–60). Besides the hero theme, the two poems have rather clear affinities with the mythic pattern outlined by Campbell and possess in embryo the cosmology that makes its appearance in many of Ibsen's later plays. The pattern of Campbell's monomyth is one of separation, initiation, and return; the hero removes himself from ordinary society, passes through a number of trials in a mysterious region, learns a secret or acquires a talisman, and returns to improve the lives of the people he has left. Campbell identifies the mysterious regions this way (emphasis mine): "This fateful region of both treasure and danger may be variously represented: as a distant land, *a forest, a kingdom underground*, beneath the waves or above the sky, a secret island, *lofty mountains* or a profound dream state." [22]

"The Miner" presents the poet metaphorically hewing his way downward into the earth, raining blow after blow on the rock, never stopping until he reaches the point at which he hears the metal sing. As he works his way down into the ground he finds there peace and silence from "eternity" and concludes that he must continue probing into the secret chamber of the heart (*det dulgtes hjertekammer*). Yet the miner has doubts. He has still not succeeded in discovering the answer to life's eternal riddle. No light has streamed up from the ground to reveal the secret of life. For a moment he wonders whether he has made a mistake, whether he should have sought his answer on the heights, but at last he reaffirms his decision:

> No, I must down into the depths;
> There is peace from eternity.
> Break your way my heavy hammer
> To the heart's secret chamber. [23]

On one level the poem can be interpreted as expressing Ibsen's determination to probe into the very depths of human psychology, but on a more profound plane it can be seen as evidence that Ibsen saw his own task as poet in mythic terms, as requiring him to separate himself from humanity and probe into unknown and possibly dangerous regions for the answer to life's riddle.

"On the Heights" adds to the pattern of separation, initiation, and return another traditional mythic element, the strange companion, guide, or teacher who leads the hero to the secret or gives him a weapon or tool which will help him to win it. The story is of a young man who takes his gun and knapsack, bids farewell to his mother, sweetheart, and home, and sets off to wander in the mountains. Early in his journey he meets a mysterious hunter who urges him on and constantly reproves him for looking back. Even when the young man sees his native village in flames, his mysterious guide urges him on. As in "The Miner," the young man feels strongly drawn to the world he has left behind and is not always completely sure of his call, but at last he decides that he has no more connection with the life of those in the valleys.

> Now firm as steel I follow the call
> That bids in the heights to wander!
> My lowland life I have lived out;
> Here on the heights are freedom and God,
> Down there fumble the others.[24]

Once again, on the realistic plane, the poem can be explained by Ibsen's disillusionment with his native land or his awareness of his separation as a poet from the concerns of everyday society. Undeniably, however, the poem follows the mythical pattern, or at least that part of it involving separation from society and the search for something greater. In this poem, as in "The Miner," the hero has not yet found his goal but the determination to continue searching is not weakened. The sense of call or hero's task which Ibsen has attributed to many of his leading characters is here applied to the poet himself.

Much of Ibsen's early work has its roots in folklore, legend, and myth. Before writing the three most significant plays of his early period, he had another opportunity to expose himself directly to such material. In May of 1862 he embarked on a walking tour through the country districts of Norway, passing through Lillehammer, Gudbrandsdal, Sogn, and Romsdalen, returning to Christiania about the first of August. In the course of this tour he met Peder Fylling, who was engaged in collecting folktales in the district of Skodje. Ibsen spent several days with him, listening and writing down as much as he could. Four of the tales he thus collected were published in the *Illustreret Nyhedsblad* in October and November of 1862. He had also arranged with a publisher and bookdealer for a collection of these tales, to run about two hundred and fifty pages. The book was never published but much of the material that Ibsen then collected was to reappear a few years later in *Brand* and *Peer Gynt*.[25]

In both content and form these two plays adhere closely to the pattern of Campbell's monomyth. The hero goes in search of something that he either finds or does not find, and in the course of his search he passes through a number of experiences and trials. In these two plays the search is for the "self," though not only in the narrow psychological sense.[26] *Brand* and *Peer Gynt* are only partly stories of individual self-discovery. In certain important ways both of the title characters represent man — man, perhaps, as he should be and as he is, man the doer and man the dreamer, man responding to or failing to respond to the call of life. In a sense each play is a study of the search for salvation yet each ends with a paradox, and when the two are put together the paradox is even more painfully apparent.

At the very beginning of *Brand* the title character is working his way down from the heights of "Paa Vidderne." He has a message of salvation to bring to the villagers in the valley: "All or nothing." Brand's God demands everything of him, and he, in turn, demands everything of his parishioners. Yet he does not even promise any kind of immediate redemption or eternal life for the individual; only the salvation of the race. The redemptive force, in Brand's view, is *will* — man's ability to will himself a higher form of existence. Irving Deer indicates that Brand symbolizes "man in his most God-like aspect in search of the absolute." [27]

This goal requires the sacrifice of everything — his mother, his child, his wife, and, at last, the very church he had caused to be built in his village. Brand has his temptations; at times he is nearly ready to turn back and desert his goal. But he also has his guide, the half-mad gypsy girl, Gerd, who repeatedly calls him back to his goal and at last leads him into the heights once more, to her ice church where he is buried in an avalanche.[28] Such demands, however, are too great for the ordinary man. The same people who had clamored for Brand to lead them desert him when they learn the real price of his leadership, and go scampering off in search of a nonexistent school of fish.[29] Nor is it sufficient that they desert him; they must stone him and cast him out. Thus, Brand becomes associated with a long line of scapegoats who suffer and sacrifice for their people only to be turned upon and destroyed or banished. He awakens echoes of both the Hebrew prophets of the Old Testament and of Christ, an equation that is specifically made by Gerd.

> Let me look at your hands!
> . . . .
> Nail scarred!
> Drops of blood I see in your hair
> Drawn forth where the thorns' teeth
> Have cut your brow.
> You have certainly borne the cross!

Brand vehemently denies this equation with the Saviour, but it is precisely the role that he has tried to play for his people and the violence with which he is met is perhaps always the lot of those who try to save humanity. (Ibsen treats this same theme with comic irony in *An Enemy of the People* when Dr. Stockmann has his trousers torn in the attempt to ennoble mankind.)

And yet there is some doubt whether Brand has chosen the right way to save mankind and, in the process, himself. This is the ultimate question of the play as Brand phrases it in his last speech:

> Answer me, God, in the jaws of death! —
> Is not one mite of salvation
> To be found in man's will?

The meaning of God's answer, "He is the God of love," has been endlessly debated, and an analysis need not be provided here. In fact, it would seem, as Deer suggests, that paradox is the desired effect. If Brand fails to find the absolute for which he has sought, he fails simply because he is man and not God. This is his tragedy and also, paradoxically, his salvation.[30] What is clear, however, is that Ibsen is once again dealing with the mythic pattern, the heroic searcher who is also a scapegoat and who carries his quest all the way to God himself.

Peer Gynt is also a searcher, but in every other respect he is Brand's opposite. Brand seeks for the self in the absolute and in following what seems to be a clear call to transcend himself; Peer avoids the call and seeks for the self in adventure and self-indulgence. Like Brand, Peer has his guides, but they are all negative ones. At the wedding feast Peer meets Solveig, who could help him to find his goal, but he runs off up the mountain with the bride and follows a series of other guides — the three cowherd girls, the Green-Clad One, the trolls, the Great Boyg. A motto that could very well be Brand's, "Man, be yourself!" is deliberately juxtaposed against the troll motto, "Troll, to yourself be — enough!" [31] Peer diligently follows the latter motto throughout most of the play: He is not evil, merely will-less and self-absorbed. He dreams and runs from responsibility. He cannot set a goal and strive toward it whatever the cost as does Brand. The goals he does set are short term and involve only his immediate gratification. He follows the advice of the Great Boyg — "Go round about."

Ultimately Peer, too, comes to Brand's position. He must face death, one confrontation from which he cannot flee. For him, however, there is not to be the dignity of burial under an avalanche; he is to be melted down like a lump of human trash into a metal button. As the Button Moulder makes clear, Peer, like most men, has not been himself. He has refused life's call, and in following the troll motto he has denied his essential humanity. But if Peer Gynt has not been himself, what is the meaning of the human motto? It is clear what Peer has not done, but not nearly so clear what he should have done. Should he perhaps have been another Brand and sacrificed himself to save others? The Button Moulder's answer, "To be one's self is to slay one's self," seems to suggest this, but though the statement is full of biblical overtones, it remains at last a riddle.

The paradox of the two plays is heightened by comparing the endings. The question of Brand's salvation is ambiguous, but it seems fairly clear that Peer is saved, though his salvation must be accomplished through another. His true self has always resided in the image that Solveig has had of him. She has had the faith and steadfastness that he lacked, and his one virtue perhaps lies in the fact that he has been able to inspire such love in another. George Groddeck insists that Solveig and Aase are versions of the same archetypal figure and in a production should resemble each other.[32] The paradox of the two plays is retained down to the final curtain. Brand, the saint and striver, is buried under an avalanche; Peer Gynt, the wastrel, finds refuge in the arms of Solveig. If the two plays represent the myth of the hero in search of an ideal self, it might be said that Brand has sought what he did not find and that Peer has found, through love, what he did not seek.

Both plays follow the mythic pattern, but in *Peer Gynt* especially Ibsen has drawn on a substantial body of mythic and folkloric material. Peer Gynt himself is the hero of a folk tale from Gudbrandsdal which is included in Asbjörnson and Moe's *Norske Folke og Huldre-Eventyr*. In his introduction to the play in the *Hundreaarsutgave* Koht traces the source of the cowherd girls, the ride over Gjendineggen, the encounter with Boyg Etnedal, and the Green-Clad One also to Asbjörnson.[33] The supernatural elements in *Brand* are less clear and are suggested rather than presented. They remain, so to speak, offstage, but the audience is nonetheless aware of their presence.

If this reading of the two plays is correct, *Brand* and *Peer Gynt* are of vital importance for the drama that follows. In a sense they mark a turning point in Ibsen's work. The implicit confidence in the possibility of attaining the ideal that seemed to be present in *Love's Comedy* and *The Pretenders* and even, perhaps, in the two poems discussed above becomes clouded by paradox. Two diametrically opposed ways of life are presented — a pure idealism and a selfish hedonism. Brand's way leads him to the ice church, a fitting symbol of its coldness; Peer's way leads him to the bosom of Solveig. Yet Brand is praised, Peer is condemned. Good and evil, idealism and selfishness, the rewards and punishments for each, are ambiguous. Man lives in a world in which the alternatives are clouded and the rewards uncertain. In many of the later plays Ibsen seems to be struggling to make sense out of this very ambiguity. He is pulled now one way, now the other, and concludes his career with the mystery only partly solved.

After the writing of *Peer Gynt* and the somewhat unfriendly critical response with which it was met, Ibsen sent his angry letter to Björnson, threatening to become a photographer and to "come to grips" with his enemies in the North. His first attempt as a dramatic photographer was *The League of Youth*, in which he viciously satirizes meanness, provinciality, and political opportunism in Norway, taking as his principal target, some critics feel, Björnson himself. He could not yet, however, bring himself to forsake the larger concerns. For four years he worked on the play that he later described as his masterpiece, finally publishing *Emperor and Galilean* in October of 1873. He subtitled the play "A World-Historical Drama," and it is clear that he was concerned with the powers or forces behind the operation of history, powers which he saw at work in his own day. On October 14, 1872, in a letter to Edmund Gosse, he said of *Julian the Apostate* (his first title for the play): "It is a part of my own spiritual life that I am putting into this book. What I depict I have under different conditions lived through myself, and the historical subject I have chosen has a much closer connection with the movement of our time than one might at first imagine."[34] Later he commented similarly in a letter to Ludvig Daae: ". . . The work that I am now bringing out will be my chief work. . . . The play deals with a struggle between two irreconcilable powers in the history of the world — a struggle that will always repeat itself and because of this universality I call the book a 'World history play.'"[35]

The two five-act plays published under the title *Emperor and Galilean* deal with the Emperor Julian, originally a Christian, who falls away from his faith and seeks to re-establish ancient paganism in the empire. The two "irreconcilable forces" that Ibsen spoke of are indicated in the title, but they must be taken to mean more than just the conflict between emperor and church. Julian wishes to restore paganism with its joy of life and its love of beauty and learning. He objects to Christianity because of its death worship, its solemnity, and its intolerance. Thus, two principles are opposed to each other, the principle of life-affirmation, beauty, and joy, and the principle of death, asceticism, and life-denial. In a sense this is merely a deepening of the conflict of *Brand* and *Peer Gynt*: an idealism which, however admirable, is nevertheless cold and inhuman versus a hedonism which, however pleasurable, is in the last analysis self-defeating. In terming the play a world-historical drama Ibsen indicated that he had seen those principles in conflict throughout human history just as, on the evidence of his letter to Gosse, he saw them in conflict in his own soul. Indeed, much of Ibsen's later drama, even his "social reform" plays, seems to indicate that he saw the struggle also in modern terms, between the new liberal and scientific ideas and the stuffy Victorianism and conservative Christianity of the nineteenth century. Thus, as Valency indicates, Nora's revolt against her husband can be seen as the playing out of this cosmic struggle on the individual scale.[36]

Out of the clash of these two forces, however, Ibsen envisioned a kind of synthesis which he labeled the third empire and which is perhaps best described by Julian's mentor and guide, Maximus, in the third act of the first play: "There are three empires. . . . First that empire which is founded on the tree of knowledge; then that which is founded on the tree of the cross. . . . The third is the empire of the great mystery; that empire which shall be founded upon the tree of knowledge and the tree of the cross together, because it hates and loves them both and because it has its living sources under Adam's grove and under Golgotha."

Under the tutelage of Maximus, Julian mistakenly concludes that he is to be the predicted founder of that empire, and once he gains control of the government he actively sets about trying to establish it. In the course of his campaign he turns into a tyrant, a dogmatist, and a persecutor of Christians. Yet for all of his cruelties he becomes, even more clearly than Brand, a sacrificial victim. Behind both Julian and the forces of the Galilean that oppose him is the world-will working out the future of mankind in its own way and at its own price. Julian's real role in the establishment of the third empire is as one of the "three cornerstones under the wrath of necessity," the "three great helpers in denial," the first two of whom were Cain and Judas Iscariot. He tries to reject this role, but in the final scene of the second play the full significance of the prophecy becomes clear. Julian is killed by a Christian, a representative of the principle that his persecution has only served to strengthen. But Christianity too is only a stage on the journey. Maximus sums up, in the key lines of the play, the meaning of Julian's sacrifice:

> The world-will shall answer for Julian's soul!! Led astray like Cain. Led astray like Judas — Your God is a spendthrift God, Galileans! He wears out many souls. Wast thou not then, this time either, the chosen one — thou victim on the altar of necessity? What is it worth to live? All is sport and mockery. — To will is to have to will. . . . The third empire shall come! The spirit of man shall re-enter on its heritage — and then shall offerings of atonement be made to thee and to thy two guests in the symposium.

Julian, then, has been chosen by a power beyond him for a task beyond his comprehension. Under the guidance of his tutelary spirit he has gone forward, doing what he was compelled to do, even though it led him to his own destruction. He has been a sacrifice in the working out of an inscrutable and inexorable will.

The scope of the drama has certainly been mythic. It ranges, as Ibsen said in another of his letters, from earth to heaven [37] and deals with the whole history and destiny of mankind. Ibsen has not been interested in history per se, but has used history as a vehicle to make an all-inclusive teleological statement about man. Yet there is a more personal way in which the play may have functioned as myth for its author. In September of 1871 he wrote to Brandes: "There are . . . moments when the whole history of the world reminds one of a sinking ship; the only thing to do is to save oneself. . . . The whole human race is on the wrong track. That is the trouble." [38]

It was perhaps in answer to this mood of profound despair over the course of history that Ibsen offered what he called his "positive philosophy." [39] Paulus Svendsen argues that the writing of *Emperor and Galilean* helped him to impose an order on what frequently seemed to him to be chaotic. It helped to clarify for him the relation between the individual and the world-will and between freedom and necessity. It strengthened his belief that a moral will works in history and will suddenly appear to "sweep the board clean" of all corruption, lies and deceit. [40] Under even a superficial analysis, the philosophy presented in the play seems to be little more than warmed-over Hegelianism, but Ibsen was, after all, a poet, not a philosopher. Whatever he may have borrowed from Hegel he wove into an imaginative design that made it possible for him to cope, at least temporarily, with the pressures of his time, of history, and of his existence and that, in the final analysis, is the task of the mythmaker. [41]

After *Emperor and Galilean* Ibsen began in earnest with his series of realistic plays, writing within the next nine years, *Pillars of Society* (1877), *A Doll's House* (1879), *Ghosts* (1881), and *An Enemy of the People* (1882). Even though these plays represent a rather sharp departure in form and subject matter from *Brand* and *Peer Gynt*, it is not beyond possibility to discern, even in them, the displaced mythic patterns. As I have previously indicated, one can see not only in *A Doll's House* but also in *Ghosts* and *An Enemy of the People* a repetition of that cosmic clash which animates *Emperor and Galilean*. It is also possible to discern in *Ghosts* an attempt at ritual exorcism of evil with its concomitant purification by fire, an attempt which is doomed to failure since the evil lives on in Oswald's bloodstream. Dr. Stockmann of *An Enemy of the People* can be viewed as a mythic hero who has lived long away from mankind (his long sojourn in "the North") and has returned to bring a boon to his fellow townsman, a boon which consists of the revelation, first, of physical, and later of spiritual pollution. Nevertheless, in all of these plays the mythic pattern is thoroughly

33

displaced in the direction of realism. They operate in a human world in which the supernatural is absent and causes and effects are, in large part, realistically determined. In each case the event which precipitates the chain of circumstances leading inevitably to the conclusion is a human action and in that sense preventable.[42] As this implies, the adversary or antagonist in each of the plays is human. (*Ghosts* can be made an exception if one regards Oswald's disease as a fatalistic force.) Of each play we can say with some confidence that if conditions had been different, there would have been no catastrophe and hence no drama. In the same way, the symbolism of the plays is rather confined. The symbols used (Nora's Tarantella, the "ghosts," the diseased baths) have fairly direct and tangible referents. There is little of the quicksilver quality of the wild duck or the white horses and little sense of mystery that cannot be psychologically or sociologically explained. In short, even though mythic patterns can be discerned in those plays, myth has been so thoroughly displaced as almost to disappear completely.

Yet Ibsen was always the poet. He could not persevere long as a photographer if, indeed, he ever really was one. In *The Wild Duck* his concern for the larger issues of life begins to reappear. Slowly the powers behind the universe, the feeling of mystery in existence, make their re-entry onto Ibsen's stage, until, in the later plays, the mythic structures and themes have re-established themselves as almost supreme.

THE WILD DUCK AND *ROSMERSHOLM* · THE
RE-ENTRY OF THE MYTHIC

❡ THOUGH myth dominates some of Ibsen's earlier plays and can
be found to be implicit even in those of his "realistic" period, it
does become displaced behind a facade of direct concern with social problems in the plays from *The League of Youth* through *An
Enemy of the People* (with the exception of *Emperor and Galilean*). *An Enemy of the People* was, however, the last play in
which Ibsen dealt directly and primarily with a social problem; it
can be regarded as the last of his polemical plays.[1] It is perhaps significant that the playwright has Dr. Stockmann specifically reject
one of the major myths (to use the term in a slightly different
sense) of nineteenth-century liberalism — that of the rightness of
the majority. Ibsen was from now on not to be concerned with
the condition of society and its institutions except as this reflected
his larger concern, the condition of man. He addresses himself to
the universal human condition as he finds it embodied in the tormented individuals that people his last plays.

In the two plays to be dealt with in this chapter Ibsen's expand-
ing concern with the metaphysical rather than the social aspects
of existence begins to reappear. From now on the question posed

35

by Maximus the Mystic, "What is it worth to live?" is never very far from the center of the dramatist's attention. At the same time, the dimension of the supernatural and nonhuman which had lurked in the background from *Catiline* through *Emperor and Galilean* but which was largely absent from the intervening plays begins once more to make its presence felt.

But Ibsen was not yet ready to take the complete step into myth. He still used the social world as a framework upon which to build the larger drama. In *The Wild Duck* the frame is marriage and family life, as in *A Doll's House* and *Ghosts*; in *Rosmersholm* it is politics, as in *An Enemy of the People*. Behind the social framework of both plays, however, there are other more ancient and archetypal patterns which give them a greater depth and richness than his immediately preceding work.

The Wild Duck · The Sustaining World of Illusion

Ibsen's correspondence relative to *The Wild Duck* seems to indicate a distinct change of mood and a deliberate rejection of the social problem drama together with a search for a new form. In a letter to Georg Brandes, for example, he says: "My head is full just now with the plot of a new dramatic work in four acts. In the course of time a variety of crazy ideas [*galskaper*] are apt to collect in one's mind and one needs an outlet for them." [2] Approximately a year later, when the draft copy of the play was completed, he wrote to Theodore Caspari, "I spent all winter spinning some new follies [*galskaper*] in my brain until they assumed dramatic form and in the last few days I completed a play in five acts." [3] The Norwegian word *galskaper* here rendered as *crazy ideas* and *follies* is a word that is difficult to translate precisely into English. Suggesting madness, foolishness, recklessness, frenzy, playfulness, it is a term that Ibsen has never before used to refer to any of his dramatic works. Indeed, these references to *The Wild Duck* are reminiscent of a remark made twenty years earlier in a letter to Björnson. Just arrived in Rome, Ibsen indicated that he was not drawn to classic art because it lacked a sense of personal and individual expression. He added: "I understand Michelangelo and Bernini and his school better. Those fellows had the courage to do something crazy [*göre en galskap*] once in a while." [4]

There is, of course, no way of proving that Ibsen meant the same thing by his use of the word *galskap* on these widely separated occasions, or even what he meant by his use of it in connection with *The Wild Duck*. If, however, one thinks of Michelangelo's vision as represented, for example, in the ceiling of the Sistine Chapel, one could safely conclude that Ibsen favored a visionary art in broad scope on a large surface, a conclusion which the nature of his earlier drama, especially *Emperor and Galilean*, would seem to reinforce. Thus, his use of it in connection with *The Wild Duck* might well suggest that the poet and visionary who had created *Brand* and *Peer Gynt* was beginning to find the strictures of realism too confining.

In the letter to Brandes and in another to Hegel he specifically denies any intention of dealing in *The Wild Duck* with social or political problems.[5] In a later letter to Hegel he makes the following statement: "In some ways this new play occupies a place of its own among my dramatic works, its plan and method differing in several respects from my former ones . . . I also think that *The Wild Duck* may perhaps entice some of our younger dramatists into new paths which I hold to be desirable." [6]

The exact nature of this new departure and plan of development has been interpreted by critics in various ways. One thing that seems obvious to most is that Ibsen is here severely questioning the position of the idealist, turning him into a meddling and destructive busybody.[7] Some critics have asserted that in this play Ibsen is castigating himself or at least that part of himself which was characterized by puritan reformist zeal. Yet the ambivalence toward the idealist was already apparent in *Brand*, and Ibsen's comic treatment of the reformer, Dr. Stockmann, in his previous play would suggest that the playwright had never been completely committed to the idealist position. On the surface the formal departures from Ibsen's earlier work do not seem to be so great, yet Koht indicates that upon the play's first appearance readers and audiences reacted to it with puzzlement.[8] Arne Duve suggests that in this play Ibsen for the first time deserts realism and openly devotes himself to symbolism.[9] Jorgenson comments that in *The Wild Duck* the playwright makes a symbol rather than a character central to the action,[10] and Northam points out that this is the first of Ibsen's plays in which the symbol is physically present or at least near enough so as to suggest its physical presence on the stage.[11] One of the most interesting theories, however, is to be found in Else Höst's monograph. She suggests that Ibsen wrote on one level a comedy and on another a tragedy, causing the two to intersect in the person of Hedvig.[12]

In this context, however, the significant difference between this play and those immediately preceding it is not the mere employment of symbolism but the manner in which a whole mysterious and uncanny world of symbolism interacts with the human world. When we add to this the presence of underlying archetypal patterns, it is easy to see the play as once again representing a movement toward myth. This time, however, the dramatist is attempting to present his myth not through the romantically distanced events of folklore and history but in the recognizable present—in the world inhabited by both his characters and his audience.

The plot of *The Wild Duck* can be easily summarized. It is the story of what happens when a well-meaning young idealist meddles in matters that do not concern him. Gregers Werle discovers that his boyhood friend Hjalmar Ekdal has entered into a marriage based on a falsehood. Devoted to the "claim of the ideal," he decides that it is his responsibility to refound the marriage on truth and thus bring about the salvation and ennoblement of the Ekdals. His task, then, is in a small way similar to Brand's. And like Brand, he has grossly overestimated the material with which he is working. Truth of the sort that Gregers brings to the Ekdal family is not for the ordinary man, a fact of which Hjalmar is dimly aware though Gregers is not. In his attempt to bring about a "true marriage," he causes the death of Hjalmar's daughter and very nearly destroys the marriage that exists. The play, then, can be seen as an attempted exorcism of evil, the story of a would-be saviour who fails grotesquely because the people he would save are neither desirous nor capable of salvation.

This bald statement of plot, however, leaves much out of account. In this play especially, *what* happens cannot easily be separated from *where* it happens and to *whom* it happens. The world or worlds of the play act almost as characters in the action, and the characters are intimately connected with the worlds which they inhabit.

There are three worlds on the stage in *The Wild Duck*, two of them human and the third a world of mysterious nonhuman forces, a world of poetic symbolism and strange fantasy that interacts in various ways with the two human worlds. The two human worlds are at nearly opposite ends of the social scale in Norway, one the world of court officials and prosperous businessmen surrounding Old Werle, the other the shabby world of the Ekdals. Though widely separated socially, these two worlds are nonetheless connected by a secret from the past, an obscure crime that has marked them both and that has symbolic connections with the third world.

Before the curtain has been up five minutes the audience is made aware of the secrets underlying the bright Werle world. Two servants are bustling about while a dinner party is in progress in the next room. Since one of them is a temporary employee, he must be filled in on the Werle household:

> PETTERSEN. Now just listen, Jensen; the old man is standing at the table proposing a long toast to Mrs. Sörby.
> JENSEN. Is it maybe true what people say, that there's something between them?
> PETTERSEN. The devil knows.
> JENSEN. Because he's certainly been a real goat in his day.[13]

The method of exposition is a familiar one from the well-made play, but Ibsen stops it at this point, leaving the audience with only hints as to the character and past life of Old Werle. A few lines later Old Ekdal enters and the audience learns of his brush with the law and his former business connections with Old Werle. Again the subject is dropped. So far the audience knows little, and though more information is provided later, by Gregers, it is important to note that the "truth" concerning these hints remains ambiguous throughout the play.

The mystery suggested in the lines is reinforced visually. In his excellent study of the visual elements in Ibsen's drama, Northam particularly stresses the lighting in *The Wild Duck*. Werle's workroom, which constitutes the main portion of the set during the first act, is lit by green-shaded lights. The subdued greenish glow cast by these lamps suggests "the half-darkness that blurs the truth," and calls to mind the green dimness of the forest and sea which play such an important part in the background of the action.[14]

The two worlds are brought together physically by the presence of Hjalmar Ekdal at Old Werle's dinner party. He is there at the invitation of his old school friend, Gregers, but he is manifestly out of place. Unable to make conversation, unaware that vintage has any effect on the quality of wine, he is the butt of the court officials' ridicule until Mrs. Sörby comes to his defense. Another suggestion of the potential evil or disaster that lurks behind the action is found in the fact that the presence of Hjalmar and Gregers brings the number of guests at the table to thirteen, a point to which I shall subsequently return. Perhaps the most ominous note, however, is the sudden appearance of Old Ekdal, with its galvanic effect on Werle and the whole dinner party.[15] Thus, from the beginning it is clear that all is not right in Werle's cheerful dining room and that what is wrong has something to do with the Ekdals.

Hjalmar Ekdal's home, though much lower on the social scale, is not squalid. The Ekdals are not well-off, but they live comfortably on a respectable middle-class diet of bread and butter, beer, smoked meat, herring. Though Gina must be careful with the household accounts there still seems to be enough left to entertain unexpected guests at lunch. Despite her grumbling about expenses and Hjalmar's occasional histrionics, the family relationships, too, seem to be good. I stress this point in order to make clear that Gregers does not bring his claim of the ideal into a sordid and miserable situation but rather to a family that seems to be getting on quite well until he makes his appearance.

This is not to say, however, that there is nothing wrong in the Ekdal household. Once again there are hints of something hidden. Old Ekdal has been involved in some kind of legal trouble that has caused him to go to the penitentiary and that has wrecked his army career. Gina reacts to the entrance of Gregers with a mixture of hostility and fright, and is deliberately evasive when she is questioned about Hedvig's age. It is also suggested that the Ekdals are still, to some degree, dependent on Old Werle. Again the audience's curiosity is aroused but not satisfied.

Behind the relatively comfortable Ekdal world, however, there is another interesting and puzzling one — the loft. Looked at in realistic terms, the loft is simply a storage room for assorted junk, most of it left by the previous inhabitant of the flat, a sea captain known in the town as the Flying Dutchman. There the Ekdals have housed assorted domestic animals, rabbits, pigeons, and the most important inhabitant, the wild duck. In it Old Ekdal plays at hunting, occasionally shooting a rabbit or a pigeon.

If the loft is looked at in poetic or symbolic terms, it takes on many additional connotations. It is a world of illusion which is both very large and very small. For Old Ekdal it is a substitute for the Höjdal forest of his youth; for Hedvig it is "the depths of the sea," where her wild duck had sought refuge from Old Werle's dog. In both cases, however, it is a pathetically shrunken world of nature. The trees of the surrogate forest are a collection of dried-up Christmas trees. The bears that Old Ekdal hunted as a young man have degenerated into rabbits. The sea is represented by an old piece of sailcloth and a fishnet.

Yet if the loft is a shrunken world of nature, it is also a microcosm of the larger world. Left in it are a clock that no longer runs, a watercolor set, and a desk containing a collection of old books, among them Harrison's *History of London*, which contains pictures of "castles and churches and streets and great ships that sail on the sea." Knight points out that the loft, thus, contains two primary Ibsen powers, nature and art.[16] For Hedvig it provides a quite adequate substitute for the "big real world," which she is not interested in seeing and which, in fact, her weak eyes may prevent her from ever seeing. Many characters in other Ibsen plays are shut away from the big real world and pine for it; significantly, the characters in *The Wild Duck* content themselves with substitutes both for the world of nature and the world of civilization.

The elements of mystery in the loft have still not been completely exhausted. The frontispiece of the *History of London* is a picture of death with an hourglass and a young girl (*jomfru*, which, like its German cognate, can also be rendered as *virgin*). The clock in the loft no longer runs, so that, as Gregers points out, time is at a standstill in the wild duck's domain. The picture and the stopped quality of time are clear foreshadowings of the fate that awaits Hedvig in the loft. Thus, if the loft contains nature and art, it also contains death.

The most mysterious element of the loft, however, is the wild duck herself. Having been wounded by Old Werle, she had headed straight for the bottom with the intention of entangling herself in the mud and seaweed and dying there. Werle, though, had an "amazingly clever dog" which rescued the duck; thus it came eventually into the hands of the Ekdals, where now it thrives in captivity. As an inhabitant of Old Ekdal's surrogate forest the duck reinforces the observations already made: the crippled bird which cannot fly and which is growing fat in captivity is a pathetic parody of the wildlife in the real forest. But it is for Hedvig that the duck chiefly takes on her mysterious significance. Hedvig herself does not seem clearly to understand what she finds so fascinating about the duck, but she tells Gregers, "Everything is so strange about the wild duck; nobody knows her and nobody knows where she came from either." Then, as Gregers adds, the duck has been to "the depths of the sea," the name that Hedvig secretly applies to the whole loft. The duck is clearly a symbol, but to say specifically what she symbolizes is no easy task. It can best be approached, perhaps, by considering the relationship of the loft and the duck to each of the major characters.

By examining the strictly visual connections between each character and the loft, Northam comes to the conclusion that it represents something different for each member of the Ekdal family. For Old Ekdal and Hjalmar it is a world of protective fantasy in which they are completely caught. Hedvig is only on the threshold of this world, and Gina is free of it altogether.[17] The observation is generally sound, but one can go beyond Northam's conclusion to note further subtle differences relating to the way each character puts the loft to use.

For Old Ekdal the loft is a safe substitute for his earlier existence. In it he can relive the triumphs of his youth as a bear hunter in the Höjdal forest without the attendant risks. Those risks, however, were not connected with the animals he hunted; Old Ekdal is not afraid of bears. Rather he fears some mysterious vengeful power in the forest itself that punishes the human interloper. Old Ekdal's disgrace and sojourn in the penitentiary resulted from his illegally cutting timber on government land while a partner in the lumber business with Old Werle. Ever since, he has feared the forest, as is made unmistakably clear in a brief exchange with Gregers in the second act.

> EKDAL. For the forest, you see — the forest, the forest! Is the forest in good shape up there now?
>
> GREGERS. Not so fine as in your day. They've been heavily logged off.
>
> EKDAL. Logged off? (More quietly, as if afraid) That's dangerous business. It catches up with you. There's vengeance in the forest.

Consequently, Old Ekdal does not mind that his forest has shrunk to a collection of withered Christmas trees and his bears have degenerated into rabbits. In fact, when Gregers suggests that he return to the real Höjdal forest, he is astonished at the thought and insists that Gregers be shown the substitute forest in the loft. Old Ekdal, in short, may be said to "believe in" the loft; he is quite happy playing great hunter among his rabbits and pigeons because it is much safer than venturing into the real world.

Hjalmar's relationship is of a different quality, and here I would differ slightly with Northam. For him the loft serves neither to rekindle past glories nor to provide imaginary new ones. That latter function is provided for him by his marvelous and imaginary invention that one day will revolutionize the whole art of photography. For him the loft is simply a means of escaping responsibility and work. He is remarkably like the little boy who will work hard for hours to build a tree house but who grumbles at mowing the lawn. Hjalmar, too, plays in the loft, but the element of belief which characterizes his father is missing in him. In fact, when he is pressed into showing the loft to Gregers, he becomes embarrassed and is eager to disavow any connection with it.

Hedvig relates to the loft in a third, more interesting way. One may agree with those who say that she is not completely an inhabitant of the world of the loft, to the extent that her attitude toward it is ambivalent. She approaches it simultaneously on two levels. She can see it realistically for what it is, and points out to Gregers that "after all it's only a loft." But secretly she thinks of it as the depths of the sea and revels in the mystery of it. For Hedvig there is a kind of consubstantiation, to borrow a term from theology, about the loft. It can be both simply a loft and a whole world of poetic fantasy at one and the same time.

Only for Gregers Werle is the loft a symbol in the conventional sense. That is to say, he is the only one who *sees* it as a symbol. For him the duck represents the Ekdal family, crippled by shot as they are by a lie, and the loft represents the swamp into which they have sunk. However, this is symbolism of the lowest order. One thing equals or stands for another, in a symbolism that an accomplished poet would find trite. In fact, it is partly his insistence on imposing upon the Ekdal family his brand of symbolism and his interpretation of the loft and their condition that brings about the tragedy of the final act.

Northam is quite correct in saying that Gina is free altogether of the loft world. For her it is a mere nuisance, but as long as it keeps her family happy she is willing to put up with it. Gina is intensely practical — in one sense, the most practical person in the play. She is perhaps not intelligent, and in Hjalmar's eyes not adequately "cultured," but without her the Ekdal family would have sunk to the bottom. She does not have time to bother about such things as the loft.

The loft, then, is an active source of spiritual support for the Ekdal family. Its existence allows Old Ekdal to go on living and to salvage a modicum of his self-respect. It is not simply a "life-lie," as is Hjalmar's invention, but a mysterious independent power. Life and death, time and eternity, nature and art are all contained behind its sliding doors.[18]

The chief mythic impact of the loft is derived from the images of nature which it contains. Forest and sea are regarded as primary mythic powers both in terms of general archetypal imagery and of Norse mythology and folklore in particular. In Frye's "demonic world" one of the major representatives of nature is the sinister forest, inhabited by wild beasts and full of danger.[19] Mircea Eliade points out that traditional societies tend to view their village or city as the world and everything outside it as "foreign, chaotic space" peopled by ghosts and demons. There is a sharp distinction between inhabited space and the unknown territory beyond its frontiers.[20] In Scandinavian folklore the forest is full of all sorts of strange and potentially dangerous creatures — trolls, giants, the *huldre* or fairy-folk, and the *underjordiske* (the underground ones). Norse myth and folklore contain many tales of human encounters with the powers that lurk in the forests, frequently resulting in man's discomfort and occasionally his destruction.[21] In Frye's apocalyptic world, water belongs to the realm of existence that is below human life, a world of chaos and destruction but also the source of life.[22] In the demonic world it is the water of death and "above all, the unplumbed, salt, estranging sea." [23] Eliade comments to much the same point: "The waters symbolize the universal sum of virtualities; they are the *fons et origo*, 'spring and origin' the reservoir of all the possibilities of existence; they precede every form and *support* every creation. One of the paradigmatic images of creation is the island that suddenly manifests itself in the midst of the waves. On the other hand immersion in water signifies regression to the preformal, reincorporation into the undifferentiated mode of pre-existence." [24] He elaborates further on the ambivalent nature of water symbolism: "The Waters of Death are a leitmotiv of palaeo-oriental, Asiatic and Oceanic mythologies. Water is pre-eminently the slayer; it dissolves, abolishes all forms. It is just for this reason that it is so rich in germs, so creative." [25]

Eliade's observations accurately characterize the use of the sea in Norse mythology. Not only is it the home of one of the chief enemies of the gods, the terrible Midgaard serpent, but at the day of *Ragnarok* it will rise and cover the earth. Out of that destructive sea, however, a new and much fairer world will emerge.[26]

Hedvig's *havsens bund* (the depths of the sea) is for her a place of beauty, mystery, and romance, but it is also the place where she meets her death. Old Ekdal's surrogate forest has been the place where he could play the great hunter in complete safety from those powers that struck him down before. But he learns that even his attic forest is not safe; death lurks there too. "The forest avenges itself —," he says after Hedvig's death, "but I am not afraid anyway." At this point he goes into the loft and closes the door, an action which Haakonsen interprets as indicating that he has at least partly cast away his illusions and is determined to embrace his fate.[27]

An examination of the relationship between the Werles and the Ekdals will further illuminate the mythic patterns underlying the drama. The most obvious aspect of this relationship is the fact that the Ekdals are largely dependent on Old Werle for their very existence. He set Hjalmar up as a photographer, arranged for him to marry Gina, and continues to provide Old Ekdal with copy work that brings in sufficient money to pay for his board and keep. He tries, in fact, to arrange for the financial security of both Old Ekdal and Hedvig for the rest of their lives. Since even the wild duck came indirectly from Werle, one could argue that the Ekdals are dependent on him even for their spiritual support. Gregers, of course, regards all of his father's charitable actions as proceeding from a guilty conscience, first, for allowing Old Ekdal to pay the penalty for what was a joint venture and, second, for having conceived a child upon Gina and then palming her off on the unsuspecting Hjalmar. A close examination of the play, however, reveals that neither of these charges is as clearly true as some critics have believed. The only person who makes a direct accusation concerning the first is Gregers himself. Neither the Ekdals nor Dr. Relling seems to have suspected any complicity on Werle's part in Old Ekdal's crime. The only evidence to support Gregers' accusation is the old man's momentary fear when he hears in the second act that "Mr. Werle" (Gregers, actually) is at the door. Even for that another plausible explanation is provided. The servants in the first act indicate that "he [Ekdal] played some kind of dirty trick on the old man [Werle]." There is no more conclusive evidence of responsibility presented. The conclusion must be that Ibsen deliberately left the issue vague.[28] The evidence for the second charge is somewhat stronger but is still far from conclusive. Gina admits that Werle did "have his way" with her, but when faced with the question of Hedvig's paternity, she replies, honestly I think, that she does not know. Since there is in the first act a subtle suggestion that she may have had premarital relations with Hjalmar also, even the fact of Hedvig's age is not reliable. The only real connecting link is the fact that both Old Werle and Hedvig have weak eyes.[29] Again, however, an alternative is provided. Hjalmar explains in the second act, when the matter first comes up, that Hjalmar's mother also had weak eyes. Had this explanation come from Gina it might have been an obvious evasion, but it does not; it comes from Hjalmar, who attributes it to his father. Probably, both Gina and Old Werle are aware of the possibility that Hedvig *might* be his child, but there is no conclusive evidence to prove that she is. Gregers' accusations of sexual philandering have a basis in fact, but the inference he draws concerning Hedvig's paternity is not warranted. Indeed, all of Gregers' interpretations of his father's conduct must be regarded in the light of his manifest hatred and, thus, they are suspect from the beginning.

Yet Gregers is determined to "save" the Ekdal family. Several critics have noted an affinity between Gregers and Brand; in fact, Gregers is nearly a negative caricature of the stern priest.[30] The most significant difference between the two, however, lies in the area of motivation. Gregers' hatred of his father is clear, a hatred so strong that he detests his own name. He must save Hjalmar, he says, "in order to find a cure for my own sick conscience." It is quite possible then that he is simply using the Ekdals as a stick with which to beat his father. At the same time, as Relling implies, he may be looking to Hjalmar in an effort to find the hero figure that he did not find in his own father. He readily admits that he must have something outside of himself to admire. So that Hjalmar might be worthy of this admiration, Gregers endows him with heroic qualities that he does not possess and expects an ennoblement of which Hjalmar is completely incapable. Indeed, Hjalmar does not even think of himself as lost and thus has no desire to be saved. Gregers' mission of salvation, then, is from the beginning sullied with selfish motives.[31]

There is yet another way in which Gregers is no Brand. Brand demanded as much of himself as he did of his villagers; he sacrificed mother, wife, child, hope of worldly success, and at last himself to what he took to be the will of his God. Even if he was mistaken, he was heroic in his error. Gregers induces Hedvig to sacrifice "the dearest thing she owns" to redeem her father's love. On the realistic plane, of course, he means the duck, but on the symbolic level the words must be taken in the double sense with which Hedvig apparently takes them. Thus, as Haakonsen points out, Gregers does not go the whole way as saviour.[32] It is Hedvig who pays the price of Hjalmar's supposed redemption. The only thing Gregers sacrifices is something he does not want in any case — the inheritance from his hated father.

If Gregers is a grotesque parody of the idealist saviour figure, Dr. Relling stands as his exact opposite. As a doctor, albeit a dissolute one, he devotes himself to fostering happiness and accommodation with life among his "patients." To achieve this end it is sometimes necessary to provide people with a "life-lie" that will render them metaphysically comfortable. The world of reality is imperfect but it is all there is, at least as far as we can be certain. There is no point, then, in burdening people with impossible claims. If Gregers can in any sense be equated with Brand, Relling must represent Brand's "deus caritatis."

Thus, the principal motif of the play is an ironic sacrifice-redemption pattern. Gregers is a highly sullied redeemer trying to bring salvation to people who have no desire to be saved, and succeeds only in bringing destruction. The sacrifice is performed by Hedvig and accomplishes absolutely nothing. Gregers tries to convince himself and Relling that her death has ennobled Hjalmar, but Relling refuses to let him off that easily. Hjalmar's grief may be sincere at the moment but as time passes it will merely become another occasion for self-dramatization.[33]

One critic has argued that there is a metaphoric relationship between Old Werle and Gregers and God the Father and God the Son. Gregers, he says, is a bringer of truth and light, and his failure to redeem Hjalmar is a consequence of the fallen condition of man. Old Werle is the greater power, the providence which has wreaked destruction on the Ekdals.[34] The lines of argument I have so far been developing have both points of contact and points of difference with this interpretation. That Gregers regards himself as a bringer of truth is evident, but his selfish motives and the highly ambiguous nature of the "truth" he brings makes it unlikely that Ibsen regarded him as such. Furthermore, no matter the degree of Old Werle's responsibility for the imprisonment of Old Ekdal and Hedvig's paternity (both of which, as I have pointed out, are inconclusive), he, in the last analysis, has not destroyed the Ekdals. As Relling suggests, neither Old Ekdal nor his son are capable of maintaining an independent existence anyway. The old man, he says, has always been a child and Hjalmar is a shiftless dreamer. Indeed, only through the good offices of Old Werle has the family been able to survive at all. Old Werle may fairly be regarded as a providence, but he is a sustaining rather than a destructive one. If *The Wild Duck* includes any kind of metaphysical statement, it is that the lot of man is a precarious and sorry one but that, despite the inadequacies of existence, he can get on well enough if left with his illusions. There are, of course, people who can manage to live with naked truth. In this play they are, ironically, Old Werle and Berta Sörby. They realize the true marriage based on absolute frankness with each other which Gregers would like to establish for the Ekdals. For most of mankind, however, Ibsen seems to endorse Relling's prescription—the sustaining "life-lie."

In addition to the general mythic patterns and atmosphere of the play, there still remain some other minor and primarily verbal symbols that deserve brief consideration. One of these is the "Flying Dutchman," the previous inhabitant of the Ekdals' flat. The nickname alludes to the famous figure from the folklore of the sea. Why Ibsen chose that particular detail is unclear. Brian Johnston suggests a connection with Wagner's opera which may well be justified.[35] At any rate, though Ibsen does not make extensive use of the symbol, it is possible that the name was deliberately chosen to enhance the element of mystery operating in the loft. The other such symbol is the "thirteenth at table" which appears sporadically throughout the play. The connotations of ill luck connected with the number thirteen seem to have arisen from two legends. During the Last Supper there were supposedly thirteen at the table, one of whom was Judas Iscariot. In Norse mythology there were twelve principal gods among the Aesir; the thirteenth was Loki, the son of a giant, perennial mischief maker, and the ultimate cause of the death of Balder the Good.[36] Both Judas and Loki brought about the death of a figure who was thought to embody goodness and innocence. This fact would seem to point out that it is Gregers and not Hjalmar who is to be thought of as the thirteenth at table, a role which he claims for himself at the end of the play. If the thirteenth is thought of as the bringer of ill luck and destruction, then Gregers' claim would certainly seem to be justified.

It is difficult to say exactly what the duck herself symbolizes. She cannot be separated from the symbolic operation of the whole loft context in which she resides. Further, she is not meant to symbolize anything directly in the sense of a one-to-one equation between symbol and referent. Rather, I think she is meant to evoke, somewhat in the manner of the Japanese *haiku* or the later symbolist poetry of France. She has power to evoke the imagination that exceeds and transcends the simplest levels of symbolism, and only Gregers sees her in such simple terms. Her very power as symbol resides exactly in the inadequacy of drawing simple connections and interpreting her as standing for anything specific.

The Wild Duck marks the beginning of Ibsen's creation of a mythology set in contemporary terms and surroundings. It does so, first, by providing a complex of mythical symbolism which suggests the operation of nonhuman powers that profoundly affects human life. Second, the play is built on an archetypal pattern involving a would-be saviour and a sacrifice — a pattern which, however, is treated in an ironic fashion. Third, it begins the development of a world view and a cosmology with which Ibsen continues to be concerned throughout the rest of his career. The possibility of any ennoblement of human existence through idealism is here brought severely into question. Man is a helpless creature in uncertain surroundings. The best thing he can do, therefore, is to endeavor to live as comfortably as possible in his precarious world with the aid of whatever illusions will contribute to his spiritual well-being. For the rest of his life Ibsen seems to be torn between such a pessimistic view and a desire to see the regeneration of man accomplished through his third empire. In fact, the latter possibility becomes the central theme of his next play.

Rosmersholm · The Avenging Spirits

In *Rosmersholm* Ibsen would seem, at first glance, to have gone back to the area of social problem drama. The subject is ostensibly the old morality and tradition against the new spirit of religious, moral, and political liberalism. The frame for the drama is the political battle between the liberal and conservative forces in Norway. Indeed, whereas *The Wild Duck* seems to have grown out of a personal mood, *Rosmersholm* seems, in part, to have been inspired by events in Ibsen's native land.

In the summer of 1885 Ibsen revisited Norway for the first time in eleven years. He arrived on the heels of one of the bitterest battles in Norwegian political history, when emotions were still running high and when the members of the liberal and conservative factions would hardly speak to one another. To make matters worse, the Norwegian Storting was, that June, engaged in a debate over whether or not to grant a literary stipendium to the novelist, Alexander Kielland. The issue brought the moderate and radical left into open conflict and its outcome, the denial of Kielland's stipendium, was regarded by Ibsen as a defeat for intellectual freedom.[37] Ibsen himself became embroiled in the conflict through a disagreement with Lorenz Dietrichson, the conservative head of the Student Association. Ibsen had refused a torchlight procession which the student group had proposed to hold in his honor and reportedly told friends that he did not like the reactionary spirit which dominated the group. When Dietrichson wrote to him in protest, he replied ". . . I do not feel myself allied to a Student Association that is under your leadership." [38]

All of this political turmoil seems to have made a profound impression on Ibsen. In a letter to Brandes dated November 10, 1886, he remarked: "The impressions I received from my journey in Norway last summer and the observations I made disturbed me for a long time. And not until I had come to a distinct understanding of my experience and I had drawn my conclusions could I think of transforming my thoughts into a work of fiction." [39] Some months earlier he had commented in a letter to Count Snoilsky that he was engaged in writing a play for which he had "made careful studies" when he was in Norway.[40] He is quoted also as having observed in conversation that his homeland was populated not by two million human beings but by two million dogs and cats.[41]

The Norwegian political situation served as the starting point for *Rosmersholm*, but by the time the play was finished it had become a work that far transcended immediate and local political concerns. His comments to Björn Kristensen in a letter written approximately a month after the play had had its premiere seem to indicate that Ibsen regarded the play's political and even moral content as of secondary importance. "The call to work is undoubtedly one of the themes running through *Rosmersholm*. But the play also deals with the struggle which all serious minded human beings have to wage with themselves in order to bring their lives into harmony with their convictions. . . . But the play is, of course, first and foremost a story of human beings and human destiny." [42]

It appears, then, that Ibsen simply used the political situation as a framework for a larger comment about human destiny, much as he had used the "true marriage" in *The Wild Duck*. Indeed, the comments contained in the above letter bear a close relation to his comments about *Catiline*, "the conflict between one's aims and one's possibilities, between what man proposes and what is actually possible." [43] The political point of departure may, however, partly explain the fact that the element of mystery and fantasy which figures so prominently in the previous play is less obtrusive here. Yet even though *Rosmersholm* may, on the surface, appear to be more realistic than its predecessor, it marks a definite advance in the direction of myth.

The plot of the play centers around the apostasy of Johannes Rosmer from the traditional teachings of the church and the conservative political beliefs of his family. As the sole descendent of a long line of clergymen, military officers, and government officials, Pastor Rosmer is the last living representative of a family that has set the moral tone for the whole local community. He had formerly been married to the sister of Rector Kroll, headmaster of the local school and acknowledged leader of the conservative faction. His wife, Beata, had, however, been ill for some years before the play opens and had committed suicide by leaping into the mill run that flows through the Rosmer property. The other member of the household at the beginning of the play is Rebecca West, a young woman of mysterious origins who had served as a sort of companion to Beata before her death. Now she acts as housekeeper for Rosmer, though there is a maid to do the actual work. All of this constitutes the outward appearance of things at the beginning of the drama.

The curtain has not been up long, however, before the audience learns that not everything is as it seems. Rosmer has not only given up his pastorate following Beata's death, he has also given up his Christian beliefs. In keeping with his new attitude toward religion he is on the point of becoming a convert to political liberalism. This revelation has two consequences. First, it precipitates a break with his brother-in-law, Kroll, who regards Rosmer's changed attitude as apostasy and treason. Second, it brings the leader of the radical party, Peder Mortensgaard, to the estate to seek Rosmer's help in the forthcoming political battle. But Rosmer is not interested in specific political causes; he wishes, like Brand and Gregers Werle, to ennoble mankind. When he realizes that Mortensgaard wishes to use his position as a Christian leader to bolster the radical cause, he refuses to go along with the deception.

Despite Rosmer's apparent devotion to truth, deception infects the very air at Rosmersholm. His new attitudes are largely the work of Rebecca, whose foster father, Dr. West, was a radical and freethinker and has left to her his library of "advanced" books. Rebecca, furthermore, has done a good deal more than merely exert her intellectual influence on Rosmer. She has, according to her own confession, planted seeds of suspicion concerning herself and Rosmer in Beata's mind and thus prompted the latter's suicide. As Rosmer slowly begins to suspect that something in his own relationship with Rebecca has contributed to Beata's act, he is attacked by a growing sense of guilt that leads him to doubt his ability to lead men to any kind of ennoblement. At the same time Rebecca has slowly fallen under the influence of the "Rosmer view of life." This development is accelerated by certain events in the play and she is at last rendered unable to seize the prize that her struggles have won her. She and Rosmer decide that some form of atonement is necessary for the wrongs they have committed, and together they leap off the footbridge, finding death in the same mill run that had claimed Beata.

To outward appearances, the plot of *Rosmersholm* could be played out entirely in realistic terms. Yet we are not far into the play before we begin to get the feeling that there are strange forces at work behind the action, forces that are only partially accessible to realistic interpretations. At the beginning of the first act Rebecca and Madame Helseth watch Rosmer returning from his daily walk and note that he still refuses to cross the footbridge from which Beata leaped to her death. Then follow the lines that give the first intimation of the mystery that lies behind the realistic action.

REBECCA. . . . . They cling to their dead here at Rosmersholm.

MME. HELSETH. Now, I think, Miss, that it's the dead who cling to Rosmersholm.

REBECCA. The dead?

MME. HELSETH. Yes, it's almost as if they can't get completely away from those that are left.

REBECCA. How did you hit upon that?

MME. HELSETH. Well, I suppose otherwise that white horse wouldn't come around.

The ghostly white horse that visits Rosmersholm when someone is about to die reappears as a recurrent symbol throughout the play. At first Rebecca treats it lightly, but as the play progresses her original attitude of skepticism changes to one of tentative belief. She herself remarks, after her confession has caused Rosmer to leave in anger and disillusionment, "I thought I saw something like a glimpse of the white horses." In the final scene Rebecca carries her white shawl out onto the footbridge and it is that which causes Madame Helseth to call out as she watches the suicide leap, "Oh God — that white thing there!" The connection with the white horse is clear and unmistakable.

The full symbolic significance of the white horse in connection with the action of the play will be considered later; here it is necessary only to examine the roots of the symbol in Norse mythology. The horse as a warning of death is a common motif in Scandinavian folklore and mythology. The *Aasgaardsreien*, the procession of riders who carry the dead off to Valhalla, has already appeared in *The Vikings at Helgeland*. They are, however, not concerned only with carrying off the slain in battle but become a generalized symbol of death. Where the *Aasgaardsreien* stop and throw their saddles on the roof someone is bound to die.[44] Even more closely related to the use of the horse symbol in *Rosmersholm* is the legend of the *kirkegrimer*. When the first churches were built in ancient Scandinavia, they were frequently consecrated by sacrificing an animal to the old gods. The most common method was to bury the animal alive near the church. The ghosts of these animals were said to wander at night and when seen they augured important events either good or evil. Some place names seem to have been derived from this practice. In the Swedish province of Skåne, for example, there is a place called Hestveda (from *hest hvite*, white horse) because a white horse was the *kirkegrim* there.[45]

Still another connection with mythology is provided in the concept of the *fylgje*, which was a guardian spirit that attached itself to a family or an individual. When that *fylgje* was seen in the form of an animal it signified death. In *The Vikings at Helgeland* Hjördis' *fylgje* was a wolf, but Turville-Petre reports that in one of the old tales a doomed man saw his *fylgje* in a dream in the form of a blood-colored horse.[46]

There is little doubt that Ibsen was here making use of a fragment of Norse mythology, especially when we consider his earlier use of a similar device in *The Vikings at Helgeland*. Probably even in Ibsen's day these ideas survived as superstition in the country districts of Norway. Pavel Fraenkl argues that not only does the use of the white horse add a deeper collective element to the "realistic" drama but that its use is absolutely essential to the play. "Without white horses, without the death-ritual that ties itself to them, and without the connected *mystic* tradition that lies behind this conception, there is no drama that can rightly be called *Rosmersholm*." [47]

The white horse is perhaps the most important mythical element in the play, but it is not the only one. Another can be found in Rebecca West herself. Her influence over Rosmer can be explained in perfectly realistic psychological terms, and yet Ibsen goes to some lengths to provide her with connections with the world of the supernatural. First of all, she is an orphan of uncertain background. Her mother has long since died, her foster father, Dr. West, is now dead, and she knows nothing of her real father. She is also an outsider, brought from the North by Dr. West. These two facts in themselves do not, of course, make her a mythic figure, but the region from which she comes is significant in this context. The district of Finmark, in the extreme north of Norway, was commonly held to be the home of demons, trolls, and witches. In one of the oldest of Norse literary works, the *Heimskringla*, there are accounts of witchcraft in Finmark and in Finland, which lies still farther north. One of the sources upon which Joseph Campbell draws in discussing the mythical journey through death and back to life is a joint volume published in Copenhagen in 1767, containing Knud Leem's *Beskrivelse over Finmarkens Lapper* and E. F. Jessen's *Afhandling om de Norske Finners og Lappers Hedenske Religion*. Both of these works contain accounts of a Finnish shaman's journey to the kingdom of the dead.[48] Rebecca's original name was Gamvik and this too may have been meant to have mythical connotations. The Norwegian word *gamme* refers to a Lapp turf hut or dugout and the morphologically similar word *gand* denotes Lapp sorcery. Thus, Gamvik may denote both the place of the Lapps and/or the place of sorcerers.[49] It would seem that Ibsen has deliberately provided Rebecca with a background that permits her to be regarded as something more than a mere human, a suggestion which is supported by his biographer, Koht.[50] The impressions created by her background are, in fact, carried out at several points in the text: Kroll accuses her of having bewitched both him and Beata, Ulrik Brendel refers to her as charmer and mermaid, and she calls herself a sea-troll which has attached itself to Rosmer's ship.

The symbolism of the white horse and the suggestion that Rebecca herself may be a witch are not mere "window dressing." They are intimately linked to the themes of the play. There are two closely related themes — indeed, so closely related that it is difficult to treat them separately. Despite the risk of oversimplification they can be labeled, first, the pattern of guilt and retribution and, second, the conflict between the traditional morality and the emancipated views of the future. Both themes are, in turn, closely related to the events leading up to the suicide of Beata.

Rebecca West is, according to her own confession, guilty of complicity in the death of Beata. Whether or not her action can be called murder depends in part on the extent to which it was under conscious control. The motive she had articulated for herself and, at first, for Rosmer was that she wished to free him from his joyless marriage so that he could become a complete and emancipated human being. It had been Rebecca's wish to wean Rosmer away from the stifling tradition of Rosmersholm, its conservative political and its orthodox moral and religious views. In many respects Beata embodies that tradition. That she is a representative of the anti-life forces is apparent from the first act. Beata could not stand flowers; their smell and their profuse colors bewildered her. Now that she is gone Rebecca has filled the house with flowers. Furthermore, Beata was barren, a fact which seems to have contributed to her "overstrained" condition. (To be fair, however, Rosmer's prissy reaction to her sexuality indicates that he may have been responsible both for her barrenness and her nervous condition.) Children, for Ibsen, tend to be, as they are traditionally, symbols for productivity and life (compare, for example, Eilert Lövborg's "child" and Rubek's). The fact that Beata is barren, plus her inability to tolerate flowers (another common life symbol) suggests the sterility of the Rosmer heritage. Consequently, in order to free Rosmer from the grip of his tradition Beata had to be removed. This Rebecca determined to do "by one means or another." But upon further self-examination, she discovers that her motives were not so disinterested as she had thought. In fact, she was in the grip of a force that pushed her forward each time she hesitated, a force she at last recognizes as an "uncontrollable passion" for Rosmer. To the extent that Rosmer did nothing to relieve his wife's condition and failed to realize the degree to which his relationship with Rebecca contributed to it, he can be said to have aided and abetted Rebecca's scheme. Indeed, after Rebecca's confession Rosmer begins to suspect his own motives and to ask himself to what degree he was unconsciously in love with Rebecca and unconsciously relieved by his wife's death.

Nevertheless, Rebecca's plan succeeded. She induced Rosmer to leave the church, to give up his former political views, and to devote himself to promoting the "new truths" of liberalism. She is, of course, not solely responsible for his "conversion," as she sees it, or his "apostasy," as it is viewed by Kroll. There is a clear suggestion that the first liberal influences upon him had come from his former tutor, Ulrik Brendel, who had been run off the place

with a horsewhip by Rosmer's father. In the scene in which Bren-
del returns one begins to suspect that young Johannes may have
had more respect for his radical tutor than for his martinet father.
At any rate he greets him with affection and falls easy prey to
Brendel's confidence game, "lending" him both clothes and money.
It is clearly Rebecca, however, who brought about the final change.

But Rosmer is not interested in specific political issues. Rather
he wishes to go from house to house ennobling individuals, perhaps creating that "nobility of character . . . of will and spirit"
of which Ibsen spoke to the workingmen of Trondhjem in the
summer of 1885.[51] The intimations of guilt surrounding him and
Rebecca, however, lead him to doubt his ability to create nobility
of character in others. He feels that one who starts out on such
work must begin free of sin. (For a former minister of the gospel
this is an interesting opinion. In orthodox Protestant theology only
Christ can claim the distinction of being free of sin.) In the final
analysis both Rosmer and Rebecca fail to achieve their goals. Despite their "emancipation" they are defeated by the orthodox morality of the Rosmer tradition.

The earthly representatives of that tradition are, of course,
Kroll and his faction, but it is not they before whom Rosmer falls.
Though he is surprised and hurt by their vindictive attitude, he is
still ready to defy them. It is, rather, the spirit of Beata, as she begins to make herself felt after Mortensgaard's visit and as she works
through Rebecca's confession, that destroys him. Beata is directly
identified with the white horse that continues to visit Rosmersholm
after she is dead. The connection is implicit throughout the play
but is made clear in Madame Helseth's final line, "Oh God — that
white thing there! The dead wife has taken them!" Beata haunts
her husband and the woman who has led her to her death, and
drives them to their graves in the same way that she died — by leaping into the mill run. Thus far, then, the pattern of the play follows
that of Aeschylus' *Eumenides*, with the difference that the Furies
do not become merciful at the conclusion of *Rosmersholm*.

However, the spirit of Beata which hovers over the action and
provides a supernatural dimension to the play is also a representa-

tive of the Rosmer tradition. Thus, she is not only an avenging spirit but one of the forces in a cosmic conflict that operates behind the realistic action. The opposing party of emancipation has as its earthly representatives Rebecca, Peder Mortensgaard, and, to a lesser degree, Ulrik Brendel, but it too has a spirit hovering in the background. The deceased Dr. West has an enormous indirect influence on the action. When Rebecca came to Rosmersholm she could be said to be her foster father's intellectual creation. He was solely responsible for her education and had left her his library of emancipated books, her only earthly possessions. Kroll's thinly veiled hints suggest that she may have been his physical creation as well; Dr. West may have been her real father. (The fact that he seems also to have been her lover, with its implications of incest, is apparently the final blow that causes Rebecca to capitulate to the Rosmer morality.) The uncontrollable passion which pushed Rebecca to her crime came over her, she says, "like a storm at sea" and such storms, as Professor Haakonsen points out, usually come from the west.[52] Indeed, the west as a source of destruction and evil is a part of Christian tradition. In the Byzantine Church, Eliade indicates, the altar is in the east and the west is "the realm of darkness, of grief, of death, the realm of the eternal mansions of the dead, who await the resurrection of the flesh and the Last Judgement." [53] Thus, two spirits seem to be hovering behind the action, Beata as representative of the Rosmer tradition and Dr. West as a representative of a different, more pagan spirit.

Valency would seem to be correct, then, in asserting that *Rosmersholm* is a playing out of the conflict of *Emperor and Galilean* in contemporary terms.[54] On the one hand is Christianity and traditional morality represented by the Rosmer tradition, by Kroll, and by the spirit of Beata. On the other there is paganism, embodied in Rebecca, perhaps in Brendel, and in the spirit of Dr. West. If this is so, Rosmer, who is torn between the two traditions, is the equivalent of Julian and the role of Maximus is divided between Rebecca and Brendel. In this connection it is interesting to note that Brendel functions in much the same manner as the mythic guide, appearing at two crucial points in the action to urge Rosmer onward.

In this play, however, both traditions are presented in a less flattering light. The Rosmer tradition is anti-life and anti-happiness. As embodied in Kroll and in Rosmer's late father it is what Nietzsche would have referred to as a morality of the whip. Transgressors such as Mortensgaard, Brendel, and, ultimately, Rosmer himself are driven from the fold with no thought of forgiveness or understanding. As embodied in Rosmer the tradition is less severe but it is also weak. Like Gregers Werle, Rosmer has a sick conscience. He agonizes over his lost innocence to a degree that is hardly justified by the actual extent of his guilt. Indeed, his very assumption that innocence is obtainable by man is a bit presumptuous. Despite his supposed "liberation," the Rosmer morality does not permit him to enjoy life even to the mildest degree without pangs of conscience. In fact, if one examines his final scene with Rebecca without presuppositions about his nobility, it is difficult to repress a shudder. There is something sick and sadistic about a man who deliberately taunts another person to her death, something which, as in the case of Gregers, belies the nobility of his declarations.

The emancipated view of life represented by Rebecca is little better. Whereas the Rosmer view lacks strength and joy, the alternative is not tempered by any form of morality. Dr. West, as the guardian spirit of the emancipated view, is far from being a savory character. Rebecca's own desire to free Rosmer is unaffected by any considerations of the worth of Beata as a human being — she is simply in the way and must be got rid of. As long as Rebecca can attribute her actions to an unselfish motive, however, she remains sure of herself. It is under the influence of the Rosmer morality that she begins to examine her motives and to discover that they are tainted by a strong admixture of sexual passion and selfish desire. At the same time, she is marked by her relationship with Dr. West and doubly so by the suggestion that he may have been her father. Thus, she stands guilty by the stern judgments of the Rosmer morality. Her realization of her own guilt may have, as she says, ennobled her, but it has also destroyed her capacity for happiness. The two traditions destroy each other; Rosmer and Rebecca leap off the footbridge to their deaths, leaving the field to the "lord and leader" of the future, Peder Mortensgaard.

I am not convinced that Ibsen meant the judgment of Mortensgaard which he put in the mouth of Ulrik Brendel to be taken negatively, at least not entirely so. Again, a careful examination of Mortensgaard's actions, as opposed to others' opinions of him, will indicate that he has not acted unscrupulously. Beata's letter had provided him with an ideal political weapon against the conservative camp, but he has not used it. Even the sexual misadventure which had originally made him a figure of scandal in the community is somewhat mitigated by Madame Helseth's account of it. True, he can live without ideals, but so can Dr. Relling; furthermore, we have seen both the tainted nature of Rosmer's ideals and the place to which they have ultimately brought him.

If my reading of the play and of the character of Mortensgaard is correct, the continuity with *The Wild Duck* is not broken. Man, even the noblest of men, is not free from guilt, and only a few men, those who do not make too great demands on life, are capable of facing it and surviving. The Galilean and the pagan views cancel each other out, but the third empire that emerges is of a more modest nature than that envisaged in *Emperor and Galilean*. The Rellings and the Mortensgaards can live, and can even, if listened to, point the way to a reasonably comfortable if unheroic existence. At the same time, however, Ibsen seems to be somewhat more sympathetic with his idealists than he was in the previous play. Both Rosmer and Rebecca somehow transcend their guilt and limitations. Implicit in *Rosmersholm* is a suggestion, to be more fully developed in subsequent plays, that there are people who *must* seek ideals no matter to what destructive heights or depths that search may take them.

In *The Wild Duck* and *Rosmersholm*, myth is still implicit rather than obvious. The powers of the loft, the white horse, and the spirits of Beata and Dr. West with all they represent still operate outside the main action. They are not physically present on the stage. As Ibsen continued to write, he became even more interested in the occult and actually introduced it onto the stage in some of the later plays. The first experiment of this sort was the play that immediately followed, *The Lady from the Sea.*

THE LADY FROM THE SEA AND HEDDA
GABLER · MYTH AND PSYCHOLOGICAL STUDY

⁋ IN THE writing of *The Wild Duck* and *Rosmersholm* Ibsen had still made use of the social problem as a kind of framework upon which to build a larger and more significant action. The question that lies behind the problem of the "true marriage" in the former is no less than, How can man manage to live in the world? Behind the relatively insignificant local political struggle of the latter there is the same cosmic conflict between opposed principles that had animated *Emperor and Galilean.* In his next two plays he was to turn from the social problem and embark on the course that he was to follow for the rest of his career — the intensive psychological analysis of a single human being. This is not to suggest, however, that Ibsen became clinically interested in mental and personality aberrations. Rather, it reflects his shift from concern with the individual functioning in society to the individual for his own sake. No longer were the problems social, legal, or medical nor were the struggles mainly with other characters. More and more the struggles came to be with the universe, both outwardly and as it is contained microcosmically within man, and the problems became problems of meaning, of significance, of the value of human life and action. These later plays are autobiographical, perhaps, to the extent that they reveal a kind of struggle that had been going on in Ibsen himself for some years, as suggested by the first two lines of a quatrain he wrote in 1878:

> At leve er — krig med trolde
> i hjertet og hjernens hvaelv.
> (To live — is to battle with trolls
> in the vaults of the heart and the mind.)

In the two plays to be discussed in this chapter Ibsen focused his attention on two women, extending in them certain of the characteristics of Rebecca West. Ellida Wangel is a woman in the grip of a mysterious power, Hedda Gabler is woman as a destructive force. Yet the plays are not that simple. Both of them continue to develop the life-problem and the possible answers to it that were implicit in Ibsen's two previous plays. At the same time, those mysterious powers which were present offstage in the preceding plays make their appearance onstage in one of these.

The Lady from the Sea · The Lure of the Unknown

The symbolism of the sea plays an important part in several of Ibsen's earlier works and is quite evident in both *The Wild Duck* and *Rosmersholm*. Hedvig's loft is, in one poetic sense, the "depths of the sea," and its contents were bequeathed to the Ekdal family by the "Flying Dutchman." Rebecca West was overcome by a passion that swept over her "like a storm at sea," she refers to herself as a sea-troll, and Ulrik Brendel calls her mermaid. In *The Lady from the Sea* the ocean, with its almost mystic powers of attraction and destruction, becomes central to the action.

This intensification of interest in the sea may be due in part to the influence of two summers Ibsen spent living near it, at Molde, Norway, in 1885 and at Saeby, Denmark, two years later. Koht indicates that during the second summer Ibsen made a practice of sitting or standing for long hours staring out at the water.[1] At the conclusion of his stay at Saeby he is quoted as having said to Hans Jaeger: "There is something extraordinarily captivating in the sea.

When one stands and stares down into the water it is as if one sees that life which stirs about on land, only in another form. There is connection and similarity in everything. In my next work the sea shall play a part." [2]

That next work was *The Lady from the Sea*, and his notes for that play seem to reveal an ambivalent attitude toward the sea. On the one hand he speculates, as does Ellida, on whether or not the course of human evolution may have gone astray and on why it is that we have come to belong to the land rather than to the sea or the air. He predicts also that men will eventually take possession of the sea, build their cities on it, and learn to cope with its storms and stresses. [3] On the other hand he says: "The sea rules over the power of one's moods and works like a will. The sea can hypnotize, Nature in general can do that. The great secret is the dependence of the human will on the 'will-less.' " [4] In further notes Ibsen wrote, "It is the sea that attracts her with mysterious power," and refers to "the daemonic attraction of the completely unknown." [5]

The sea, then, constitutes the major part of the mythic background of the play, but other influences make themselves felt as well. During his stay at Molde Ibsen had heard an old lady from Nordland tell of a *kvaen* (a native of Finmark) who had, with the troll-power of his eyes, lured a pastor's wife away from her husband and children. During the same summer he was told of a seaman who had been missing so long that he was presumed drowned, yet who suddenly turned up to find his wife married to another man. Two years later at Saeby he heard of a local girl who, apparently out of frustration and unfulfilled longing to get out into the world and be a poet, had shot herself. This incident so fascinated Ibsen that he called at her home, obtained pictures of her, read the books she left behind, and even visited her grave. [6] During the same period, Koht reports, Ibsen became intensely interested in hypnotism and other phenomena that we would today call extrasensory perception. [7] All of these impressions, stories, and obsessions he seems to have combined into the plot for *The Lady from the Sea*.

There are three plots in the play, one main plot and two subplots. The main plot revolves around Ellida Wangel and the return of her mysterious sailor lover to persuade her to leave her husband and follow him. The second involves the marriage of Arnholm and Dr. Wangel's older daughter, Boletta, and serves as a parallel and an ironic comment on the main plot. The third involves the tubercular artist, Lyngstrand, and his dreams of artistic achievement which the audience knows will never be realized because of his lung condition. All three plots are woven together in such a way that they comment upon one another.

Some years before the play opens Ellida had married Dr. Wangel, coming to preside over his home and act as stepmother to his two nearly grown daughters. The couple have no children of their own, their one son having died in infancy. Ellida is, for a variety of reasons, not happy in the home of Dr. Wangel. In the first place, she was a lighthouse keeper's daughter, and in the little village at the head of the fjord where she now lives she feels cut off from the sea which had been so much a part of her earlier life. Second, she has no real task in the Wangel household since Boletta manages the domestic duties and Ellida does not feel old enough to act as stepmother to the young girls — even if they wanted her to function in that role, as she is convinced they do not. Furthermore, she seems to have little communication with her husband. In short, to use a modern term, Ellida is alienated. She is cut off from her natural element, from any meaningful task in life, even from the people who surround her.

It is not her position in the Wangel household alone, however, that is to blame for Ellida's distress. Her present situation is intimately bound up with a previous experience. Some time before her marriage (the exact amount of time is unclear) she had had an affair of sorts with the second mate of an American ship that was in port in her home community. One morning the sailor revealed to her that he had killed the captain of his ship and had to flee. He urged Ellida to wait for him and attempted to assure her compliance by attaching their two rings together and flinging them out into the water, thus "marrying" them to each other and to the sea. After the sailor had gone Ellida wrote him two letters attempting to break off the relationship. These letters he ignored and continued to write to her. After a while, though, the letters stopped and Ellida, assuming he had finally forgotten her, married Dr. Wangel. For a time everything seemed to go smoothly, but during her pregnancy with their child Ellida dreamed she saw her seaman standing at the foot of the bed and staring at her. When the child was born she imagined that it had the seaman's eyes and refused to sleep with Wangel.[8] Now, feeling useless in Wangel's household, she is tormented by her recollections of her earlier experience.

So far this reads like a classic case history in psychology: the wife, unhappy with her marriage, begins to dream of her former lover and that dream eventually becomes an obsession. It is at this point that the Stranger, as he is called, returns for Ellida, and it is at this point that the play begins to diverge from the form of a purely psychological drama. The Stranger is a mysterious figure, almost unreal, and Ellida is terrified of him even though she is at the same time strongly drawn to him. At the conclusion of his first visit the Stranger leaves, warning Ellida that he will return the next day and at that time she had better be ready either to go or to stay. She now begs Wangel for her freedom, which he is reluctant to grant. On the following evening the Stranger returns as he had promised; Ellida is on the point of going with him when Wangel decides to accede to her request and grant her her freedom, but "with responsibility." It is this simple phrase that seems to save her. She rejects the Stranger, telling him that she can now let him go precisely because she was free to choose him.

As we examine the strange triangular relationship among Ellida, the Stranger, and the sea further, the sense of mystery deepens and the simple psychological explanation becomes less and less plausible. Ellida herself is closely related to the sea and the symbolism of the play continually reinforces that connection. She is, as has been indicated, a lighthouse keeper's daughter who feels uncomfortable, indeed, sick, away from the sea. She is named after the legendary Viking ship of Frithjof the Bold that had the power to understand human speech.[9] On that account the pastor in her home community had nicknamed her "the heathen." The people of her new community have little to do with her and call her the lady from the sea.

This name, in Norwegian *fruen fra havet*, is close in form to *havfrue*, mermaid. The latter had, in fact, been Ibsen's original title for the play. By changing it he retained, in Norwegian, the associations of the original title without making the metaphor quite so direct. (Ibsen had done something very similar before and was to again. The original title for *Rosmersholm* was *White Horses* and that for *When We Dead Awaken* was *Resurrection Day*.)

The mermaid metaphor is actually introduced in the opening scene of the play. A minor character, Ballested, is painting a picture of a mermaid who has been washed up from the open sea into the shallow waters of the fjord and is dying there. The subject, he says, was suggested to him by the lady of the house. Only a few minutes later Ellida makes her first entrance, coming from her daily swim in the fjord and is greeted by Wangel as the mermaid. Immediately she complains that the water in the fjord is never fresh but always tepid and sickly. Thus, it is immediately suggested that Ellida is a sea creature who is perishing because she is separated from her natural environment. Later, the scientifically oriented Dr. Wangel tells Arnholm that she belongs to the special race of the sea people who cannot bear transplanting. He is, in fact, ready to give up his local practice and move nearer the sea in order to cure her of her restlessness.

Yet Ellida's relationship with the sea is not so simple as it at first appears. She does seem to regard it as her natural environment and the source of her being, and she speculates, as had Ibsen, about whether people might have been happier had they evolved as sea rather than as land creatures. At the same time, however, she is frightened of the sea; she refers to it as *det grufulde*, a term which can be rendered roughly as "the terrible." The terrible, she explains to Wangel, is that which both frightens and attracts. This fear prompts her to tell Wangel, when he proposes to move to the seacoast, of her affair with the strange seaman.

Being a sailor the Stranger has a literal relationship with the sea, but he is symbolically connected with it in a number of other mysterious ways. In describing her love affair Ellida herself comments on this relationship. They used to sit, she says, for long hours talking of the sea:

> ELLIDA. About storm and about calm. About dark nights on the sea. We also talked about the sea in glittering sunshine. But mostly we talked about whales and porpoises and seals that lie out on the reefs in the midday sun. And then we spoke of gulls and eagles and all the other sea-birds, you know. — And think — isn't it strange — when we talked about such things it seemed to me that he was related to both the sea animals and the sea birds.
>
> WANGEL. And you?
>
> ELLIDA. Yes, I almost felt as if I were one of them too.

To reinforce this impression there is the fact that the Stranger's eyes changed with the condition of the sea; they were bright and clear when it was calm, cloudy and gray when it was stormy. This quality of the eyes was what frightened her so much when she thought she saw it in her own child. A further connection is provided by the Stranger's pearl stickpin, which Ellida describes as resembling the eye of a dead fish. In fact, Ellida's relationship with the Stranger is very like that with the sea; he both frightens and attracts her.

This attraction-repulsion conflict is perhaps explained by the dual nature of the Stranger. First of all, he is a highly mysterious figure. In this play Ibsen resorts to a device that he has not employed since *Peer Gynt*. The Stranger has no biography, no name, not even a clear-cut identity. When Ellida knew him he was a mate on an American ship. Some years later when Lyngstrand knew him he was a boatswain on a Norwegian ship but claimed to be an American by nationality. When he finally appears, he is a passenger on a English tourist liner. He is given two names, Friman and Johnston, but denies the latter and never directly admits to the former. All we really know about him is that he is a *kvaen* — like Rebecca West, he comes from Finmark, though he claims to have emigrated there from Finland. This mysterious effect is exactly what Ibsen desired. In connection with a Berlin performance of the play he wrote to Julius Hoffory: "I must object to having the character listed on the program as 'Ein Seeman'; or 'Ein fremder Seeman,' or 'Ein Steuermann.' Actually he is none of these. . . . No one is supposed to know what he is just as no one is supposed to know *who* he is or what his real name is. This uncertainty about him is the essential element in the method I have deliberately chosen." [10] Moreover, on both occasions when he appears, it is dusk, not only suggesting mystery in itself but also providing the stage manager with an excellent excuse for keeping the lights down and preventing the audience from getting a clear look at him.

In addition to the air of mystery there is an aura of danger surrounding him. He has killed the captain of his ship, a crime which carries overtones, however slight, of regicide or parricide. He carries a revolver. True, he insists that he means to use it only on himself but the mere possession of the weapon makes him potentially dangerous. Third, he may have come back from the dead. Lyngstrand is sure that he had drowned in the same shipwreck that gave Lyngstrand his lung lesion. To reinforce this impression there are the words that Lyngstrand heard him utter when he read of Ellida's marriage: "And she will follow me, if I must come to fetch her as a drowned man from the black sea."

Dangerous and mysterious though the Stranger may be, there must be something attractive about him. At any rate he succeeded in causing Ellida to fall in love with him, or at least to think she had, in a very short time. When he returns, she is at first terrified but later is ready to leave her home and husband to go with him. A part of this attraction must, of course, be attributed to the strange hypnotic power of his eyes through which he was able to bend Ellida to his will in spite of her resistance. Whatever the source of his power, the term that Ellida applies to the sea, *det grufulde* — that which both frightens and attracts — applies equally well to him.

But with all of this mystery, this aura of danger, this hypnotic power, what exactly does the Stranger (and by virtue of the close connection between them, the sea) symbolize? One critic has suggested that he represents death.[11] An argument can certainly be made for this interpretation. First, is the Stranger's association with murder and the revolver that he carries. Second, there are the suggestion that he may have returned from the dead and the extreme fright that he engenders in Ellida. Third, and more subtle, is the fact that Ellida's child, which she thought had the Stranger's eyes, died in infancy. It is quite clear, furthermore, from all that has been said above, that the Stranger is closely identified with the sea and that from the sea — while he was on the same ship as the Stranger — Lyngstrand acquired the lung lesion that the audience and other characters know will kill him. Despite all these associations, however, the symbolic significance of the Stranger must be somewhat more subtle. If he simply represents death, his line to Ellida when she rejects him presents certain difficulties: "It can never be repeated then, Ellida. I will never come to this country again. You will never see me again, nor hear from me again either. I shall be as dead and gone from you forever." Death, even if it is avoided on one occasion, certainly returns. Peer Gynt's Button Moulder, though he is temporarily put off, promises to meet Peer at "the next crossroads." Unless we are willing to credit Ibsen with some arcane form of Christian symbolism, the simple association, Stranger equals death, is hard to maintain. His connection with death must be explained in some other way.

There is another aspect of his character, though, that provides a clue to that connection. His name when Ellida first met him was Friman. He later denies the name of Johnston but not of Friman. The symbolic significance of this name is reinforced not only by his insistence that Ellida come to him in full freedom, but specifically by two lines in the text, one of Ellida's and one of his own. When Wangel tells her that he can protect her from the Stranger by the simple expedient of turning him over to the police for the murder of his captain, she replies, "No, he shall not be caged. He belongs out there on the open sea. That's where he belongs." Later, when Wangel makes the same threat to him, he produces his revolver saying that he will kill himself first for, "jeg vil leve og dö som en fri mand." (I will live and die as a free man.) In Norwegian the *d* on *mand* would not be sounded, so that the words, *fri mand* would sound exactly like the name by which he had earlier been introduced. It is clear, then, that Ibsen intended the Stranger to have a connection with freedom.

Another critic comments that the sea has something to do with love, for it is to the Stranger that Ellida is most strongly drawn and he in turn is associated with the sea.[12] It is interesting, however, that Ellida never says that she loves the Stranger; in fact, she is not sure that she ever loved him. She does indicate on more than one occasion that she loves Wangel, both to him directly and to Arnholm. The power that the Stranger exercises over her must be explained in some other way, and again the explanation is closely tied up with the idea of freedom.

Ellida feels cut off from the real source of her being, the sea; she is alienated in her new home. Insofar as she has no real task to perform and she has no real communication with her stepdaughters or her husband, she feels useless and a prisoner of the bargain she has made in marrying Wangel. This concept of the bargain is important, but not quite so simple as some critics seem to have made it. It is true that Ellida says that she has sold herself to Wangel, and it is true also that the motif of a woman selling herself to a man or vice versa appears in many of Ibsen's plays. Whatever may have been the case at the time of her marriage, however, the marital relationship is not now loveless. The problem, then, lies deeper than an unsatisfactory marriage. The crucial factor is the imprisonment which Ellida feels is her lot. Indeed, imprisonment is the condition of the whole community and household as Boletta makes clear with her metaphor of the carp pond.

Yet Ibsen's treatment of the freedom theme is highly ambiguous. If the sea and the Stranger represent freedom, they also represent a dangerous unknown. Ellida has never, for all her longing for the sea, ventured out on an actual sea voyage. The Stranger is a murderer and the sea has destroyed Lyngstrand. Arnholm suggests, also, that the poor "house fish" would not actually thrive in the open sea. Thus, full freedom, the only condition under which the Stranger will accept Ellida, is fraught with peril. When one ventures out onto the open sea he must be prepared to face dangerous, even fatal, consequences. Ellida is faced, therefore, with a choice between a stifling life of security with Wangel and a dangerous life of freedom with the Stranger. Ultimately, Wangel meets the Stranger's challenge by granting her freedom but adding to it the concept of responsibility. This suddenly changes Ellida's idea of her condition and makes it possible for her to reject her demon lover and all that he represents. Valency feels that this combination of freedom, the pagan principle, with responsibility, the spirit of the Galilean, is the equivalent of the establishment in Ellida's spiritual state of the third empire.[18] Arild Haaland also provides an interesting insight when he points out that the freedom problem does not involve Ellida alone. By granting her her freedom Wangel also takes a chance on the unknown; he makes a complete commitment to her as a person, something which he had not previously done. Such a commitment is the equivalent of what Kierkegaard called "life at forty thousand fathoms," a completely engaged life of which one cannot know the final consequences.[14]

And yet, tempting as it may seem to conclude that Ibsen was recommending a modest accommodation with life, the ambiguities are not yet finished. The Stranger's threat to Ellida which has been previously cited strikes an ominous note — "It can never be repeated then, Ellida." If the Stranger represents a kind of freedom, however dangerous, Ellida has only one last chance at it. If one does not seize his freedom when the opportunity arrives, "it can never be repeated." When the Stranger's kind of freedom and Wangel's are put into the balance, which should be chosen is unclear. Perhaps, as the two preceding plays seem to imply, freedom is for those strong enough and brave enough to take it, whereas others must work out an accommodation with life in more modest terms. Yet the course of freedom with responsibility which Ellida follows may be on a slightly higher plane than the cynicism of Relling or the opportunism of Mortensgaard.

The two subplots and the minor characters simply provide variations or comments on this same theme; in a sense, they suggest alternative ways of coming to terms with existence. The Arnholm-Boletta subplot has been cited by many critics as a parallel with the

Wangel-Ellida marriage (and Arnholm has frequently been interpreted as another Dr. Wangel, equally good-hearted and understanding). In fact, it is nothing of the kind, but, rather, an ironic commentary on it. From the moment Arnholm enters his express purpose is to marry Boletta. There is, of course, nothing wrong about a man of his age exhibiting an interest in a young girl, except that he is in various ways dishonest about his intentions. He frequently makes comments about Boletta, then amends them so that they apply to both of the sisters. Even this would not be negative conduct but for the fact that it is part of a larger pattern. Under the mistaken impression that she was longing for her old tutor, Wangel has invited Arnholm to visit. Arnholm previously proposed to Ellida and was rejected, yet when she asks him whether he has since looked around for anyone else, he assures her that he has been true to his memories. Coming on the heels of his obvious interest in Boletta, this line is ironic at best. Furthermore, he is so jealous of the time that Boletta spends with Lyngstrand that he goes so far as to try to discredit the artist with Wangel. This is hardly ethical conduct; it is, in fact, in direct contrast to the action of Wangel who, in order to help Ellida, deliberately invites for a visit the person whom he assumed to have been Ellida's former love.

The Arnholm-Boletta proposal scene only reinforces these observations. There are actually two relevant scenes. In the first of them Boletta reveals her frustration, her sense of imprisonment, and her desire to get out into the world. Arnholm promises to help her by broaching the subject of her higher education to Wangel. At this point the audience already knows of his special interest in Boletta. Following this scene the tutor has only two conversations with Wangel — a five-minute whispered exchange at the end of the fourth act, and a continuation of an offstage conversation in which the subject seems to have been principally Ellida and her problems. But before Arnholm proposes, he tells Boletta that he and Wangel have discussed the subject and that she can hope for no help from her father. There is no absolute proof that Arnholm is lying, but neither is there firm evidence that he actually kept his promise and spoke to Wangel.

The second scene, the proposal itself, is equally interesting in the way in which the offer of marriage is presented. Boletta's hopes of possibly going away to school have been dashed. Arnholm then makes what appears to be a disinterested offer of help. Only after Boletta joyfully accepts does he reveal the string that is attached — the matter of marriage. When she refuses he renews his offer of help, but the proposal has placed Boletta in a different relationship with him. She can no longer accept his help. He then proceeds to apply the pressure by reminding her of what a dull and uninteresting life she will lead and of the fact that when her father is dead she will be alone in the world and may have to turn for help to some other man whom she does not love either. At this point Boletta accepts. In a sense she does sell herself into a marriage with a man she does not love in order that he may provide her with a means of escape from her confining situation. It seems difficult to argue, however, that she does so cold-bloodedly and deliberately. Rather, she is subtly but deliberately forced into her action by a man who knows how to manipulate and apply pressure. In the light of Arnholm's earlier equivocal conduct, it may even be doubtful whether he will keep his end of the bargain. Recall that Arnholm observes that the carp are better off in captivity, that they would not thrive in the open sea. This suggests that he is far more likely to turn out to be another Thorvald Helmer than another Dr. Wangel.

Another approach to life is represented by Lyngstrand, especially in his relationship with Hilda. As an aspiring artist he lives in a fantasy world, dreaming of the great masterpiece that he will create after he gets to Italy where the climate is more congenial. All the while, however, the audience and the other characters know that he will not live to create any masterpiece. He too, of course, knows about his lung lesion but his fantasy life triumphs even there. He is able to rationalize it out of existence, to convince himself that it is merely an annoyance that will disappear once he gets to Italy. In short, his whole life consists of dreaming and pretense.

He approaches love in the same fashion. He does not really want a woman but merely the thought that a woman is waiting for him and thinking about him. Originally he looks to Boletta to fulfill that role, but when she becomes involved with Arnholm he quite readily switches to Hilda. Lyngstrand, like Peer Gynt and Hjalmar Ekdal, lives quite contentedly in a world of self-created fantasy.

Though not a part of one of the subplots, Ballested too provides a comment on the life problem. Originally a touring actor who got stranded in the community, he has become a local jack-of-all-trades — barber, dancing master, horn player, and leader of the local music society. He has, as he says, "acclimatized" himself. The deliberate irony with which Ballested is handled is apparent in a number of ways: in the incongruent coupling of trades — artist and barber; in the fact that he cannot even pronounce the word that describes his adjustment to the community; and in the fact that he speaks three languages, two of them badly.

There are, then, five alternative ways of life offered in the play. The first is the life of dangerous and anarchic freedom held out to Ellida by the Stranger. She rejects that life in favor of what is ostensibly the better choice, the life of freedom with responsibility. However, in choosing the latter, as the Stranger points out, she forfeits her last chance at the former. The third is that of the realist, as exemplified by Arnholm. He knows what he wants out of life and how to get it, using a carrot-and-stick technique alternately to lure and force Boletta into marriage. She, too, might be said to take a realistic approach in marrying Arnholm so that he may help her escape, but in fact she may be deceiving herself. Fourth, there is the helpless dreamer, Lyngstrand, so adept at pretense that he can even rationalize away his impending death. Last, there is Ballested, the dilettante who keeps himself busy with all kinds of activities, at none of which he excels. None of the alternatives is presented in a very favorable light. The Stranger's course is fraught with danger and possible death, Arnholm's seems to be ethically questionable, and Lyngstrand's is a "life-lie." In a sense, Ballested's way seems the most foolish of all, but there may be a connection between it and the way of life chosen by Ellida. She too "acclimatizes" herself; she adjusts to the life she has, and the audience must hope — indeed, is led to hope — that Hilda will at last look upon her as a mother and that now some communication will be established between herself and her husband. If so, she has achieved a kind of victory, but a modest and unheroic one which would hardly satisfy Brand or some of Ibsen's later idealists.

Clearly, Ibsen has used the Ellida Wangel story to conduct yet another examination of the problem of how one should live in the world. Ellida is in search of a meaningful existence, one that will give her satisfaction and a sense of identity, and the positive ending of the play suggests that she has found it. The mood is less bitter than *The Wild Duck* and less somber than *Rosmersholm*, but the problem dealt with is essentially the same. In that sense, Ibsen continues the development of his mythic world view; he presents another perspective on a teleological problem. He goes further in the direction of myth, however, than he had in his two previous plays. The elements of the occult which have lurked in the background in the earlier plays are here introduced onto the stage, chiefly in the person of the Stranger.

The Stranger is a figure of mystery, and that is what Ibsen wanted him to be. We are constantly faced with the question of his reality. Those who wish to interpret the play as a psychological study have frequently taken the Stranger to be a projection of Ellida's psyche.[15] There is, unfortunately, a real difficulty with this conclusion. Both Hilda and Lyngstrand see the Stranger and Lyngstrand is able to recognize him as a man he had sailed with years before. A figment proceeding from Ellida's tortured psyche could hardly make itself so corporeal as to be seen and recognized by other characters. But if he is simply a real sailor, what accounts for his strange power over Ellida, for the air of mystery which surrounds him, for the frightening quality he communicates when he actually appears? Archer is, I think, correct when he suggests that Ibsen's method here is similar to that of Hawthorne. He is deliberately ambiguous as to whether the Stranger is a real or a supernatural character or both.[16] Ellida's problem, then, appears to be more than merely psychological or even philosophical. She may very well be the victim of supernatural powers intervening in the universe. Ibsen's notes for the play indicate that he was less interested in aberrant psychology or in a philosophical question than he was in the mysterious powers residing in nature, the same powers that had made themselves felt in *The Wild Duck*.

Indeed, the very structure of the play is formed out of legendary material that appears in variant forms throughout Europe. Pavel Fraenkl traces the story of the husband or lover returning from the dead to claim an unfaithful wife or sweetheart to a ballad entitled "Lenore," written in 1773. It also appears in a Polish folk ballad and in a Czech ballad entitled "The Wedding Shirt" by Karl Jaromir Erben.[17] An American ballad, actually a version of an English ballad, found in the hills of Kentucky and West Virginia presents a similar story of a returning lover, though his demonic qualities are more pronounced in the English than the American version.[18] The story also had a wide currency in Scandinavian folklore. In Nicolaisen's *Sagn og Eventyr fra Nordland* there is a story of a dead lover who visits his sweetheart at night and urges her to follow him. In a second story by J. Qvigstad the lover is a soldier rather than a sailor; he visits his sweetheart on her wedding day and spirits her away. Still a third variant on the story comes from Troms and Finmark; in it a captain lost at sea while fishing visits his fiancée on a white horse and requires her to go with him.[19]

To summarize, then, it can be said that Ibsen has constructed a drama on three levels. The first is the psychological plane; *The Lady from the Sea* is the story of a disturbed young woman and, as such, reveals some acute insights into the nature of emotional disorder. Valency feels that as a psychological study Ellida's case is unduly complicated and could not be cured so easily as it is in the concluding scene.[20] This would be true were the story purely a case study, but it exists, as Valency recognizes, on a philosophical plane as well. It embodies an idea of how one can live in the world and attempts to discover a way that is neither the futile idealism of Gregers and Rosmer, the cynical compromising of Mortensgaard, nor the simple-minded dwelling in illusion of the Ekdals. There is a sense, however, in which one could say that a teleological question embodied in a story or drama is moving from the purely philosophical to the mythical. Ibsen has constructed his play on this third plane by throwing over it a veil of mystery, by using the sea and its creature, the Stranger, as mysterious and potentially dangerous forces, and by basing his drama on an old and common folk tale. Thus he takes advantage, as he did with the white horse in *Rosmersholm*, of the poetic and mythic resonance that such symbols possess.

The Lady from the Sea has never been regarded as one of Ibsen's best plays. Knut Hamsun referred to it as "higher insanity" (*höjere vanvid*),[21] and Henry James felt that it should have been "tinted and distanced." [22] If one insists upon regarding the play as a realistic psychological study, one can legitimately share the annoyance of Hamsun and others at Ibsen's hocus-pocus about the Stranger's eyes and his insistence that the audience make the connection between the carp in the pond and the Wangel family. If, however, it is regarded as allegory or myth, one can much better appreciate what Ibsen was attempting to do. The faults of the play do not lie in the fact that Ibsen wrote an imperfect realistic play, but rather in that he was not skillful enough in writing an unrealistic one. The symbolism is irritatingly obvious and the ambiguity over the Stranger is difficult to resolve simply because the playwright was so careful to make him real. If the hypothesis that Ibsen was searching for a form, for a means of embodying mythic material in a contemporary framework is correct, his earlier attempts might be expected to be somewhat clumsy. In *The Wild Duck* and *Rosmersholm* he had not wandered far from the boundaries of realism; in *The Lady from the Sea* he was more daring and paid the price in producing a less polished work. That Ibsen himself may have been aware of some of these difficulties is perhaps suggested by the fact that in his next play he completely banished any indication of the occult and ostensibly returned to straight realism.

Hedda Gabler · Woman as a Destructive Force

The method I have so far been following appears at first glance to meet with complete frustration when it encounters *Hedda Gab-*

ler. Here there is no mysterious duck, no shadowy world of the unknown, no white horse, no demon lover from the sea. Edmund Gosse went so far as to say that there is no symbolism at all.[23] Although this conclusion is untenable, the symbols in *Hedda Gabler* do at first seem once again to have the rather tangible referents of *A Doll's House.* Those who regard the play as a realistic psychological study of a perverse woman find a measure of support in a letter that Ibsen wrote to Moritz Prozor: "It was not really my intention to deal in this play with so-called problems. What I principally wanted to do was to depict human beings, human emotions and human destinies upon a groundwork of certain of the social conditions and principles of the present day." [24]

In spite of all this, however, Rolf Fjelde maintains that in this play "the mythological content is traditional and close to the surface of the text." [25] The comment implies that the mythic content in *Hedda Gabler* does not lie in the intrusion of supernatural forces but rather in what Frye calls the shape of the story. The shape is concealed behind the realistic events in an archetypal pattern of action and in archetypal relationships among the characters.

The search for such patterns must begin with Hedda herself, since she, like Ellida in the previous play, is the absolute center around which all of the action revolves. Furthermore, the patterns may emerge more clearly if one begins not with a psychological examination of Hedda but with observation of her main actions in the course of the drama.

The principal action of *Hedda Gabler* is the temptation and destruction of Eilert Lövborg. If, for the moment, all poetic resonances are removed from his character Lövborg can be described simply as a reformed alcoholic. Sober he is a brilliant scholar and writer, but drink is his weakness and he must stay away from it. For some time before the play begins he has successfully avoided alcohol. He has published one book that has brought him a great deal of acclaim and has another in manuscript which promises to be even more sensational than the first. Hedda tempts him with his one great weakness — drink. In the manner of a small child she plays on his vanity; she dares him in such a way that he cannot refuse. As a result he goes on a binge, loses the manuscript of his new book, and ends the carouse in a brawl with the police at the apartment of a local woman of loose reputation. When he returns contrite to Hedda the next day, she hands him a pistol and suggests that he kill himself "beautifully." Her motives in all this are complex and must be examined in detail later. For the moment it is sufficient to observe her action, the temptation and destruction of a man.

As destructive female Hedda is clearly an archetypal figure with antecedents as far back as Eve. Maude Bodkin points out that the destructive female is one of four standard female archetypes.[26] Like Eve, Hedda tempts Eilert. She attacks him, as Delilah does Samson, at his one weak point. Hedda bends Eilert Lövborg to her will as Omphale enslaved Hercules. At last, like Clytemnestra and many others, she kills him, or forces him to kill himself, which amounts to the same thing. Obviously also, the destructive female is an archetype within the corpus of Ibsen's work. There is Furia in *Catiline*, Hjördis in *The Vikings at Helgeland*, the ambiguous figure of Gerd in *Brand*, the various female temptresses in *Peer Gynt*, and Rebecca West in *Rosmersholm*. Again, in three of the four plays that follow *Hedda Gabler*, a woman appears as the agent or at least the precursor of a man's destruction. If one wished to admit the Rat-wife to this company, one could say that such a figure appears in all of the last four plays.

The second principal action, closely related to the first, involves the struggle between Hedda and Thea Elvsted for the domination of the soul of Eilert Lövborg. Hedda and Eilert had once enjoyed a considerable degree of intimacy as "comrades," spending long hours together in conversation, though she threatened him with a pistol when he attempted sexual advances. At the time of the play, however, Thea is Eilert's "comrade." She is his inspiration and his source of strength. She has reformed him, kept him away from alcohol, and made it possible for him to write his new book, which both refer to as the "child" of their spiritual union. She has, indeed, left her husband and her stepchildren in order that she can stay near Eilert and keep him safe from the temptations of the city.

Hedda's jealousy is immediately aroused and her action is at least partly motivated by the desire to win Eilert away from her rival. In the struggle between two women for one man we can again readily glimpse an archetypal pattern, especially when we consider the opposed natures of the two women in question. Hedda is a temptress and a destroyer. Although her sex drive is apparently low (indeed, some critics have argued that she is frigid [27]), there is little doubt that her sexual charm exceeds that of Thea, a fact that is obvious in her relationship with Judge Brack. In addition, she represents Eilert's connection with the life of excess and debauchery, about which he seems to have told her in detail during their long conversations. Thea's chief characteristic is her motherliness. She cares for and inspires Eilert and enables him to resist temptation. Thus, she is clearly associated with one of Miss Bodkin's other archetypal figures, the Divine Mother, sustainer of man and fount of life.[28] Such a figure is frequently combined with the virgin or potential bride and represents one pole of a dichotomy between "the lady of duty and the lady of pleasure." [29] The contrast between the two women is heightened by the fact that Thea is symbolically fecund with Eilert's book but physically barren. Hedda is unable to bear the kind of symbolic "child" that she does want and is physically pregnant with a child she does not want. The difference is suggested also in the two women's hair, Hedda's being brown and sparse whereas Thea's is blonde and abundant. Implicit in the struggle between the two women is the struggle between the two cosmic forces that operated behind the action in *Rosmersholm*: Hedda can be seen as representative of a pagan principle with which she consistently associates Eilert's "untamed" life.[30] Thea, with her motherly qualities, can be more readily associated with the Galilean. The former destroys Eilert physically; the latter makes it possible for him to work. Yet Eilert suggests when he returns from his carouse that Thea's beneficent influence is not totally free of detrimental side effects. In a line interestingly reminiscent of *Rosmersholm*, he tells Hedda, "It is the courage and daring for life that she [Thea] has broken in me."

The third action, quite as important as the other two, though not so prominent in terms of stage time, is the burning of Eilert's manuscript. In a sense this can be seen as a part of the destruction of Eilert, since the manuscript is an extension of him. Ibsen, however, takes great pains to establish in the audience's mind the equation manuscript equals child. Hedda specifically destroys the child of Eilert and Thea: ". . . Now I'm burning your child, Thea! — You with the curly hair! . . . Your child and Eilert Lövborg's. . . . Now I'm burning — burning the child." The primary motif here, then, is a symbolic form of that *Kindermord* which one critic sees as central to all of Ibsen's plays after *Brand*.[31] Child murder, of course, also has its archetypal echoes in myth and folk and fairy tales. Both Jung and Kerenyi have discussed the significance of the child archetype. The essential feature of that archetype is "potential future"; and for that reason, many of the mythological saviour figures are child-gods. This child-god is, furthermore, frequently delivered into the hands of its enemies and placed in grave peril if it is not, in fact, destroyed.[32] Now, of the two books that Eilert has written, the first is a historical study of the development of civilization down to the present, and the second, which is burned, is a projection into the future of the historical trends that the first book had noted in the past. Thus in a sense, the second is a book of prophecy. Even more interesting is the completion of the fate of the symbolic child. Its father is killed and it is burned, but at the end of the play it is to be resurrected from Eilert's notes through the efforts of its "mother," Thea, and a kind of "stepfather," Jörgen Tesman. The irony here is sharp and clear when one considers the contrast in character and scholarly ability between Eilert and Jörgen.

In summary, Ibsen has woven together three archetypal patterns to form the action of *Hedda Gabler*. It may certainly be true, as Archer indicates, that he conceived his idea from two different stories that he had heard from Christiania gossip or read about in the newspapers. In one of them the wife of a young Norwegian composer had burned the manuscript of his new symphony; in the other a young wife had tempted her alcoholic husband by giving him a keg of brandy for his birthday, with the predictable result.[33] These, however, are only raw material for a much more significant story. In spite of what Ibsen said in the letter quoted on page 81, there are indications in his correspondence and his notes for the play that he wished to emphasize the temptress aspect of Hedda's character. He says, for example, "It is in proximity with Hedda that the irresistible need for excesses always comes over E. L.," and again, "When Hedda beguiles T. into leading E. L. into destruction it is done to test T.'s character." [34] (Both motive and method disappear in the completed play. Hedda does her own leading and seems not to do it to test anyone's character but simply to exert her influence.) Later, in writing to Hans Schröder about the casting of the play, he comments, ". . . Hedda should be played by Miss Bru[u]n, whom I trust will take pains to express the demoniacal basis of her character." [35] We have no way of knowing for certain what Ibsen meant by "demoniacal basis," but in the light of his other comments it seems logical to assume that he was referring to this tempting and destructive quality.

However, the complexity of Hedda and her motives give the play its richness. Almost any single interpretation of her character is an unfortunate reductionism which ultimately weakens the play. She is not simply this or that, not even destructive temptress, but rather, as Henry James indicates, "various and sinuous and graceful, complicated and natural; she suffers, she struggles, she is human, and by that fact exposed to a dozen interpretations, to the importunity of our suspense." [36] To get at the deepest levels of meaning in the play, the character of Hedda must be examined more closely in terms of the facts that are presented about her and the ways in which she interacts with other characters.

A reasonably accurate picture of her earlier life may be extrapolated from the relatively few hard facts in the text. First of all, she is a general's daughter, and her character is strongly marked in various ways by the personality of her father, a point which Ibsen emphasizes by using her maiden name as the title for the play. A general, especially in an army as small as that of Norway, is a person of social consequence, so Hedda must have moved in the highest of social circles, at least the equivalent of those which surrounded Old Werle. She seems also to have been reared largely in a man's world; since there is no mention of a mother she presumably died when Hedda was very young. The skills in which she takes the greatest pride are masculine — riding and shooting. Yet, though General Gabler was at the top of Norwegian society he cannot have had much money, for Hedda is entirely dependent on her husband's income.[37] She has had a reputation as a local beauty and has attracted a great many admirers but she had not, until Tesman, found anyone she wanted to marry or who wanted to marry her.[38] Nor does she seem actively to have sought the connection with Tesman; she seems mostly to have used him as an escort home from parties and, out of sympathy for his shyness, made the remark about the Falk villa that led eventually to their engagement and marriage. She was not, of course, blind to the prospect that Tesman might gain a professorship and thus an acceptable social position, but it appears primarily to have been his own importunities that led to her unenthusiastic acceptance of him.[39] She had, as she tells Judge Brack, danced herself tired and Tesman perhaps provided a suitable escape from a wearying round of parties and balls. By the time the six-month European "honeymoon" is over, however, her attitude of mild acceptance has changed to one of contempt. Tesman is certainly not the witty companion that she had found in Judge Brack and the other males of her former circle. He is instead a "specialist," full, all his waking hours, of the domestic industries of Brabant in the Middle Ages. If she married Tesman to escape a way of life that was beginning to weary her, she discovers on her wedding trip that she has only given herself over to a still more irritating source of boredom.

The extent and nature of this boredom is revealed most clearly by an examination of the Tesmans and Hedda's relationship with them. Like Hjalmar Ekdal, Jörgen Tesman has been brought up by two maiden aunts who seem to have showered him with praise and affection and to have given him an inflated sense of his own importance. At the age of thirty-three, as Else Höst points out, he is still a *tantegut*, the connotations of which can best be rendered by the related "Mama's boy." [40] His position as scholar and doctoral candidate seem to have won him entrance into Hedda's social circle though nothing in his breeding or native gifts qualifies him for admission. The Tesmans are, in fact, extremely bourgeois, however good-hearted they may be. This quality is illustrated in several ways. There is, for example, the inordinate pride that Berta and Aunt Julianne display in Tesman, a pride which far surpasses his actual worth. There is also Julianne's pathetic purchase of a new hat (apparently in poor taste) "so that Hedda won't be ashamed of me if we happen to walk together on the street." A clear suggestion of the prosaic dullness of Hedda's husband is found in his constant iteration of "*Hvad?*" and "*Taenk det.*" [41] The most telling indication, however, is the object that is associated with Tesman in much the same way as her father's pistols are associated with Hedda, his old house slippers. It would be hard to find a sharper and more ironic contrast. A man who longs for his half worn-out slippers on his wedding trip is hardly a fit companion for a woman who amuses herself by playing with pistols.

Yet Hedda has married into this family and she is to be compelled to exist on their level. An examination of their attitudes toward her further reveals the nature of her plight. At the very beginning of the play Berta and Aunt Julianne are congratulating themselves and Jörgen on his marriage to Hedda Gabler. Both women regard this as a triumph won by the adored nephew, a triumph comparable to the earning of a doctor's degree. That Tesman himself shares this attitude is clearly indicated in dialogue shortly after his first appearance:

> MISS TESMAN. . . . No, but just think, Jörgen, that you've become a married man! — And then that it was you who carried off Hedda Gabler! The lovely Hedda Gabler! Think of it! She who had so many cavaliers around her!
>
> TESMAN. (Humming a little and smiling complacently) Yes, I rather imagine I have several good friends around town who envy me. What?

Thus, the Tesmans' attitude is clearly one of pride in a new possession. The aunts' little Jörgen has not only earned a doctorate, he has also acquired a wife who comes from the top level of the local society and who has been the object of local admiration. This is an obvious feather in his cap and can only reflect favorably on those who brought him up and scrimped and saved for his education. As Miss Höst points out, Tesman has not sought a wife who was his intellectual equal or who shared his interests; on the contrary, he has chosen that which glittered the most brightly and cast a glow over his career.[42] Actually, it is even doubtful that Tesman has deliberately sought social advantage in his marriage. He seems too naive even for that. His innocent pride in her resembles that of a small boy in having the finest bicycle on the block. Among the fragmentary jottings in the *Efterladte Skrifter* is a comment which lends support to this interpretation. "She thinks that Tesman basically only feels a vain pride in having won her. His solicitude for her is like that which one shows for a valuable riding horse or an expensive hunting dog. This, however, does not disturb her. She merely regards it as a fact." [43]

Despite this comment, there are indications in the script that Hedda is disturbed by the Tesmans' attitude. The sophisticated Hedda Gabler has married into a family that puts slipcovers on the furniture and spends much of its time wondering how people make their livings. She has become attached to a man who longed for his old slippers on his wedding trip, who does not realize that marriage frequently results in children, and who is so delighted by his wife's calling him by his first name that he feels he must ask his aunt if such a thing is usual with young wives.[44] These people take a possessive pride in her and regard her as a tangible symbol of Jörgen's success in the world. To feel owned by such a family would be uncomfortable for one of Hedda's background, even if she were the most psychologically well-balanced person in the world. If this is the way she understands her position in the Tesman household, the business with Julianne's hat that otherwise seems a gratuitous cruelty becomes a tiny act of rebellion. Tesman has just been given his old slippers which have so many fond memories for him and insists on showing them to Hedda. When she replies, supported by his aunt, that they can hardly have the same associations for her, he says, "Yes, but I think now that she belongs to the family —."

At this point, Hedda interrupts with her uncomplimentary remark about the hat, seizing upon it as a device to put the Tesmans in their place relative to her. A few minutes later Jörgen is trying to convince her that she should use the familiar *du* to his aunts and again he uses the argument that she now belongs to the family. Once more Hedda uses a prop to escape, demanding that her piano be moved into the inner room.

This instinctive resistance to being owned, on Hedda's part, is carried out in the setting. Ibsen describes two rooms in his stage directions; the inner one is Hedda's refuge. It contains all the possessions of her youth, her piano, and a large portrait of her father. Even the color of the hanging lamp matches her complexion.[45] There, too, she kills herself. The inner room seems to symbolize some part of herself that Hedda must keep inviolate from the Tesmans. Its contents represent all that her life had been before her marriage. Furthermore, when Hedda learns that Tesman's professorship is in doubt and that the couple may have to confine themselves socially to the company of his aunts, she indicates that she still has her father's pistols with which to amuse herself. The pistols are another means of warding off the invasion into her life of hostile forces.[46]

Ibsen's correspondence contains one comment which indicates that this polarization into two camps was exactly what he wanted. In January of 1891 he wrote to Kristina Steen: "Jörgen Tesman, his old aunts, and the faithful servant, Berte, together form a picture of complete unity. They think alike, they share the same memories, and they have the same outlook on life. To Hedda they appear like a strange and hostile power aimed at her very being. In a performance of the play the harmony that exists among them must be conveyed."[47]

If the Tesmans strike Hedda as her natural enemies, it would seem that Judge Brack is her natural ally. Before her marriage he was apparently a regular member of her social circle. In dress, in manners, and in sophistication he clearly fits Hedda's circle much better than does the bumbling Tesman. To Brack she can reveal herself as she cannot to her husband. With him she feels free to engage in the kind of sophisticated banter, full of double entendre, that was apparently the substance of her conversation with her former friends. This kind of conversation was what she missed most on her wedding trip, and this fact is frequently cited as evidence of Hedda's essential sterility. The observation is not without merit. Granted that six months of discourse on the cottage industries of Brabant would be boring, there is little of greater value in her conversations with Brack. Furthermore, the ambitions that she reveals to Brack are of a negative sort that finds an outlet not in what she can do but in what she can make others do. Her disgust with her pregnant condition reveals that she lacks even the "normal" feminine ambition for motherhood.

Yet Brack is not Hedda's equal and she resists him as she does the Tesmans. He is an arranger, a man of affairs, a rake. Although there is no hint of dishonesty in his business dealings with the Tesmans, in his private life he is not so scrupulous. His stag parties are well known but he has managed to escape the kind of reputation for dissolute conduct that Eilert Lövborg has acquired. The key to this lies in the fact that Brack is in complete control of himself; whatever he does is handled discreetly. Before her marriage he had been one of Hedda's admirers, though he had not been interested in a serious relationship. Now that she is safely married he seeks to work himself into a position where, as trusted friend of the family, he can engage in a careful adultery without running any risks thereby. Moreover, he does not balk at applying any available pressures to attain that end. Miss Höst calls him evil personified.[48]

Hedda recognizes the threat to her freedom posed by Brack just as clearly as she recognizes that posed by the Tesmans. The discreet adultery which he desires has no part in her plans. This is symbolically indicated by the use of the pistol at the beginning of the second act. The conversation with Brack is to be a kind of duel and the fact that he takes the pistol from her may foreshadow the power that he ultimately achieves over her through that same weapon.[49] Hedda's resistance to Brack can, of course, be explained by fear of scandal but there is an obvious objection to that conclusion — Brack takes scrupulous care to see that no scandal attaches to his name. Hedda's real reason for shrinking from a liaison with him is revealed in her own lines when she learns that he knows that her pistol killed Eilert Lövborg. "In your power all the same. Dependent upon your will. Unfree. Unfree then! . . . No — that thought I can't stand! Never!" Once again Hedda sees that she is in captivity and she is aware that this time the captor will not be so easily managed as the guileless Tesman. She is caught in a dilemma; on the one hand is the possibility of a police investigation, scandal, publicity; on the other the revolting captivity to Judge Brack. In desperation she even turns back to her husband, who is busy with Lövborg's notes for the destroyed manuscript. "Is there nothing the two of you need from me now?" she asks, and is told, "No, nothing in the world," and sent back to the very captor from whom she is trying to escape. Under such circumstances she has no choice but to shoot herself.

It is in her relationship with Eilert Lövborg that, paradoxically, both the best and the worst sides of Hedda Gabler are revealed. Through that relationship we see most clearly her aspirations for freedom and a higher form of existence and at the same time her imperfect understanding of the nature of that freedom and the destructive path into which it leads her.

Like Tesman, Lövborg is a scholar but otherwise the difference between the two men could not be sharper. Tesman is presumably laboring on a weighty tome dealing with his favorite subject, the domestic industries of Brabant in the Middle Ages. From what we know of Tesman there is little doubt that he will get the book out and that it will be thorough, meticulously researched, dull, and of little use to anyone but other "specialists" of his own type. Eilert has already written one book tracing the course of civilization and his second speculates boldly on future developments. Tesman is a pedant, a caricature perhaps, but still an example of a type who is to be found both in Europe and America. Lövborg, on the other hand, is a visionary, one who adds to his scholarship the fruits of his own insight and who dares to venture intellectually into uncharted areas. There is little doubt which of the two will make the greatest contribution to knowledge, a fact of which Tesman is painfully aware. Tesman's comment and Hedda's when they hear about Lövborg's new book clearly reveal the difference between the two men and reveal also which of the two most impresses Hedda.

TESMAN. Remarkable! It would never have occurred to me to write about such things.
HEDDA. . . . Hmm — No, of course not.

Yet there is another important difference between the two men. Tesman, for all his dullness, is stable; he will finish his work, such as it is. Lövborg is in constant danger of dissipating his creative energies in carousing and revelry.[50] He seems to need the stability provided by Thea Elvsted.

In her younger years Hedda and Eilert had been close friends and had held many long conversations in her father's parlor. Hedda drew Eilert out, encouraging him to talk about his bohemian exploits, inducing him to recount the details of the revels in which he had participated. This, she admits, gave her vicarious enjoyment of the uninhibited life from which her social position barred her. The strictures of her father's home could be escaped in her companionship with Lövborg; she could indulge her "thirst for life" in perfect safety. Had she actually ventured into his existence, through a sexual union perhaps, she would have exposed herself to all sorts of uncertainties, but when that threatens Hedda retreats behind her father's pistol. Like Ellida Wangel she will not risk a "dangerous freedom."

Yet Hedda's understanding of the nature of that freedom is misdirected and limited. Whether or not she truly appreciates Eilert's intellectual gifts is not clear, but she does recognize the difference between him and her husband. Miss Höst argues that her very association with Lövborg indicates that she possesses a vague sense of a life that is richer than that lived in father's household.[51] Her understanding of that richer life, however, is directed at Eilert's dionysiac energies as they are reflected in his orgies with Mademoiselle Diana rather than at his intellectual powers as they are revealed in his two books. Thea Elvsted is the one who has recognized that latter part of his character and made him productive, but she has done so at the cost of his life energies.

Thus, Hedda's motives in destroying the "reformed" Eilert Lövborg must be mixed. She is certainly jealous of Thea and of the part she plays in his life. There is, however, also the fact that the romantic Eilert "with vineleaves in his hair" whose image she had carried in her mind has been tamed by this creature who, as Eilert himself admits, is too stupid to share with him the kind of companionship that he had with Hedda. This is the meaning surely of her boast that at ten o'clock he will return "fiery and bold" with vineleaves in his hair. Hedda is attempting to free Lövborg from his bondage and restore her old dream of the dionysiac rebel and embracer of life. This time, of course, she learns that the vineleaves were, after all, a dream, that the bacchanalian revels are sordid rather than romantic, and that in the midst of his revel Eilert was still thinking of her who inspired him.[52] In her eyes there is now only one thing for him to do — kill himself "beautifully" and thus salvage at least some of her dream. But even that goes awry. Eilert does not shoot himself deliberately but dies by accident, and the bullet lodges not in his brain but in his bowels. Thus, Hedda learns that what she is not able to do for herself — that is, free herself from a life that is too small for her — she cannot accomplish vicariously through someone else. Like Old Ekdal she learns that there is danger and death even in her dream world. She has destroyed Eilert and his "child," but instead of freeing herself she has only delivered herself into a worse captivity.

In short, Hedda is a woman of aristocratic breeding and background with a highly developed sense of the fitness of things. She has sold herself into a marriage with a naive and pedestrian man and is compelled to exist in a suffocatingly bourgeois milieu, the whole nature of which offends her. She has a vague sense of a richer life, but nothing in her upbringing and previous life has fitted her to realize her greater potential. In struggling to free herself from any kind of bondage she succeeds only in destroying herself.

Directly contrasted with Hedda is Thea Elvsted, stolid, unimaginative, not very intelligent. She lacks the wit or the skill to fight for Eilert and must stand helplessly by while Hedda destroys him. Yet her very solidity allowed her to serve as an anchor for Eilert and to give him the sense of security which he apparently needed in order to pursue his work. At the same time her limited intelligence and lack of imagination have destroyed, as he tells Hedda, his strong sense of life. The tragedy and irony of the play is heightened by the fact that the two couples are so mismatched.

In fact, the match between Thea and Tesman that occurs at the end of the play is the perfect one. They suit each other. He has found the ideal task for one of his pedantic nature. There is no doubt that he will painstakingly reconstruct Eilert's book, though some of its brilliance may be obscured in the process. Thea will make no demands on him; she will not ask him to be witty, brilliant, or amusing. She has found a new man to "inspire" and that is enough for her. Hedda and Eilert are also suited to each other though, given Hedda's personality, that match might well not work out as smoothly. Had she a clearer understanding of her own nature, of her own needs and drives, she might have been able to provide Lövborg with both the security and the "joy of life" which he needed. Indeed, an association with Eilert might have broadened and deepened her understanding. Had she not driven Eilert away with her pistol years before, Hedda Gabler might have been a quite different woman. That match, however, never occurred and in her present circumstances Hedda can retain any shreds of her dignity only by killing herself.

Hedda is not, then, purely a destructive force. Like Johannes Rosmer, she is a potentially creative force that has become aborted. She lacks the strength, the understanding, the moral qualities to realize whatever vague sense of nobility and higher purpose she possesses. At the same time there is that in her breeding which makes it impossible for her to accept life on the terms offered by the Judge Bracks of this world. This is the meaning, surely, of Brack's last line, "But good God, people don't do such things!" People of Brack's sort do not, but Hedda Gabler is made of different stuff. Incomplete and warped though she may be, she has an innate sense of dignity that will not allow her to compromise with an existence that is less than she wishes. Thus, choosing death rather than a life of captivity and compromise she triumphs but, as in *Rosmersholm*, the triumph is negative. Hedda lacks the power to change her life; she can only escape it.

There is a sense, I think, in which *Hedda Gabler* is more modern, less Victorian, and perhaps less Norwegian than any of Ibsen's earlier plays. Hedda is a type that could and does exist in many an American or European provincial community even today. She has affinities with Strindberg's Miss Julie, with Emma Bovary, and in some respects, perhaps, with the heroine of Lewis' *Main Street*. In a larger sense she has affinities with modern man, trapped, as Ibsen had suggested in the preface to *Catiline*, between what she sees as desirable and the limits of the possible. The condition of Hedda Gabler is an extension of the landbound and alienated condition of Ellida and Boletta Wangel, with the difference that Hedda has greater aesthetic and intellectual gifts than either.

Camus has said that the only important philosophical question is whether or not to commit suicide. In the narrow world in which Hedda Gabler is forced to exist she comes to the conclusion, intuitively if not intellectually, that this is her most important question. Unwanted, unfulfilled, doomed to one captivity or another, she has no other choice and in taking that step she raises herself above the society that hems her in. Hedda has great possibilities; she has a faint vision of a larger world than the one she now occupies, but, like modern man, devoid of any easy access to divinity or a secure place in the social order, she does not know how to realize her possibilities and in groping for a means she brings only destruction.

In these two plays Ibsen has used mythic and folkloristic materials and built his dramas on mythic frameworks, but he has done still more, taking an additional step in the direction of the creation of a myth of modern man. The alienation, the rootlessness, the lack of purpose and direction that characterize Ellida Wangel and Hedda Gabler are very modern problems. Indeed, they form the basis of much of modern literature. This desperate condition of man has been implicit in most of the earlier plays, in *Brand* and *Peer Gynt* certainly, and especially in those beginning with *The Wild Duck*. In those which follow *Hedda Gabler* Ibsen makes it explicit, following his misfits, Solness, Borkman, and Rubek, through their frenzied attempts to realize themselves against the limitations of society and existence to their eventual and inevitable doom.

THE *MASTER BUILDER* · PROMETHEUS AND
THE DYING KING

⁋ TRADITIONALLY there have been two ways of approaching *The Master Builder,* the biographical and the psychological. In some cases the two have been applied together. Thus, the play is commonly seen as a kind of capsule autobiography of Henrik Ibsen, with parallels between Solness' meeting with Hilda Wangel and Ibsen's acquaintance with Emilie Bardach, and between Solness' churches, homes for human beings, and castles in the air and Ibsen's early dramas of high idealism, his plays of social realism, and his later plays of poetic symbolism.[1] The problems of Solness — his sense of guilt, his fear of the younger generation — become those of his creator, disguised only slightly by the alteration of detail. The psychological approach is usually couched in Freudian terms, focusing on the truncated sexual development of Hilda Wangel and on the phallic symbolism of the towers and spires that play so important a role in the drama. A combination of these approaches suggests that the play is a kind of atonement in which Ibsen acts out his guilt over what seems to have been largely mental infidelity to his wife.[2]

The problems of conscience that afflict Solness can be explained in still another way within the autobiographical frame-work. Else Höst maintains that the meeting with Emilie Bardach set off in Ibsen a strong internal conflict between his artistic call-ing and the desire for the free life of the senses on which his duty or vocation made no demands.[3] Thus, Solness' attraction to Hilda is an attraction to the youth and joy that he felt had been denied him by his vocation.

There is no doubt that all of these approaches have value and are probably in varying degrees correct. They are all limited, how-ever, in that, whatever they reveal about Ibsen's life and personal problems, sexual or otherwise, they do not say a great deal about the play as a finished work of art. The reader or the spectator in the theater does not necessarily bring with him a detailed knowl-edge of Ibsen's life or of Freudian psychology.[4] The effect that the play has in the theater must be independent of this specialized knowledge. Autobiographical and psychological details are work-able in this respect only if they tap the depths of universal human experience.

That the play did have such an effect on at least one viewer is attested to by Maurice Maeterlinck's comment in his famous essay, "The Tragical in Daily Life."

> "What is it that, in *The Master Builder*, the poet has added to life, thereby making it appear so strange, so profound and so disquieting beneath its trivial surface?" The discovery is not easy, and the old master hides from us more than one secret. It would even seem as though what he has wished to say were but little by the side of what he has been compelled to say. He has freed certain powers of the soul that have never yet been free, and it may well be that these have held him in thrall.[5]

Various critics have noticed the mythic element in the play. Like Maeterlinck, they have seen that there is something intensely troubling and at the same time, perhaps, exhilarating, that operates beneath the realistic surface of the play.[6] The mythic element in *The Master Builder* becomes more obvious and at the same time more troubling and mysterious than it has been in any of the plays considered in the chapters thus far. The play is, however, a continuation of the world view that Ibsen has been developing since early in his career.

I shall not here repeat the story of Ibsen's relationship with Emilie Bardach or any of the other young ladies that may have served as models for Hilda Wangel, since it is fully recounted in all the standard biographies. There is no doubt that these encounters did have a profound effect on him, as the correspondence with Fräulein Bardach illustrates. Yet the problem which appears in *The Master Builder* and even the one which is expressed in the inscription he wrote in Miss Bardach's autograph book — "hohes schmerzliches Gluck — um das Unerreichbare zu dringen!" — are not new to Ibsen. Brand, Rosmer, and even Hedda Gabler struggle toward the same unattainable. The conflict between joy of life and sense of mission is as old as *Catiline*. It is only natural that these problems should trouble Ibsen more strongly as he grew older and began to weigh in the balance his own accomplishments. Yet for all its autobiographical impetus, the play is not, in the last analysis, bound by Ibsen's own life.

The story of Master Builder Solness can be approached on several levels. The most obvious of these is the simple, realistic plane, the encounter between Solness and Hilda. Looked at in this way the play is the story of a middle-aged man who loses his head over a young girl and lets himself be dared into taking a suicidal chance which does, indeed, prove fatal. Even on this level, however, there are some strange elements that bear further examination.

When the play opens Solness is a middle-aged builder who has reached the peak of his profession. He has three employees, one of whom he has, in essence, deposed from a position very similar to his own. He has people actively seeking him out with commissions, but he is in the enviable position of not having to build anything that he does not like. He is described in the stage directions as healthy and vigorous (*sund og kraftig*). In short, he seems to have achieved all, or almost all, that any man can hope to achieve in life.

But Solness is not happy. There are certain things lacking in his life, the most obvious being children. There are three nurseries in his house, all of them empty. Earlier he had had twin boys, both of

whom perished from an infection communicated to them through
their mother's milk, an infection which she acquired as the result
of exposure following a fire which destroyed her ancestral home.
Aline Solness herself has become a shadow figure. She is in a constant state of melancholy and performs her daily tasks without enthusiasm, simply because they are her duty. Furthermore, the fire
which destroyed the Solnesses' original home seems to have been
the precipitating factor in his success as a builder.

This situation could provide the starting point for a television
drama or a Hollywood film. Here is a man who has made a great
success in business but has done so at the expense of losing love,
wife, and family. Moreover, this same loss made his success possible
and, as a result, he bears a burden of guilt. At this point in the melodramatic formula a young girl should appear, who would offer him
love and happiness and show him that he is tormenting himself
over something that is not essentially his fault. And a young girl
does, in fact, make an appearance.

From the moment she does, however, we are aware that Hilda
Wangel is no ordinary young lady and this is no ordinary story
of May-September love. She has come not to offer something to
Solness but to demand something from him. She has come to claim
the "kingdom" that he allegedly promised her ten years before.
We soon begin to suspect, furthermore, that she represents mysterious forces working, as in *The Wild Duck* and *Rosmersholm*,
behind and through the ostensibly realistic action.

The precise nature of her "kingdom" remains vague, as does
the question of whether or not Solness actually promised it. Except
for the climbing of the church tower and the fact that there was a
party afterward, the whole story of the events at Lysanger is told
by Hilda. Not only does Solness not remember it, he emphatically
denies parts of it:

HILDA. (Looks intently at him) You took and kissed me, Mr.
Solness.
SOLNESS. (Open-mouthed, gets up from his chair) I did!
HILDA. Yes, you did. You took me in both arms, bent me back-
ward and kissed me. Many times.

SOLNESS. But my dear Miss Wangel — !
HILDA. You're not going to deny it?
SOLNESS. Yes, I most certainly am going to deny it!

Yet only a few minutes later he is manipulated into admitting that something of the sort may have happened:

Miss Wangel . . . Don't stand there like a statue. This that you've said, it must be something you dreamed. . . . Now listen. . . . Or — ! Wait! — There's something deeper to this, you'll see! . . . I must have thought about all this. I must have wanted it. Wished for it. Had a desire for it. Doesn't that make sense? . . . Oh, all right, damn it, then I did it too!

This is the response that Hilda has desired and she now proceeds with an interrogation that forces Solness to admit every detail of the story, exactly as she recounted them. The question, then, is, is Solness right? Did she merely dream the events? Or is Solness' memory failing him, or alternatively, was it merely an episode that was not important enough for him to remember? Critics disagree on the answers. Weigand maintains that Hilda's whole story is a figment of her imagination and this conclusion goes along with his interpretation of her condition as being basically a case of arrested sexual development.[7] Downs disagrees directly and asserts that such a conclusion is an unnecessary complication, especially since Solness eventually comes to believe the story himself.[8]

If, however, one approaches the story on a realistic level, there are some basic improbabilities that cannot be avoided. It is highly unlikely, for example, that a man who must at least have been in his forties would have behaved in the fashion that Hilda describes toward a thirteen-year-old girl. It is even more unlikely that, had he done so, he would have forgotten in a mere ten years an incident associated with a day of considerable triumph, every detail of which he would remember. If Solness were the senile old man that he is sometimes taken to be his forgetfulness would be more probable, but the text clearly indicates that he is not really that old. One can, of course, conclude with Weigand that the whole story of the events at Lysanger is something that Hilda fantasized and wished for so strongly that she actually came to believe in its reality. At this point, however, one is faced with the question of why Solness comes to believe her story, at first grudgingly but more and more willingly and completely as the play goes on. The only alternative, if one insists upon a realistic explanation, is to conclude that both characters are, in varying degrees, mad, and that seems to be the position to which Downs is forced.[9]

If the play is viewed from the standpoint of myth the simple answer to these improbabilities is that they do not matter. Hilda Wangel is, as Valency recognizes, a total enigma. She has a recognizable background, a real father, a home, connections with other characters, and we have even seen her in a previous play. Yet here she takes on mysterious connotations which go beyond any realistic interpretation.[10] The kingdom which she demands of Solness can be achieved only by his repeating the heroic feat which he performed ten years before, even though its repetition means his death. Thus, Hilda has affinities with the Norns of Norse mythology who presided over the fate of men and tempted them to heroism and to death.[11] This connection is further reinforced by the fact that her name closely resembles that of one of the six most commonly named of the Valkyries.[12] In a still wider sense, Hilda is the guide that appears to urge the hero onward, to lead him through the dark regions. She has had many forebears in Ibsen's drama. Such guides have, as we have noted, tended to be ambivalent, urging the hero on to a great task which proves to be his destruction. Female versions are to be found in Furia, in Gerd, in Rebecca West, even, perhaps, in Hedda Gabler, though in the latter case the destructive element is clearly predominant. Male versions are to be found in Bishop Nikolas (who encourages Skule Bardson), in Maximus, in the strange hunter of "Paa Vidderne," and in Ulrik Brendel. Always these characters attempt to work their influence over others, and frequently they appear mysteriously at just the right moment. Only once does a character successfully refuse the call (Ellida Wangel); in all other cases the heroes, or victims, are encouraged to some form of perilous action. Thus, the pattern of many of Ibsen's plays coincides again with the hero's quest as outlined in Campbell.[13] Valency points out that Solness' death, over which Hilda presides, takes on, through her, the nature of a sacrament.[14] Her function in the play is not a realistic one but rather, as Valency again asserts, "to tease the mind of the hero, and with it the mind of the spectator, not toward any certainty but into the doubtful labyrinth of surmise, which is, for the symbolist, the *locus* of the poetic experience." [15]

Similar indications of the workings of the mysterious are apparent in Solness. He is not an ordinary man, but a man possessed of strange fears and fancies. He has an inordinate fear of youth that is hardly justified by his age and position. Second, he is more than half convinced that by merely willing something he can cause it to happen, a fact which is revealed by his first response to Hilda's story. He seems also to believe that he is attended by a class of guardian spirits that he refers to as "helpers and servers," who assist in bringing about the things for which he merely wishes. Fourth, he is burdened by a sense of guilt over the fact that his success has been purchased at the price of the death of his children and the virtual death of his wife, though he was in no way physically responsible for the fire which brought about those deaths.

Again, the obvious realistic explanation of all this is that Solness is mentally deranged and there is even a suggestion of paranoia in his conversation with Dr. Herdal. If this is so, Hilda, the church tower at Lysanger, and all of the events surrounding them can be regarded as hallucinations or psychic projections. If we say this, however, we must recognize a more drastic departure from realism in the play than Ibsen has employed since *Peer Gynt.* If, on the other hand, these events are real, we are faced with the same improbabilities as before, the only escape from which is the conclusion that Hilda is also mad. This reduces the play to a kind of freak show, a study of two pathological characters, one of whom destroys the other. However interesting this sort of thing may be in itself it is not the type of drama with which Ibsen has previously been concerned.

Looked at mythically, what appear to be aberrant symptoms become suggestions that mysterious forces are actually at work in some way to direct and govern the destinies of men. Solness' helpers and servers may exist; perhaps they have ordered his life in the way he wished, with the proviso that such ordering would cost something. Perhaps, too, Hilda is one of those forces come either to exact retribution or to force onward Solness' flagging will. The helpers and servers certainly bear a close relation to the *fylgjur* or *kynfylgjur* of Norse mythology who were supposed to attend a man or a family and to bring good fortune.

There are, however, at least two other levels of myth built into the design of the play, two levels which correlate closely with traditional mythic patterns. In order to uncover those mythic levels, we must first examine Solness' position in relation to the other characters and second, scrutinize the stages of his career as he relates them.

Solness is a prosperous builder who has three persons in his employ: Knut Brovik, his son Ragnar, and Ragnar's fiancée, Kaja Fossli. When the play opens, the three stand in awe of Solness, though except in the case of Kaja, their awe is mixed with resentment. Knut Brovik is an old man on the point of death. It was he who trained Solness in the builder's trade, but at some time in the past Solness deposed him and the roles of employer and employee switched. Ragnar, the son, is himself a highly promising builder, but Solness does not wish him to strike out on his own. The young man is extremely clever at figuring stresses, cubic content, and other details with which his employer does not wish to be bothered. In order to keep him Solness has employed his fiancée as bookkeeper in the firm, reasoning that as long as she stays so will Ragnar.

The relationship between Solness and these people is more than that between employer and employee; it is that of father to children, king to subjects, or master to slave.[16] In a sense Solness can be said to own them. Kaja is in love with him and is completely dependent on his will. She came to him, he tells Herdal, in response to an unspoken wish, and she is ready to do whatever he tells her. Ragnar must have Solness' sanction to set himself up as an independent builder, that sanction consisting, first, of Solness' relinquishing to him a commission which the former does not want in

any case and, second, Solness' written approval on a set of drawings that Ragnar has prepared.

Knut Brovik is even more basically dependent on Solness than
the other two. On the realistic level he is dependent in the sense
that he is an old and sickly man and no one else is likely to hire
him. Indeed, there *is* no one else to hire him; Solness is the only
builder in the town. Symbolically, his dependence runs deeper still.
In the first act Knut comes to Solness to beg that his son be given
a chance. The latter curtly refuses. Knut, however, begs further,
using his illness and approaching death as an additional appeal:

> BROVIK. Am I to die, then, without certainty? Without any
> happiness? Without faith and confidence in Ragnar? With-
> out having seen a single piece of his work? Is it to be that
> way?
> SOLNESS. (Turns half aside and mutters) Hmmm — don't ask me
> any more now.
> BROVIK. Yes, answer me. Am I to pass out of life in such com-
> plete poverty?
> SOLNESS. (Seems to struggle with himself; finally says in a low
> but firm voice) You shall have to pass out of life in the best
> way you know how.

What Knut Brovik is basically asking for here is a means to face
death, some assurance that Ragnar is talented so he can die content,
knowing that he has accomplished something with his life. Thus,
the relationship between Solness and his employees becomes more
even than that between king and subjects; it takes on overtones of
the relationship between God and man. Indeed, this aspect of their
relationship is given visual stress when Kaja declares her un-
bounded loyalty to Solness with outstretched, folded hands — a
gesture, as Northam points out, of prayer.[17] Later Kaja falls on
her knees before him, calling on God, and Solness accepts her
homage almost like the God she invokes.[18]

This line of reasoning can be pursued a bit further by considering Solness' occupation and the way he carries it out. He is a
builder — more specifically, a master builder — and he builds houses
in which people can live and be happy. In other words he is one
who creates, or so he has once thought, the means for human hap-

piness. In order to do this he has declared his independence from God and placed himself on an equal footing with Him. On top of the church tower at Lysanger he shouted: "Now listen, almighty One! From now on I'll be a free builder too. In my domain. Just as You are in Yours."

In relation to other men, then, Solness is master, king, creator, god. He is above others, and because he is he is vulnerable to attack from below. There are upstart gods, upstart builders who would challenge his supremacy, and for this reason he is dreadfully afraid of youth. His fears arise not because he is old and feels his own powers waning, but rather because he knows that the old king or god is challenged always by the new.

In this case the challenger is the young apprentice, Ragnar Brovik, whose talent, Solness knows, is as great as his own. Solness' position in relation to the Broviks emphasizes the ritual pattern of the play. Knut, on the one hand, is the deposed king, displaced by Solness who now occupies the throne. Ragnar is the challenger awaiting his opportunity. Realistically, as old Knut says, there must be room for more than one master builder in the town, but mythically there is not room for more than one king. The sacrament over which Hilda presides, then, is the ritual sacrifice of the old king to make room for the new. The connection between Ragnar and Hilda in bringing about the destruction of Solness is made clear by a number of related facts. Hilda urges Solness to climb the tower, she induces him to write on Ragnar's drawings, and she and Solness are alone on the stage when Ragnar brings the wreath that is to be the literal cause of the master builder's fall. After the fall Ragnar and Hilda are the only characters to comment. In a sense, they pronounce a kind of epitaph upon him now that the way has been cleared for Ragnar's ascension to the throne.

This pattern is so familiar in myth that it is hardly necessary to comment upon it. The archetypal tale perhaps is that of the priest at Nemi, who bore the title King of the Wood. He retained that title until someone younger, craftier, and stronger could kill him. But before the would-be king could kill the incumbent he had to pluck the golden bough from the tree that the priest was guarding.[19] That such a legend is neither unique nor even unusual is attested to by the fact that Frazer recounts similar practices in places as widely separated as Cambodia, southern India, central Africa, and ancient Scandinavia. Of particular interest is the indication of a tradition that at one time Swedish kings were allowed to rule for only nine years, after which they were put to death or had to find a substitute victim.[20]

The myth of the fall of the king belongs to that stage of the Ur-myth which Frye calls the autumn phase and which corresponds in literature to tragedy.[21] Taken literally, one of the extremely vexing anomalies in the play is the churchlike tower on Solness' new house. Looked at mythically, however, and considered in connection with what Frye says about the tragic hero it takes on a new and more interesting coloration. "The tragic hero is typically on top of the wheel of fortune, halfway between human society on the ground and something greater in the sky. Prometheus, Adam and Christ hang between heaven and earth, between a world of paradisial freedom and a world of bondage." [22]

Such is Solness' position. He must seek his kingdom at the top of his perilous tower, and in finding it he falls to his death. That death comes moreover, not only as a deposition by a new king but as a kind of destiny, perhaps as a kind of vengeance. Solness fears retribution for several reasons, his defiance of God on the church tower at Lysanger, his supposed crime against his wife and children, and his deposition of Knut Brovik. The mythic correspondences may, indeed, be taken a step farther. The very building of the tower or steeple on the new house suggests, in this context, the biblical myth of the tower of Babel. The erection of such a structure implies the aspiration to share the domain of God and brings punishment for man's arrogance. Again Frye's comment is instructive. The mythos of tragedy, he says, usually involves a vision of the operation of an impersonal natural law: "In its most elementary form, the vision of law (*dike*) operates as *lex talionis* or revenge. The hero provokes enmity, and the return of the avenger constitutes the catastrophe." [23]

Actually, we have seen the operation of such a *lex talionis* before in Ibsen's drama, certainly in *Rosmersholm*, perhaps in *Brand* (whose "crime" against his wife and child is similar to that of Solness), and perhaps also in *Ghosts*, though the nature of Helen Alving's "crime" is more obscure. It is not difficult to see Ragnar as such an avenger nor is it difficult to see Hilda Wangel as a force come to lure Solness to his destiny. One other comment by Frye, not unrelated to those already cited, casts additional light on the mythic significance of the play: "The tragic hero usually belongs, of course, to the alazon group, an imposter in the sense that he is self-deceived or made dizzy by hybris. In many tragedies he begins as a semi-divine figure, at least in his own eyes, and then an inexorable dialectic sets to work which separates the divine pretence from the human actuality." [24]

Solness' bold claiming of the position of god has already been noted, but several incidents have occurred and others occur in the course of the play to "separate the divine pretence from the human actuality." First, Solness becomes literally dizzy in high places —this dizziness nearly cost him his life ten years before in Lysanger. Thus, even while Solness was defying God from the top of his tower, he was conscious of his own precarious humanity. That same dizziness, of course, causes his final and fatal fall from the tower of his new house. By the time of the play's opening, too, he has come to fear for his position and to doubt the validity of the mission he took upon himself at Lysanger. This he confesses to Hilda in a speech full of bitterness and disillusion.

> SOLNESS. This building homes for human beings, it's not worth five cents, Hilda.
> HILDA. Do you say that now?
> SOLNESS. Yes, now I say that. People have no use for these homes of theirs. Not to be happy in. I wouldn't have found a use for such a home either, if I'd had one. (With a quiet, embittered laugh) So that's the sum total as far back as I can see. Nothing built at last. And nothing sacrificed for the chance to build anything. It's nothing, nothing —all nothing. [25]

Solness, then, has come to the point so frequently faced by the tragic hero, where he recognizes his own weakness and suspects that all he has done is folly and futility. He has claimed the king-ship by usurping the position of Knut Brovik, he has dared God and set himself to the task of building homes for human beings, a task the value of which he now questions, and he feels himself threatened by the son of the man he deposed. His position is not unlike that of Macbeth, but also a situation that has become so common in modern literature as to be almost a cliché. Solness has tried to create a life for himself and now believes that life to have been a futile one, devoid of meaning and satisfaction.

The tower is an objective representation of Solness' position of king/god, both in its height and in its precariousness. With the coming of Hilda he has no choice but to climb it. The wreath that Ragnar brings him and the signature that he must obtain from him have an interesting parallel with the golden bough that had to be plucked from the tree by him who would challenge the priest at Nemi. The mythic implications of the play are given even deeper significance by the fact that Ragnar is, in a sense, Solness' own cre-ation. The master builder trained him in his craft, just as he, in turn, was trained by Ragnar's father. Thus, Ragnar's deposition of Sol-ness might be regarded as the destruction of his spiritual father, in the same way that Solness removed the man who stood in that same relationship to him.

Beyond the tale of the death of the king there is yet another level of myth which is closely related to the world view emerging in the earlier plays. Solness is not only a sacrificial king, he is also a Promethean rebel, defying God for the well-being of man. Ac-tually, the two myths intersect and constitute together another ex-amination of the problem of freedom and idealism which has been a recurrent theme in the earlier plays.

To examine Solness' Promethean role it is necessary to go back to the stages of his career as he relates them. He began as a builder of churches, feeling that such service to God was the greatest goal to which he could aspire. Yet God's reward for this service was to beset him first with the troll that dwelt in him and the devils that surrounded him, and, second, to bring about the death of his chil-dren and, for all practical purposes, of his wife. Solness then perceived that the God he served was indeed a jealous and a selfish God. He wanted Solness all to Himself; He would brook no divided loyalties in His church builder. At this point Solness decided to declare his independence, but, significantly, not for himself alone but for the sake of other human beings. He would dedicate himself to building houses in which men could be happy. Thus, he stood on the tower at Lysanger, a feat he had never before been able to accomplish, and shook his fist at God. Like Prometheus, he defied God for the sake of man.

Yet unlike Prometheus, Solness was allowed to discover that the building of homes for human beings was not the glorious task that he had envisioned. They had no real use, as he says, for such homes. Like Brand, he has learned that human beings do not appreciate what is done for them. His rebellion has been incomplete — he has not really declared his freedom but only devoted himself to another ideal, one which, perhaps, is too small for him. At this stage of his frustration Hilda Wangel appears as an objectification of that triumphant day at Lysanger. Her talk of a kingdom and his of castles in the air is a recognition of the fact that his ideal has been too limited; for service to God he has merely substituted a facile humanism. Hilda helps him to understand that in order to reclaim his ideal and expunge the guilt he feels he must once more climb the tower, face God again, and declare his complete independence. Like the guide in Campbell's monomyth she comes to remind him that his hero's task is incomplete and to urge him on.

This is the significance, I think, of Hilda's disgust with the word *duty*, and of all the talk of weak and robust consciences. Solness has not been like the old Vikings who took what they wanted from life without fear or scruple. He has declared himself independent of God, but he cannot follow a life of freedom and joy without a sense of guilt and a compensating sense of duty to others. He cannot pursue his ideals without reservations and "climb as high as he builds." The coming of Hilda, however, reawakens in him his desire and his ability to climb. The fact that he falls to his death from his tower is of less ultimate significance than the fact that he climbed it, as the final lines of the play indicate.

RAGNAR. This is terrible. So he couldn't do it after all.
HILDA. (As in a quiet, dazed triumph) But he got all the way to the top. And I heard harps in the air. (Waves her shawl overhead and cries with wild intensity) My — my master builder.

Hilda heard harps in the air on that other occasion, when Solness climbed the tower at Lysanger. The two towers become, in Frye's terminology, points of epiphany, points of contact between the human and the divine.[26] Solness' building and climbing of the tower is an act of hybris and of blasphemy,[27] but in the last analysis it is also an act of triumph. This is so not merely because he has conquered his fear of heights and dared to climb a literal tower, but because Solness the artist/idealist has reasserted himself. He has escaped the earth and the prosaic business of building houses and sought his visionary kingdom in the air.[28] In his very destruction he has achieved something and this, as one critic points out, is the significance of Hilda's line as Solness reaches the very top of the tower. In Norwegian the line reads, "For nu, nu er det fullbrakt." Fjelde's translation suggests the mythic significance of the line, ". . . because now, now it's fulfilled." The words suggest an affinity with Christ, through the repetition of his last words from the cross. Solness, however, is not merely a Christ-figure. The line, and the whole last scene, evoke a variety of ideas and associations.[29]

Solness, then, has more affinities with Brand than he does with Rosmer, for he is able to transcend his weakness in an act of daring comparable to Brand's final struggle up the mountainside, and he faces God from the top of his tower in much the same way as does Brand in his ice church. The difference lies, perhaps, in the fact that whereas Brand poses a question Solness delivers a challenge and thus, in spite of his vertigo, may be said to be the stronger figure.

The Master Builder is one of the richest, most complex, and most evocative of Ibsen's plays. To isolate a single theme would be to do it an injustice. On the one hand Ibsen seems to affirm that, though life may be futile and idealism ultimately destructive, there are men who must climb their towers. Solness defies God but his human weakness (his dizziness) causes him to fall at the very moment of his triumph. Yet he should no more have humbled himself to God than he should have devoted himself to the service of humanity. The presence of Hilda and her whole effect within the play suggests that he should not have modified his heroic stance at all, but should have ventured completely into that "dangerous freedom" that Ellida Wangel and Hedda Gabler both rejected, even at the risk of his own destruction.[30] This seems clearly to be a reversal of the position taken in *The Lady from the Sea*. However, Ibsen is not finished with the question of freedom and idealism versus life and compromise; he continues to examine the problem from various angles in his subsequent plays.

Aside from plot, theme, and symbolism there are other changes in the form and structure of the play that take it away from psychological realism and in the direction of myth. One of the most notable of these is in the nature of the characters. Northam notes that the information provided about the characters through visual means is more generalized than in previous plays. This tends to make them types, or even archetypes. They are, as Northam puts it, "exemplars of a universal process in various stages of completion."[31] A look at the physical juxtaposition of the characters bears this out. There are three stages of chronological development in the play; old age, as represented by Knut Brovik; middle age, as represented by Solness; and youth, exemplified by Ragnar, by Kaja, and especially by Hilda.

Even more significant, however, may be what we actually know about the characters. In most of his previous plays Ibsen has provided a capsule biography of his characters. We know something about their childhoods, their parents, their social positions, and so forth. They may be said to have an identity outside the play. In *The Master Builder* almost no such information is presented. All the spectator or reader knows about Solness is related in some way to his position as builder, as idealist, and to his mythic position as king. The same is true of Hilda Wangel. She has a father, she comes from Lysanger where, ten years before, she met Solness, she has just been on a walking tour of the mountains. Beyond that we know nothing about her. The Broviks and Kaja

Fossli also are uncharacterized except in terms of their relationship with Solness. Aline is less a real person than she is a ghost, a woman who has died years before the play opens. These people, then, almost literally have no life outside the immediate contexts of the play.

A similar observation can be made about the action, as Henry James recognized on the occasion of the London production of *The Master Builder*. "The action," he commented, "at any rate is superficially simple, more single and confined than that of most of Ibsen's other plays." [32] Unlike *The Wild Duck*, *Rosmersholm*, or *Hedda Gabler*, there is in this play no social or political world to form a frame for the action. There are, to be sure, people who want houses built but they are only talked about; they never make themselves felt in the action. Dr. Herdal, the only extraneous character, functions merely as a confidant through whom Solness can reveal his obsessions. [33] The town of Lysanger is important only as the scene of Solness' earlier climbing feat and is thus symbolically connected with the main action of the drama. Everything is focused on the single action toward which the play leads and that action can be regarded as almost completely a ritualistic one — the apotheosis, sacrifice, and death of Halvard Solness.

In an article on Cocteau's handling of myth in drama and film, Chester Clayton Long makes the interesting observation that myth is essentially a narrative form, sketchy in detail of action and in development of character, leaving both in a sense to be experienced in the reader's mind. [34] This observation casts an interesting light on another shift in technique that seems to occur in Ibsen's later plays, a gradual movement from action to words. In *The Master Builder* there is one principal action, the offstage climbing of the tower and the fall from it. There is no other minor action and no direct clash of forces as there is, for example, in *Rosmersholm*. What does occur, primarily, is a verbal evocation of a situation and a spiritual condition which leads inevitably to the one final action on the tower of the master builder's new house. [35]

Northam has also recognized this aspect of changing technique. He notes that in this play Ibsen turns to the spoken word rather than to visual suggestion for his poetry, and he recognizes that what he calls "Solness' mania and Hilda's wildness" free them from the bonds of realism.[36] Certainly the language here loses much of the quality of cryptic hinting that was characteristic of the earlier plays and launches itself into the realms of poetry. Especially in the second act, all the talk of trolls, of dark and light devils, of helpers and servers, of kingdoms and castles in the air takes on colorations of mystery, of madness and of poetry. Solness and Hilda talk as no other Ibsen characters have talked (except as objects of parody) since *Emperor and Galilean.*[37]

With *The Master Builder* Ibsen seems, both in form and in content, to leave the social world almost completely behind and to enter firmly into the world of myth. This play is the most successful blending of mythic material and realistic convention of all of Ibsen's later work. From now on the Ur-myth, the death-rebirth cycle, becomes central to his drama, as does the hero's quest, and both continue to be tied to the question of how to live in the world, with the heights of idealism pitted against the lowlands of everyday life. We feel in these last plays, furthermore, a sense of greater personal involvement on Ibsen's part.[38] He cannot view Solness, Borkman, or Rubek with the same detachment that he could Gregers Werle and Johannes Rosmer. This substantiates the body of criticism that has viewed these last plays as heavily autobiographical. Ibsen's concerns, however, go far beyond his own personal problems or even those of artists, as is indicated by his straining at the bonds of realism and his entry into the world of myth. All of these questions must be explored in further detail in the remaining plays, but it is, I believe, in the above senses that Ibsen was speaking when he said, in a letter to Moritz Prozor, "You are quite right when you say that the series which ends with the epilogue really began with *The Master Builder.*" [39]

LITTLE EYOLF · THE MYTH OF SACRIFICE
AND REDEMPTION

❡ IF *The Wild Duck* marks, roughly, the beginning of a gradual attempt on Ibsen's part to interweave myth into realistic form and to set it in a contemporary context, *The Master Builder* represents the nearly perfect combination of realistic form and mythic content.[1] In *Little Eyolf* Ibsen continues to conceal under the apparently realistic surface a layer of mythic import. The combination here, however, is not such a happy one. The post-Victorian critic must question whether the obviously moralistic conclusion of the play can be taken seriously, given the character of the persons involved. This has led at least one such critic to argue that Ibsen was playing a grim joke on his audience, a joke very like that which Professor Rubek perpetrated on those who commissioned his portrait busts.[2] Yet if the myth which underlies the action is discerned and its relationship to Ibsen's previous work discovered, the meaning of the play is deepened and enriched, and the melodrama and Victorian moralizing which seem to dominate it become less annoying.

The most obvious layer of myth is that which involves the title character. Northrop Frye assigns *Little Eyolf* to the phase of the tragic mythos that he calls the tragedy of innocence, which may involve the cutting off of a youthful life and typically does involve an adjustment on the part of the central character to a new and more mature experience. In this play, he points out, it is the older characters who are educated through the death of the child.[3] Because of this supposed enlightenment or education on the part of Rita and Allmers it is appropriate to call the play a myth of sacrifice and redemption. A closer examination, however, reveals additional levels of myth that relate *Little Eyolf* quite closely to the *Weltanschauung* that Ibsen has been developing since *The Wild Duck.*

The story of the play can be summed up rather briefly. It involves a marriage between a young man of ascetic temperament and noble ideals and a passionate and intensely possessive woman. In some ways the pair are reminiscent of Rosmer and Rebecca, though Rita Allmers certainly lacks Rebecca's intellectual depth and there is reason to question whether Alfred really has the moral sensibilities of Rosmer. These two have a child who, when he was a baby, fell from a table where he was lying unwatched and was so severely injured that ever since he has had to use a crutch. The fact that the parents were engaged in sexual intercourse at the time of the accident heightens their sense of guilt and leads them, in large part, to neglect the child. His existence, moreover, has caused an estrangement between them, principally because of Allmers' sense of guilt. When the play opens Allmers has just returned from a walking trip in the mountains, taken on the advice of his doctor. While on this trip he claims to have undergone a kind of moral transformation that has made him see life in a new light. He had previously been engaged in writing a book on "human responsibility," but during his sojourn in the mountains he decided that the writing of books is vain and that responsibility needs to be worked out in life. Consequently he rushed home to devote himself to the upbringing of his crippled son. The day after he returns, however, the family is visited by a strange and frightening old woman whose profession is ridding houses and villages of rats by luring them out to sea.[4] The little boy, Eyolf, is both fascinated and frightened by her. When she leaves he follows her down to the dock to watch her row away, becomes dizzy, falls in the water and drowns. The poor boys who play around the dock make no attempt to save him, and his parents learn that he is the victim by hearing them shout, "The crutch is floating." This is the end of the first act.

The second act consists of a series of conversations in which each parent tries to shift the blame for Eyolf's drowning, and for his earlier crippling, to the other. Both of them are aware that for the rest of their lives the memory of Eyolf will haunt them with a sense of guilt. The act proceeds to an examination of their past way of life and to the proposal of various alternatives which might provide release from the guilt they feel. The third act continues in much the same vein until, prodded by her sense of remorse and apparently won away from her own selfish egotism, Rita decides to devote her life to providing love and happiness for the poor boys who did nothing to save Eyolf from drowning. Allmers joins her in this resolve, and the play ends with a ringing moral declaration that is reminiscent of the end of *Pillars of Society*. Thus, if the play is to be taken seriously, it is simply the story of how two people are saved or ennobled by the sacrificial death of their child. This level of myth bears further examination.

Little Eyolf is in a double sense his parents' victim. Their neglect led to his initial crippling, and their guilt over that incident has led them to neglect him still further. Allmers' half-sister, Asta, seems largely to act as mother for him, whereas Allmers keeps him locked away at his books and, incidentally, out of sight.[5] Eyolf is his parents' victim also in the sense that he has stood as a barrier between Rita and Allmers and therefore she, at least, has wished him out of the way. She in fact implies such a subconscious wish just before his drowning. There are suggestions here of that "thought-murder" which Strindberg emphasized so strongly in *There Are Crimes and Crimes*.

In spite of the fact that he is a victim, Eyolf seems to maintain his innocence, to harbor no bitterness toward his parents, and to be completely unaware of the strain in their relationship. He seems even to be unaware of his own crippled condition and its implications for his future life. Few generalizations can be made about Eyolf, since we see so little of him, yet it is perhaps safe to say that, in his fascination with the Rat-Wife, he shares some of that poetic sensitivity which characterized Hedvig Ekdal. Like her, too, he dies as a sacrifice in the depths of the sea, but presumably with better and more lasting results.[6]

On the level of the main plot, then, there are two principal actions in the play: the drowning of Little Eyolf and his parents' subsequent decision to devote themselves to altruistic causes. Moreover, a rather direct cause-effect relation is drawn between them. Rita decides to take the poor boys into her home to, as she puts it, "flatter myself into the good graces of the great open eyes" of Eyolf. Although this desire to appease the spirits of the dead has its roots in paganism, the notion that one person may be saved or ennobled through the death of another is most familiar to us from the Judaeo-Christian context. This sacrifice-redemption theme is symbolically suggested by one of Allmers' lines in the first act. When his family expresses amazement that he is giving up his work on the book on human responsibility, he strokes Eyolf's hair and replies, "There is one who comes after me who will do it better." The suggestion is a subtle one, and may be purely accidental, but the words resemble those of John the Baptist. When asked if he were the Messiah he replied, "There cometh one mightier than I after me the latchet of whose shoes I am not worthy to stoop down and unloose."[7] John's reference, of course, is to Christ, who died to save men, and Eyolf's death, in a slightly different sense, apparently saves his parents.

Little Eyolf is, as the title indicates, the dominating figure of the play and his death constitutes its most important action, even though he is on stage for only a few minutes of the first act.[8] Like the wild duck, he functions as a symbol which exists simultaneously on several levels. The level of symbolism with which I have so far been concerned is that of the sacrificial victim. If, however, we examine Eyolf's crippled condition, it is safe to say also that he suggests the crippled condition of his parents' marriage and perhaps of their lives. On this level, too, the figure of the Rat-Wife has its most immediate connection with the action of the play.

Both Rita and Allmers can be said to have lived their lives, up to the time of the play's opening, in complete self-absorption. Rita is a beautiful woman of intense sexual passion, a passion which must have played a principal role in attracting Allmers to her. Once married she is extremely possessive. The idea of sharing her husband with anything, even his work, is abhorrent to her. He exists, it seems, entirely for her satisfaction. Modern psychologists might say that such a woman is compensating for a deep-seated sense of inferiority, but the reason for her behavior is less important here than the fact of it. Allmers, on the other hand, has little of the passionate and much of the ascetic in his nature. Though he seems to have been sexually attracted to Rita in the beginning, he is now frightened and repelled by her ardor. This attitude is, of course, heightened by the fact that in a moment of passion with Rita the unattended Little Eyolf suffered his crippling fall.

Allmers' attitude toward sex, however, constitutes only part of his crippled condition. To fully understand it requires a look at his relationship with his half-sister, Asta. The two were orphaned early in life, but at an age when they were capable of looking after each other. Since, as far as Allmers knew, Asta was his sister in blood, the two became very close. Their relationship has overtones of both incest and transvestism in that Asta used to dress up in Allmers' clothes and play at being his little brother, Eyolf, the name she would have borne had she been a boy. The real crippling factor, though, in this strange and possibly perverse relationship is that it represented for Allmers a kind of idyllic life in which the outside world did not exist. In that sense it might be regarded as the very antithesis of the human responsibility about which he proposed to write. Since his maturity and marriage, he has been unable to cut himself off from this relationship with Asta, continuing to cling to it as a dream of childish purity. The fact that he named his own son Eyolf symbolically suggests this adherence to the essentially childish mode of existence which he enjoyed with his supposed sister. If Rita is overly possessive, Allmers is equally guilty in that his loyalties are divided. He cannot really come to Rita as a husband because he still clings sentimentally to his relationship with Asta. (In this respect he can be compared with both Ellida, who clings to her seaman lover, and Dr. Wangel, who clings to his dead wife's memory.) His guilt is further compounded by the admission that Rita's money and the opportunity it offered to provide for his sister made up a large part of her attraction for him.

The crippled little boy, then, is first a living symbol of his parents' neglect and second, on a more profound level, a symbol of their unwillingness to abandon their own egotistical interests and assume real responsibility. What is undesirable about Rita's passion is not, as some critics have suggested, its physicality, but rather the fact that it is self-centered. What is perverted about Allmers' relationship with Asta is not primarily that it is incestuous, but rather that it is essentially childish. There is about it, perhaps, something reminiscent of the illusion on which the Ekdals lived, though in this play the illusion is not sustaining but limiting.

When the Rat-Wife appears, in what is perhaps one of the most richly suggestive scenes that Ibsen ever wrote, she says that she can free the house of things that creep and crawl and gnaw. On the most literal level, of course, she means rats and other vermin. On the first level of symbolism she may mean the reminder of Rita's and Allmers' guilt, Little Eyolf. On another level, however, she perhaps means that she can free them of those limitations which prevent them from becoming truly human. If the ending of the play is to be taken seriously, that is precisely what the death of Eyolf accomplishes. Halvdan Koht compares her function in the play with that of Ulrik Brendel in *Rosmersholm*. She comes in briefly, speaks in a riddling fashion, and drives the action forward.[9] The analogy can, in fact, be extended in that Brendel, too, indicates to Rebecca and Rosmer the nature of the sacrifice that must be made if man is to be ennobled.

The basic mythical pattern on which the play is built is, therefore, that of sacrifice and redemption. Eyolf dies that others might live more abundantly; this is a reworking of the scapegoat pattern that finds its most obvious manifestation in the Christian gospel.

Yet one cannot be content with that, accepting one critic's assertion that *Little Eyolf* is simply a sad, sweet ethical exhortation.[10] Though the surface seems simple, the play is a good deal more complex than that.[11] It proceeds to deal, much more profoundly than is at first apparent, with the same life-problem with which Ibsen had been concerned since *The Wild Duck*. To discover the way in which these problems are handled, we must further examine the characters, the relationships between them, and the cosmological symbolism which appears more obviously in this play than it has in Ibsen's previous work.

Allmers is a scholar of sorts and a man of letters. He is supposedly writing a book on human responsibility. Yet his own ability to assume responsibility is sadly limited. The most obvious indication of this is the book itself. So far as the reader or spectator knows, he has done no writing. The ream of paper he carried to the mountains came back completely unmarked. Of his work before the trip we know only that he brooded over his book alone in his room till late at night. However, Hjalmar Ekdal also "worked" on his invention by locking himself in for long periods of time. Thus, the book is a "life-lie" akin to that invention, and there is no evidence in the text to prove otherwise.[12]

Like Hjalmar, too, Allmers seems to enjoy indulging himself in his own emotional states. He torments himself first because Eyolf is dead, later because he has not grieved enough — and in the midst of his breast-beating he wonders what he will have for dinner.[13] Though the caricature is not so broadly drawn as in the case of Hjalmar, Allmers' rhetoric and actions strike a distinctly similar note. He makes a theatrical attempt at suicide from which he is rather easily dissuaded. In his long scene with Rita in the second act, he tries desperately to shift the blame for what happened to Eyolf to her shoulders. In short, Allmers grieves extravagantly for his lost son but seeks in every way to avoid responsibility for what happened. He seems in love with his own grief, as Relling indicated Hjalmar Ekdal would be.

In the same scene, Rita directly charges him with continuing to dwell in his romantic idyll with Asta while at the same time taking his pleasure with her. Again Allmers tries to shut out the reality:

> RITA. . . . It was Asta, nevertheless. . . . Or no – it was Little
> Eyolf. Little Eyolf, my dear!
> ALLMERS. Eyolf —?
> RITA. Yes, you used to call her Eyolf didn't you? I seem to re-
> member your telling me so once – in a moment of confi-
> dence. Do you remember it – that entrancingly beautiful
> hour, Alfred?
> ALLMERS. I remember nothing! I will not remember!
> RITA. It was in that hour when your other Little Eyolf was
> crippled for life.

Immediately after this exchange Allmers "discovers" that he cannot stay any longer with Rita and seeks escape by returning to his childlike relationship with Asta. Such a return is impossible, however, for Asta has discovered, through her mother's correspondence, that she is not really his half-sister, but rather the product of an extramarital affair between her mother and another man. Her relationship with Allmers is thereby placed on an entirely new footing. The societal bars to a sexual union between them are now removed, but Allmers again dodges responsibility by refusing to recognize that it was a sexually based love that really united them. In the beginning of the third act he asks her to remain with him and Rita as a substitute for Little Eyolf, something that, in view of the changed basis of their relationship, she clearly cannot do.

Thus, the life of responsibility of which Allmers talks is, in the last analysis, an illusion. His whole life has been an attempt to avoid responsibility. He has, moreover, wronged both of the women in his life – Rita by marrying her largely out of mercenary consid-erations, and Asta by refusing to recognize the real basis of the feelings that have united them. Asta should have been his true "traveling companion," but when he is given a chance to correct the situation he flees from it.[14]

If this analysis of Allmers' character is correct, what of his experience of transformation in the mountains and the "law of change" that runs like a leitmotif through the play? Close exam-ination will reveal that this also is mere pretense. During his sojourn in the mountains. Allmers supposedly became lost and, as he wandered trying to discover his way again, he felt that death was his "traveling companion." The experience of that night on the heights, face to face with death, revealed to him that his real duty lay in devoting himself to the upbringing of his son. This appears to be a noble resolution, but his behavior when he returns is full of contradictions. He proposes first to bring Eyolf's desires into harmony with what is attainable to him and agonizes over the boy's desire to learn to swim and to climb mountains. Yet a few minutes later he tells Borgheim, "I intend to make a real open-air boy out of him"; this is precisely what Eyolf's crippled condition prevents him from being.[15] A few lines later he goes even further, asserting that "Eyolf shall be the complete man of our race," a curiously noble ambition for a crippled boy.[16] Another interesting facet of Allmers' devotion to Eyolf is the fact that, as Rita points out, it will provide him with an additional excuse for not being a complete husband to her; Eyolf takes the place of the unwritten book as a handy escape mechanism. Allmers' constant invocation of the "law of change," then, is merely a pious slogan, and his mountaintop transformation is more imagined than real. He has, in fact, changed very little, and his continued selfishness is revealed at the end of the play when he wishes to tear down all the hovels and drive the poor people away from the waterfront because they did nothing to save Eyolf.[17]

Though Rita is equally egocentric, she is, in one respect, the exact opposite of Allmers. He seeks to escape responsibility in lofty moralizing, whereas she remains, as she says, earthbound. It would perhaps be a bit strong to call her a hedonist, but she sees little value in ideals. She feels sympathy for Eyolf because Allmers makes him study so hard but she does not really wish to be bothered with motherhood. She is jealous of Allmers' work, which keeps him away from her. Her strongest interest is the erotic one.

The loss of Eyolf brings about a crisis for Rita and Allmers. Their feelings of guilt over having neglected him now come clearly to the fore and the additional fact that their marriage has been largely a sham during the nine years following his crippling cannot now be ignored. The problem, however, is not merely personal or psychological but metaphysical as well. Rita and Allmers are at the end of their tether, so to speak, and must search for a means to face life.

This aspect of the problem is pointed up sharply at several spots in their second act conversation. To begin, Allmers recounts a dream he has had in which Eyolf was still alive and in which he realized that the drowning was really a dream. He concludes, "Oh how I thanked and blessed . . ." and at that point breaks off. Rita then challenges him:

> RITA. (Looking at him) Whom?
> ALLMERS. (Evasively) Whom —?
> RITA. Yes, whom did you thank and bless?
> ALLMERS. . . . I was only dreaming, you know.
> RITA. One whom you yourself do not believe in?
> ALLMERS. That was how I felt all the same. Of course I was sleeping.
> RITA. You should not have taught me to doubt, Alfred.
> ALLMERS. Would it have been right of me to let you go through life with your head full of empty fictions?
> RITA. It would have been better for me; for then I should have had something to take refuge in. Now I don't know where to turn.

Following this suggestion that religion does not provide a viable means of dealing with their predicament, Allmers suggests that suicide might be the alternative. They could both go, he says, to join Little Eyolf, but they both openly admit that they could not do it.

> RITA. . . . I could not. — I feel it. No, no, I never could! Not for all the glory of heaven!
> ALLMERS. Nor I.
> RITA. No, isn't that true, Alfred? You couldn't do it either!
> ALLMERS. No, for it is here in the earthly life that we human beings are at home.
> RITA. Yes, here is the kind of happiness that we can understand.

Their conceptions of earthly happiness are, of course, vastly different, but the suggestion is made that perhaps they could try to forget Eyolf and the guilt they suffer on his account. They propose several possible means of so doing:

RITA. Couldn't we try traveling — far away?

ALLMERS. Away from home? You, who cannot live anyplace but right here?

RITA. Then let us have many people about us. Keep open house! Plunge into something that can deaden and dull our thoughts.

ALLMERS. Such a life would be impossible for me. No, I would rather try to take up my work again.

RITA. (bitingly) Your work — That which has stood like a wall between us.

ALLMERS. (Slowly and looking fixedly at her) There must always be a wall between us from now on.

Thus, several alternatives to their present mode of existence are posed and rejected. Travel, friends, work, even, by implication, love and sex are found wanting. Allmers, of course, still has one escape route in mind, his relationship with Asta, but he soon discovers that that too is closed to him.

If neither religion, nor work, nor travel, nor love, nor even suicide are acceptable alternatives to their predicament, what is left? A partial answer may be found by looking at the one character who has so far not been discussed. The road builder, Borgheim, represents an alternative mode of existence that Allmers and Rita have not considered. He lives the life of earth also, but in a different way than Rita. As an engineer he is engaged in the world, at the service of his fellow men. This is not to say that Borgheim is a conscious idealist; he himself says nothing of the kind. Nevertheless, his work of pushing roads over the mountains and through the wilderness is of direct benefit to humanity. He could, in a sense, be said to be the living embodiment of the human responsibility about which Allmers only talks.[18]

In respect to "human responsibility," however, Borgheim differs drastically from Allmers. He simply does not bother himself with such abstractions, but builds roads because he finds enormous joy in the work. This is clearly indicated shortly after his first entrance when he tells Rita and Allmers that he has completed his work in their district and has accepted a new commission in the north: "It's a big road-job — up in the north. With mountains to cross and with the most unbelievable difficulties to overcome. (Breaking out) Oh, you big beautiful world — what a joy it is to be a roadbuilder!" Borgheim's work, then, though beneficial to humanity, is not an obligation to mankind, but rather a series of challenges, "unbelievable difficulties" to be met zestfully and overcome. Nor is this joy in life to be confined to his work; it overflows to encompass all of life. When Allmers tells Borgheim that he proposes to make an open-air boy out of Eyolf, the latter's response is one of total approval: "Yes, that's right! Out into the open air with him also, the poor boy! Good Lord, one can't do anything better than to play in this blessed world. I think, myself, that all of life is like a game! . . ." It could be argued that Borgheim is just as shortsighted as Allmers concerning Eyolf's possibilities, but such an argument is difficult to sustain. Allmers, as has been indicated, is inconsistent and sentimental about Eyolf's handicap. If the boy's education were left to Borgheim, he would be taught to accept his crippled condition as another of those "unbelievable difficulties" with which all men are faced, and urged to struggle to overcome it just as Borgheim struggles to push his roads through the mountains. Thus, in this case too, Borgheim would do what Allmers only talks about doing.[19]

The young road builder also rejects the "law of change" to which Allmers is committed. In the first act, for example, Rita tells him that Allmers' "furlough," like everything else in life, must come to an end. Borgheim takes issue and argues that there are some things in life that do not end. He is referring, of course, to his love for Asta, but the statement can be taken, nonetheless, as an article of faith in life. In the third act his boyish exuberance has been somewhat modified by the death of Eyolf, but he is firm in his conviction that one can overcome difficulties and sorrows by oneself — it is joy that needs sharing. Asta then describes to him her life with Allmers, which ended, she says, because of the "law of change." Borgheim's response is again an assertion of faith in the permanence of things, "Ah, — what a stupid law that must be! I don't believe at all in such a law."

Borgheim, then, stands in sharp contrast to both Rita and All-mers. He differs from Rita in that, though he is wedded to the life and happiness of the earth, his concept of that happiness is not, like hers, selfish. Joy, to him, does not mean possession and self-satisfaction, but, rather, challenges boldly met and overcome and an un-bridled pleasure in existence that must be shared in order to be fully possessed. Rita does not wish to share anything, but to clutch things to herself. She could not be Borgheim's wife or mistress as she threatens, for she would be jealous of every minute he spent building roads and of every word he said about it at the end of the day's work. To her, the only allowable joy is that in which she can be involved.

Unlike Allmers, Borgheim does not seek idealistic justification for what he does. The fact that he is alive in the world is sufficient reason for him to try to master it. The work he does benefits others but he has no time to speculate on its effects. He simply does it and finds joy in it. He has no time for either indulging himself in his own sorrows or lamenting about how things change. Life may be a game to Borgheim, but the game demands all of one's ener-gies. The contrast between the two men is pointed up most sharply by the fact that Asta stands between them as Allmers stands be-tween the two women. When she discovers that Allmers will not take the responsibility of accepting their old relationship on its new footing, she agrees to go with Borgheim.

If we note the affinities between Alfred Allmers and Hjalmar Ekdal — their tendency to dream rather than to work, their ten-dency toward self-dramatization — and if we observe the resem-blance, in their asceticism and futile idealism, between Allmers and Johannes Rosmer, it is possible to see in Borgheim the "new man." In *Rosmersholm* Ibsen had identified Peder Mortensgaard with the wave of the future. In *Little Eyolf* he presents a more positive figure, for Borgheim is completely without guile. He is able to accept life on its own terms but he does not suffer any de-filement in the process. If Rita, with her passionate nature, repre-sents the pagan principle and Allmers, the Galilean, Borgheim seems to stand for a third empire fusion. He serves mankind, but he does not do so deliberately and consciously. He lives as he does simply because he exists, and he lives with that joy which Ibsen had so often in the past seen as lacking in Christianity.[20] In spite of all this, however, Borgheim lacks plausibility as a character. He is too good to be true and believable. Despite his boundless enthusiasm he is, as a person, uninteresting. The possessive and jealous Rita or even the weak and vacillating Allmers exercise more fascination over the audience than does he. In the last analysis he becomes a sort of walking moral, an embodiment of health both physical and spiritual, but not an interesting character. An actor would have to exercise great care to keep him from becoming a comic caricature, an Adam Trueheart hero of melodrama. This difficulty with Borgheim is, I think, closely related to the difficulty which even Ibsen sensed in the end of his play, a point discussed below.

In *Little Eyolf* Ibsen, for the first time, unites elements of the natural world that have appeared in earlier plays in a hierarchically ordered cosmos. The three levels, in this play, are the heights, the lowlands, and the sea. The mountains or heights are found in *Brand*, in *Peer Gynt*, in the narrative poem "Paa Vidderne," and, of course, in *The Master Builder*. In the poem the mountains seem to represent freedom and God. The narrator leaves the lowland behind to follow his guide and wander in the mountains; his act is an idealistic transcendence of the life led by those who "fumble" in the valleys. In *Brand*, written seven years later, and in *The Master Builder*, the heights are still a challenge and a calling but they are also destructive. Both Brand and Solness die when they reach their high places.[21] Like his predecessors Allmers climbs the mountain and meets there a strange "traveling companion" whom he interprets to be death, and as a result of this meeting he undergoes a transformation. This "traveling companion" seems clearly to suggest the mysterious guide of myth, perhaps the one who appeared earlier in "Paa Vidderne." Allmers, however, does not follow the guide. He comes scurrying down from the mountain full of rhetoric about transformation and the law of change. Both Solness and Brand purchased their moment of transformation at the cost of their lives, but Allmers tarries only long enough to glimpse death, and flees. Furthermore, the real extent of his transformation is somewhat dubious. In fact, Ibsen takes some pains to point out that Allmers did not really scale the heights at all. If his story is carefully examined, it becomes clear that he was not actually climbing a peak but wandering through the valleys and along the shores of a mountain lake. In the very beginning of the play Asta comments that the mountain air may have been "rather too sharp" for Allmers, and what we subsequently learn of his character suggests that the clear air of idealism is indeed too sharp for him to breathe.

The lowlands are the natural habitat of man and if he fumbles there, as Ibsen suggested in "Paa Vidderne," that is perhaps his natural lot. In the life of the earth, as Rita suggests, most men find the happiness that they can understand. Yet man is not completely secure there either, as the intrusion of the Rat-Wife indicates; he cannot, therefore, lead a completely self-centered existence. Indeed, if Allmers thought to escape death by fleeing from the mountains, she demonstrates that he was simply deluding himself. The lowlands are no more secure from death than was Old Ekdal's attic forest. If one must live there, however, Borgheim's way seems to be the proper one. One must take life as a challenge without worrying unduly about either responsibility or reward.

The third element of the cosmos in *Little Eyolf* is the sea, which has made its symbolic appearance also in *The Wild Duck* and *The Lady from the Sea*. In the former, the destructive aspect of the sea seemed to predominate; in the latter, its fascinating or luring aspects. In *Little Eyolf* the two elements, destruction and fascination, are combined in the figure of the Rat-Wife. Schechner is correct, I think, in saying that she shares the demonic character of the Stranger in the earlier play,[22] but she strikes me as being much more sinister. Her lines are full of dark allusions to both death and sex, and some Freudian critics have made a great deal of the equation of the two.[23] The simple explanation of this equation, however, can be found without speculating upon Ibsen's psychological state. The sexual instinct is a strong one that has traditionally been thought to lure men to destruction. Sex and death have been regarded as dark chthonic powers and have been the objects of primitive worship. In *Little Eyolf*, as in *The Lady from the Sea*, the sea is most clearly identified with that dangerous unknown, a mysterious force which is both creative and destructive. The Rat-Wife lures Eyolf to his death in the sea, but on the first level of myth that death is also a kind of life, for Eyolf's death makes possible a meaningful life for Allmers and Rita. This is symbolically indicated at the end of the second act, when Asta brings Allmers a handful of water lilies, "the sort that shoot up from the very depths," as a last gift from Little Eyolf.

This play, then, contains more clearly than any of the earlier ones a three-level cosmos, with each level having its symbolic significance. The heights are, or may be, a place of transfiguration, but they may also be a place of death, as indicated by Allmers' "traveling companion." The lowlands are the natural habitat of man and contain the potential of happiness for those who know how to find it. They are, however, surrounded by the sea and are subject to its destructive intrusions. The sea is the source of death, as indicated by the deliberate equation drawn by Allmers between the Rat-Wife and his "traveling companion." The sea may also be the source of life, as indicated by the water lilies' shooting up from Eyolf's resting place.

Such a symmetrical, three-part cosmology is familiar from many mythologies; indeed Frye says it is itself a branch of myth.[24] The obvious example for Western culture is the Christian cosmology of heaven, earth, and hell, but the Greeks too had their Mount Olympus, earth, and the underworld. According to Norse mythology the world was created in three parts, heaven, earth, and the sea, from the body of the giant Ymir.[25] In such mythologies, also, each level has its significance. The earth, of course, is always the home of men; Heaven is the dwelling place of the gods; the mountaintop, according to Frye, is a part of the apocalyptic world[26] and is the point of contact between the human world and the gods or the animating powers of the universe.[27] The sea exists in both the demonic and the apocalyptic worlds as a source of destruction, a state of chaos, and dissolution following death, but also as a source of renewal.[28] There is, of course, no evidence that Ibsen drew directly on mythological sources for his cosmology. What is significant, nevertheless, is the fact that he created one in *Little Eyolf* and that he employs it similarly in the two following plays. By so doing he outlines the universe in the fashion that, as Frye indicates, is typical of myth.

Within this universe Ibsen has juxtaposed his characters so that, as in previous plays, they represent various ways of approaching life. Allmers appears, at first, to be an idealistic climber of heights, but in the final analysis one must agree with Weigand that Ibsen's treatment of him is ironic. His ideal of "human responsibility" is a kind of life-lie, and he resembles Hjalmar Ekdal much more closely than he does Brand or Solness, or even Gregers Werle and Johannes Rosmer. Rita is an example of a person who can be happy only in the lowlands. The type of ideal about which Allmers talks has no meaning for her. Yet her basically down-to-earth approach to existence is wrong in that it is totally self-centered. The way of life that Ibsen seems to endorse is represented by Borgheim and, to a lesser degree, by Asta. They live the life of earth both usefully and happily because they are devoted neither exclusively to themselves nor to an abstraction or visionary ideal. They are free, but their freedom seems, by implication, to include that modest but genuine responsibility which was the solution to Ellida's dilemma in *The Lady from the Sea*.

This combination of freedom and responsibility seems, indeed, to be the solution adopted by Rita and Allmers at the end of the play when they resolve to live their lives in service to humanity by caring for and loving the poor boys who live by the docks. This conclusion has led traditionally minded critics to see the play as a moral exhortation in which the baser passions are transcended by idealism. Yet, if my interpretation of Rita and Allmers is correct, their moral transformation at the end of the play is almost totally unbelievable. Thus, the critic who attempts to evaluate this play is faced with a real problem.

The most tempting way out, perhaps, is that offered by Weigand, for the irony in the treatment of Allmers is obvious. Such a solution, however, is too easy. The sacrifice-redemption theme inherent in the play must lead to a conclusion of the sort that Ibsen has provided, and there is no indication in the final scene that he was treating the resolution ironically. In the somewhat similar conclusion of *The Wild Duck*, there is a Dr. Relling to offer the author's ironic comment on the value of the sacrifice and the durability of Hjalmar's ennoblement. No such figure exists in *Little Eyolf*. There seems to be no escaping the conclusion that Ibsen meant to have the moral transformation taken seriously.

Various critics have offered other answers to the problem. Valency, for instance, asserts that Ibsen simply surrendered to the tradition of the second empire drama which demanded a sentimental and moralistic ending.[29] Knight finds the conclusion acceptable as "a brief indication signifying goodness."[30] Koht offers a more plausible explanation. He recounts that after seeing a performance of the play Ibsen asked a friend, "Do you think that Rita will carry on with the unfortunate boys? Don't you think that it is just a holiday mood?"[31] This suggests, according to Koht, that Ibsen himself was in doubt about the believability of his conclusion, but at the same time he wanted to believe in the nobility of the soul.[32]

Such an explanation is more acceptable than one which would have required Ibsen to sustain, through the entire play, a complete and subtle deception of the audience. Ibsen had been grappling with the problem of how to live in the world from his very early work, obviously so since *The Wild Duck*. The faith in the possibility of a third empire was still present as late as 1887, and in one other play out of the last eight he had attempted to take an optimistic position. Yet Ibsen's character contained a healthy dose of skepticism coupled with a keen insight into human psychology. However much he may have wished to believe in the possibility that humans could be ennobled through suffering, his penchant for looking honestly at life may have made it more and more difficult for him to write a play in which such a transformation was completely believable. The conclusion strikes a sentimental note at best, and when the characters of Rita and Allmers are taken into account, it strikes a false note — a weakness which Ibsen may have recognized in seeing the play performed. A further indication of this may be found in the fact that his last two plays contain no such facile optimism.

Little Eyolf must, I think, be regarded as the weakest of Ibsen's mature works, though it contains in the Rat-Wife sequence one of his finest scenes. The myth which underlies the play, however, is not greatly different from that which animates the plays preceding it, and the drama is another building block in the world picture which he had been creating since *The Wild Duck*. In the two plays that follow, Ibsen returned to his doomed and tragic climbers of the heights and built his dramas more obviously than ever before on the traditional mythic patterns.

JOHN GABRIEL BORKMAN AND WHEN WE DEAD AWAKEN · MYTHS OF DEATH AND RESURRECTION

❡ THE introductory chapter of this book indicated that underlying all myth there is a basic pattern or Ur-myth which recounts the combat between the god and another force, depicts the suffering and death of the god, and, ultimately, his resurrection.[1] Frye designates this basic pattern the "quest myth." It is closely related to the natural cycle of life and death, waking and sleeping, light and darkness which man shares with the rest of nature.[2] This cyclical pattern is divided into a number of stages, each corresponding to a phase of the myth, to a portion of the natural cycle, and, in Frye's view, to a type of literature. Thus, the summer represents the period during which the god-king is at the height of his powers, the autumn is the period of his overthrow and death, winter is the period of darkness, chaos, and desolation when the god-king is absent, and spring is the time of his resurrection and triumphal return.[3] Intertwined with this pattern is the myth of the hero's search, his separation from society, his passage through regions of danger and desolation, and his eventual return with a boon for his fellow men.

As Ibsen approached the end of his career, his plays came more and more to coincide with these basic mythical patterns. In the plays so far discussed I have traced the emergence of suggestions of a mysterious and nonhuman world, a powerful world which impinges upon and affects human life. The suggestion of such a world of nonhuman "powers" is reinforced by the use of symbolic material drawn from Norse myth and folklore, from classical sources, and from biblical lore. Underlying each of these plays, too, have been certain mythical patterns or themes, sometimes related to specific bits of folklore and myth, sometimes not. Beginning with *The Master Builder*, however, Ibsen seems consciously or unconsciously to have constructed a series of dramas that are clearly based on the stages of the cyclical Ur-myth. *The Master Builder* may be interpreted as a treatment of the ritual sacrifice and death of a god-king figure, represented by Solness. In *Little Eyolf* the pattern is less obvious but the death-rebirth sequence is implicitly contained within it. In the last two plays of his career the pattern becomes obvious. *John Gabriel Borkman* and *When We Dead Awaken* can thus be treated together as two stages of the cycle. The former deals with the period of darkness and desolation which corresponds to the winter phase of the myth during which the god-king and, by extension, the world is dead; the latter, as the title indicates, deals with the resurrection phase. Such a classification is, of course, arbitrary and somewhat oversimplified. Only a detailed examination of the two plays will reveal the ways in which they correspond to the myth, the ways in which they depart from it, and the intricate ways in which Ibsen has woven together his material to create the final components of his world view.

John Gabriel Borkman · The Myth of Winter and Death

Extra-dramatic sources are of little help in approaching *John Gabriel Borkman*. After Ibsen returned to Norway his correspondence drastically dwindled, so that there are only passing references in it to his last plays. The first drafts of the play found in the *Efterladte Skrifter* provide little more that is of use in determining the sources of Ibsen's material or in revealing his intentions in writing the play. Koht indicates that the basic idea for the drama may have come from an incident that Ibsen heard about during his first stay in Christiania. A high-ranking military officer was imprisoned for misappropriation of army funds and after his release he completely isolated himself, refusing to speak even to his wife.[4] Archer suggests that the play was, in a sense, based on *Pillars of Society*, in which Consul Bernick, like Borkman, gave up his real love for business advantage.[5] However valid these observations may be, they do not really provide a key to what Ibsen has done with the raw material. Even if he began with a real-life incident or with an earlier play, he has transformed the material into something far greater than the original source or sources. In many ways Borkman must be compared with Solness, and the play must be regarded as a later stage of the process that is recounted in *The Master Builder*.

John Gabriel Borkman is, like Solness, a man of uncommon gifts, though his lie in the field of finance. Even in defeat he towers over the rest of the characters in the play, with the possible exception of Ella Rentheim. In his younger days he had a great dream of becoming a captain of industry, in order, as he explains it, to free the powers of metals slumbering in the earth so that they could emerge to serve mankind. He has dreamed of building a vast financial empire in which his mines and factories produce goods and his ships span the earth carrying those goods to all portions of it. His has been a dream of conquest not much different, perhaps, from those which inspired Alexander or Tamburlaine, but it is presented in terms particularly applicable to the nineteenth and twentieth centuries. By the time the play opens that dream has long since gone down to defeat, and brought the dreamer with it. Borkman has misappropriated funds belonging to the depositors of the bank for which he was director, has been detected and convicted, and, by the time the action begins, has spent a total of sixteen years in isolation from the world — three years awaiting trial, five more in prison, and eight in self-imposed exile on the top floor of his house. Yet all the while he has maintained his faith that one day a deputation will come to him and ask him to return to the financial world "to take the reins of the bank again — ! The new bank that they have founded and can't manage." This dream is, of course, a foolish and pathetic one but there is about it also a note of nobility. Unlike Old Ekdal, for instance, Borkman has not accepted his defeat and bowed down to his conquerors. In his calm assurance of his own superiority to the forces that have crushed him, there is a heroic dignity that is borne out in other ways as well. He lives in illusion, but a grander illusion than that which sustains Old Ekdal.

This innate dignity is suggested also by his relationship with Ella Rentheim and with his only remaining friend, Old Foldal. Borkman knows the hatred which the whole world, including his wife, bears for him. This is something to which he has become accustomed, and he is able to console himself with the thought that no matter how much people may hate him they will one day come to realize that they need him. Ella Rentheim, however, comes to him with a request that cannot be borne so easily as the blows he has already suffered, nor assuaged by foolish dreams of a visiting deputation. She has come to visit the Borkmans in order to induce their only son, Erhart, to live with her and be her consolation in her few remaining months of life. She wants not only Erhart but something more significant:

> When I die the name of Rentheim dies also.
> And that is such a torturing thought to me.
> To be wiped out of existence — even to the name —
> . . . .
> Let Erhart bear my name after me.

In other words, what she asks of Borkman is exactly what she fears for herself, the complete obliteration of the name of Borkman. It is no sacrifice for him to lose Erhart, for he knows that he has lost him already. However, if a man's existence is continued in his son, Ella is asking Borkman to give up that existence, and any dreams of dynasty that he may still entertain. Borkman's answer is further evidence of the dignity already cited: "Well and good, Ella, I am man enough to bear my name alone."

The surface picture of the relationship between Borkman and

Foldal is one of two old men, each of whom has suffered a defeat, each of whom lives his own life-lie, and each of whom is dependent upon the other to sustain his own faith. Borkman dreams of the deputation that will one day visit him; Foldal dreams that the tragedy he wrote in his youth will eventually be recognized, to bring him fame as an author. Each encourages the other in his vain hope and the similarity between the two men in this respect casts Borkman and his dream in an ironic perspective. To fail to note the differences between them, however, is to do Borkman an injustice. He is not the equivalent of Foldal nor are their dreams equivalent. Borkman has, however briefly, experienced the position of authority to which he hopes to be restored. There is little doubt that, despite his crime, he is even yet capable of taking up the reins of the new bank. There is no such certainty concerning Foldal's talent as an author. Indeed, beside what Borkman has sought to accomplish, beside what he has almost accomplished, Foldal's tragedy is a puny achievement, as he himself recognizes. Furthermore, both men are despised by their families, but Foldal complains about his fate whereas Borkman bears his, for the most part, in stoic silence. If both men are, like the wild duck, wounded creatures, Foldal is the more severely wounded because he was less strong in the beginning. In fact, although Borkman sustains Foldal's faith, the reverse is not necessarily true. When Foldal calls into question his dream of a visiting delegation, Borkman's faith is not diminished; he simply treats the other's comment as a breach of loyalty and the next time there is a knock on the door he draws himself up once again into the Napoleonic pose with which he wishes to receive the emissaries from the world of finance. Thus, Foldal serves a double purpose in the play. On the one hand he serves as an ironic commentary on Borkman and his dream of the restoration of vanished glory; on the other he reveals by contrast how far Borkman stands above the characters who surround him. Indeed, Borkman is physically above all the other characters until the climactic scene of the play. Though he has taken up refuge, that refuge is on the top floor of his house.

In Borkman's bearing, then, and in the events of his life can be perceived an example of the king who has undergone struggle, symbolic defeat, and death. It is not necessary, however, to depend upon such obscure symbolism. Gunnhild specifically equates Borkman's position in the financial world with the kingly position. The words, true, are spoken bitterly but that does not alter the fact of Borkman's past position of eminence: "Oh yes, we had to put on a show. And he really put on a show! Drove with four-in-hand — just as if he were a king. Allowed people to bow and scrape for him like a king. . . . And then they called him by his first name — all over the country — just as if he were the king himself. 'John Gabriel,' 'John Gabriel.' They all knew what a great man was 'John Gabriel!'" The word *king* is used three times in this brief passage, and what we have seen of Borkman's own bearing and demeanor reinforces its application. Thus, Borkman occupied a position in the financial world comparable with that which Solness held as builder and, like Solness, he has fallen. At least two other critics interpret his position similarly. Valency, for example, notes that the destruction of such a figure is as close as we can come in the middle-class drama of modern times to the fall of a prince.[6] G. Wilson Knight comments that Ibsen had decided that the man, in his day, who wielded the power of the superman and the messiah as envisioned in *Emperor and Galilean* was the financier.[7]

If Borkman is, like Solness, a symbolic king-figure who falls, there are many indications that the play portrays a later stage of the myth than that presented in *The Master Builder*. In the earlier play Solness is physically healthy and vigorous. Though beset by doubts and threatened from below he is still very much in command of his world. What we witness in the play is the actual moment of his overthrow, as he climbs his tower, experiences a kind of epiphany, and is sent hurtling back to earth. Borkman, on the other hand, has fallen long before the play begins. In him we see only the remnants of kingship — the memory of what he has been, the shreds of dignity that still remain, the hope of restoration to which he stubbornly clings. The moment of his physical death in the last act is of less importance than the symbolic death that occurred sixteen years before when he lost his "kingdom" and was sent to prison. Since that time, Gunnhild tells him, he has been dead, and his only duty now is to lie quiet in his grave. Indeed, as Steiner indicates, all of the characters, except for Erhart, Frida Foldal, and Fanny Wilton, are symbolically dead, though they move and talk like living beings.[8]

The seasonal symbolism simply reinforces this theme. In Frye's "quest-myth" autumn is the period of violent overthrow and death of the king, and winter is the period of desolation and death that follows. The action of *The Master Builder* takes place, as far as can be determined, in the autumn, though the season is not made obvious in that play. (Hilda, however, is returning from her summer walking tour of the mountains, which indicates that the season must be late summer or autumn.) There can be no doubt that *John Gabriel Borkman* is a play of winter. It is pervaded, from the very first scene, by images of cold. A raging snowstorm can be seen through the window when the play opens, and Gunnhild sits with a woolen shawl around her shoulders. A few minutes later she tells Ella that she is always cold. Though three of the four acts take place indoors, hats, coats, and outdoor gear are prominent among the properties. The last act moves outdoors into the frozen landscape: "The snowstorm has ceased but the newly fallen snow has drifted deep around. The fir branches droop under heavy loads of snow. The night is dark with drifting clouds. Now and then the moon gleams faintly. Only a dim light is reflected from the snow." When Borkman goes out, Ella warns him that the winter air will be too cold for him. A few minutes later Foldal appears, covered with snow; he has been knocked down by Fanny Wilton's sleigh. When Borkman dies he feels his heart gripped by a "hand of ice," and the two sisters agree that the cold killed him. In addition to these images of cold, there are images of darkness. The entire play takes place in the evening. The rooms are dimly lit by a few lamps, and in the last act there is only the dim light of the moon. A specific contrast is drawn in the first act between the dimness of the Borkman house and the bright lights at the Hinkels.[9]

Thus, we have in *John Gabriel Borkman* a group of people who are, for all practical purposes, dead, who live in a dimly lit house in the midst of a cold and frozen landscape. The central figure of this group is the former financial king, Borkman, who, despite the dignity he continues to possess, has been removed from his "kingdom" long before and has entombed himself in his upstairs room, where he waits for a delegation to come and beg him to return to the world. All of these details coincide with Frye's winter stage of the mythic cycle.

In order to grasp the full significance of the play, however, it is necessary to go beyond the comparatively obvious conclusion that Borkman is a fallen king to examine the circumstances surrounding his fall. Such an examination reveals that Ibsen is once more dealing with the life-problem, with idealism versus life, and with the mythos of the heroic call.

The immediate cause of Borkman's fall was his misappropriation of funds placed in his keeping as director of a large bank. That action, however, was only the means to the realization of his great dream, a financial empire that would span the world and bring the powers of the earth into the service of mankind. Once he had established his empire on a firm footing, Borkman had every intention of returning the funds he had used to establish it. The manner in which he justifies his action demonstrates that other people are for him only the expendable means to an end, just as for the general soldiers are only an expendable means to victory. Borkman regards himself as an exceptional man to whom the strictures of ordinary morality do not apply. As far as he is concerned, the theft of the bank funds was less significant than the end for which he wished to employ them, and his downfall is due not to his own guilt but to the machinations of his enemies and to bad luck.

The precise nature of the motivations which underlay his great dream is ambiguous and Borkman's own statements contribute to that ambiguity. An examination of a few of the speeches in which he discusses his dream reveal the contradictions in them. Speaking to Foldal, for example, he says:

Yes, but think of me, who could have controlled millions! All the mines I should have controlled! Innumerable new veins! Waterfalls! Quarries! The trade-routes and steamship lines over the whole wide world. All, all that I alone would have organized!

The chief motivation here seems to have been a desire for power. In speaking to Ella, however, he adds another, more altruistic motive:

> I wanted to have at my command all the sources of power in this country. All the wealth that lay hidden in the soil and the rocks and the forest and the sea — I wanted to gather it all into my hands, to make myself master of it all, and so to promote the well-being of many, many thousands.

A few minutes later Ella accuses him of having made a bargain by which he exchanged her for the opportunity to advance his dream. His reply now casts doubt upon the credibility of the altruistic motive he has just cited:

> Yes, I did, Ella! For the love of power was so uncontrollable in me, you see! So I struck the bargain. I had to. And he helped me halfway up toward the beckoning heights that I was intent on reaching.

Still later, in the third act, another revealing exchange takes place:

> GUNNHILD. You have never loved anything outside of yourself; that is the secret of the whole matter.
> BORKMAN. (Proudly) I have loved power.
> GUNNHILD. Yes, power!
> BORKMAN. The power to create human happiness, wide, wide around me!

Thus, there are two motives presented for Borkman's dream of financial empire. The first coincides with what might be termed the folklore of nineteenth-century capitalism. The industrialist, the financial entrepreneur really serves mankind; in promoting his own interests he promotes the interests of the community, of all mankind. Russell H. Conwell merely gave a religious tone to the idea when he said, in his famous "Acres of Diamonds" speech: "Money is power, and you ought to be reasonably ambitious to have it. You ought because you can do more good with it than you could without it. Money printed your Bible, money builds your churches, money sends your missionaries and money pays your preachers. . . . Money is power, money is force, money will do good as well as harm. In the hands of good men and women it could accomplish, and it has accomplished good." [10] This motive is perhaps not entirely false. What is significant, however, is that it frequently seems to come as an afterthought and to be less vehemently expressed than the other motive – the love of power for its own sake. There are, in fact, in the lines quoted, three references to power as opposed to two concerning service to mankind. At least half of Borkman's dream has been to see himself in control of a vast empire. His is a case of hybris, a pride which has led him to place himself above all moral and human considerations.

This pride is clearly revealed in his relationships with the other characters. Haakonsen points out that Borkman has wronged both Gunnhild and Ella, in that he has devoted himself to his inhuman ideal and neglected his human responsibilities to both.[11] His crime against Ella Rentheim is the most obvious. She loved John Gabriel and he seems to have had some affection for her, but she was also loved by Hinkel, the man who was in a position to obtain for Borkman the directorship of the bank. Since this was an important stepping-stone toward the realization of his dream, he sold her – marrying her sister so that Hinkel would not stand in his way. It is this that Ella calls the one unforgivable sin, the murder of the love-life in another human being. Toward Gunnhild he is equally guilty. He married her not out of love, but because she represented no threat to his precious dream. She was merely an asset and he even made use of her at his trial by trying to shift the blame for his theft to her desire to live ostentatiously. The real core of his crime against her is most tellingly revealed by Gunnhild herself in the lines that follow those previously quoted.

GUNNHILD. You once had the power to make me happy. Have you used it?
BORKMAN. Someone must usually go under in a shipwreck.
GUNNHILD. And your own son! Have you used your power and have you lived and labored to make him happy?
BORKMAN. Him I do not know.

Borkman speaks truthfully here and in a deeper sense than he knows. Not merely has he avoided his son in the eight years since he was released from prison; he has, in fact, never recognized either his son or his wife as persons, but only, as he specifically indicates, as parts of himself. In his devotion to the happiness of the abstract thousands, he has ignored the happiness of the real people at his side, just as Solness built homes in which strangers could be happy while in his own home there was no happiness either for himself or for his wife. He complains of never having found understanding, and Gunnhild justly points out that he has never come to her in search of understanding. He has had room in his life for nothing but his dream of financial power.

Still, such a character can exist on the plane of psychological drama. To justify placing Borkman on the mythic plane, I must delve further into what made him what he is. To do so will necessarily involve dealing with one level of the play's cosmology — the underground of Borkman's mines. To put it simply, he is a man obsessed, but he is obsessed not merely by a dream of wealth. More correctly, perhaps, he is possessed, possessed by a set of mysterious powers that dwell under the earth. The first mention of these powers is in the second act, as Frida Foldal is playing the piano.

> BORKMAN. Can you guess where I first heard tones such as those?
> FRIDA. No, Mr. Borkman.
> BORKMAN. It was down in the mines.
> FRIDA. (Not understanding) So? Down in the mines?
> BORKMAN. I'm a miner's son, you know. Or perhaps you didn't know?
> FRIDA. No, Mr. Borkman.
> BORKMAN. A miner's son. And sometimes my father took me with him down in the mines. Down there the metal sings.
> FRIDA. Oh, does it sing?
> BORKMAN. (Nods) When it is released. The hammer blows which release it — that is the midnight clock which strikes and sets it free. Therefore the metal sings — out of joy — in its own way.

This singing is, to Borkman, a sign that the metal wants to get free and to serve mankind. The singing and crying of the metal have engendered his dream of financial empire and continue to lure him on. Borkman is convinced that he alone hears its cries and that he is thus uniquely chosen. He actually personifies the hidden metals and claims to have seen them as visible shapes that stretched out their luring arms to him as he stood before the vault trying to decide whether or not he should take the money that rightfully belonged to his depositors. All this, of course, could be taken as the raving of a mad old man, but in other essential respects Borkman does not seem to be mad. He is no madder, at least, than Solness with his talk of helpers and servers.

In fact, Borkman's underground powers, like Solness' helpers and servers, have their counterparts in Norse mythology. The helpers and servers have been compared to the *fylgje*; the powers to which Borkman refers can best be compared to the *underjordiske* — the "underground folk" who play an important part in Scandinavian folklore. These creatures are not necessarily evil, but they can be, and any dealing with them involves some risk.[12] There are countless tales in Norwegian folklore of children and young girls being stolen by the underground folk, sometimes in revenge against humans who had not accorded them the proper respect. In one tale it is said that they belonged originally to the party of angels that was driven out of heaven with Lucifer.[13] The belief in underground spirits, however, predates Christianity in Scandinavia. Ellis-Davidson indicates that when the gods created men they also created a race of dwarves who dwelt in hills and rocks and bred in the earth. Of some significance, perhaps, in connection with *John Gabriel Borkman*, is the fact that this race of dwarves were skilled craftsmen and metalworkers who made treasures for the gods.[14]

There is, as in most such cases previously cited, no direct evidence that Ibsen deliberately drew upon the materials of myth and folklore, but he certainly must have been familiar with these tales from his earlier reading and his walking tour through the rural valleys of Norway. More significant, however, is the relation to Ibsen's earlier poem and to the myth of the hero's quest. In "The Miner" Ibsen pictures a man delving deep into the earth, raining hammerblow after hammerblow on the rock until he hears the metal sing. The miner of the title is seeking the secret of life under the earth, and the underground is one of the common regions of the mysterious through which the mythic hero's quest leads him. In the course of his search the hero encounters powers, some of whom wish him well and others ill. In Borkman's journeys into the mines he too encountered powers and followed them, but if he took them to be beneficent guides he was mistaken. He has given himself in thrall to those powers, he follows their call, and to them, in the last scene, he still proclaims his love: ". . . I love you as you lie there spellbound in the depths and in the darkness! I love you in your life-demanding power — with all your shining train of power and honor! I love you, love you, love you!" As Ella Rentheim indicates, this is precisely Borkman's crime. He has ignored the possibilities of human love in his obsession for the powers under the earth: "Yes, down there you have your love still, John. Have always had it there. But up here in the daylight — here there was a warm and living heart that beat for you. And that heart you crushed. Yes, worse than that! Ten times worse! You sold it for — . . ."

The power for which Borkman sold his human love is ultimately destructive. The metallic spirits of the earth kill him. In the last act Borkman feels his hand gripped first by a hand of ice and a few seconds later by a hand of metal. Yet it is not at the last only that these powers are destructive. That they have always been so is subtly indicated in the beginning of the second act. In the mines, says Borkman, he first heard the metal singing in tones like those that Frida Foldal is now playing, and the tune she plays is the *Danse Macabre* — the dance of death.

Ibsen probably did not mean to suggest that the act of mining was in itself evil. However tempted a modern critic might be to read the play as an indictment of capitalism, the fact remains that Ibsen seems not to have been concerned with specific political or economic systems. Borkman is not guilty of being a miner or a capitalist or, at last, even of being a thief. His chief crime has been his failure to be a complete human being. In this sense, also, he is like Solness, but his guilt is greater in that, first, he has actually committed a crime and second, he never, even in the moment of death, recognizes the extent of his own responsibility for the direction his life has taken.[15] He remains true to his obsession to the very end. The underground powers in this play function much as do the witches in *Macbeth*; they play upon a weakness already present in Borkman. Their singing is a siren call that leads him to follow what is in fact a false ideal and to totally neglect his human possibilities.

Borkman's obsession has led him to ignore one level of the play's cosmology and to misinterpret another. He has refused to dwell on the plane of human happiness (the option elected by Ellida, Borgheim, and Asta), and as a result the lives of both Ella and Gunnhild are warped and blasted. In this play the lowland world, which is the abode of human happiness, is frozen and dead. The heights toward which he was climbing are, moreover, not really the heights of idealism. Borkman has followed the wrong guide and his dream was predominantly one of personal power. Brand, too, brought misery to those around him, but his idealism did not seem to be sullied by personal ambition. When Borkman at last climbs up to the literal heights, at the end of the play, he is not struck down from above as were Solness and Brand; he is dragged down by a hand of metal, a hand in whose grip he has been all along. Thus, there seems not to be even an ambiguous triumph in *John Gabriel Borkman*. The very possibility of attaining the heights of idealism is called into question.

Yet there is an alternative to the fate of Borkman and those who surround him. This is suggested in the secondary action of the play, the escape of Erhart. From the very beginning Erhart is the object of a struggle between his mother, who wishes him to serve as a living monument that will remove the disgrace that has adhered to the family through his father's action, and his aunt, who wishes him to serve as a consolation to her in her last days and, more importantly, to carry on the name of Rentheim. In essence, both women wish him to devote himself to an abstraction, though Ella is more concerned about his own happiness than is his mother.

Neither alternative, however, appeals to Erhart. At this point Borkman comes forward with a third possibility:

> Listen, Erhart, — will you then go with your father? It is not through anyone else's life that a man can be raised up from his fall. Those are empty dreams that have been spun for you — here in this airless room. If you were to live your life like all the saints put together it would not do me one bit of good.
>
> . . . .
>
> I will raise myself up. Begin at the bottom again. It is only through one's present and one's future that one can atone for his past. Through work — through unceasing work for all that which in my youth stood for life itself, but which now seems a thousand times greater than it did then. Erhart, will you join me and help me with this new life?

All three wish to bind Erhart to the past and to the dead, for whatever Borkman says about the future and a new life, it is clear that his own past is what he wishes to rebuild. In fact, that which "stood for life itself" is his old dream of financial empire, *his* dream, which he wishes to fix upon Erhart.

Erhart, however, has different ideas about how his life should be lived. He rejects the role of saviour of his father's name and of restorer of his father's vanished glory. He rejects the parlors of his mother and his aunt because they are airless and smell of roses and lavender, but he also rejects his father's call to work. He wants to live for his own pleasure and the symbol of that pleasure is his implied sexual relationship with Fanny Wilton. With her and Frida Foldal he will leave the frozen landscape of his parents' home and seek happiness in the southern sun.

Various critics have interpreted this subplot in different ways, but most agree that Erhart's way of life represents an alternative to that of Borkman. Payne sees the Erhart plot as an assertion of every individual's right to live his own life.[16] Thus, Erhart becomes a symbol of individualism. Valency sees him as the exact opposite of his father in that he is willing to sacrifice his career for a few years of happiness. This coincides with the theme of the play as he sees it, "the incompatibility of the desire for success and the need for happiness." [17] Raphael asserts that Erhart is another example of Ibsen's "new man," the spiritual descendent of Borgheim and the precursor of Ulfheim in the last play.[18]

All of these interpretations have validity, but some caution must be exercised in connection with any one of them. Payne's interpretation must be questioned on the grounds that Borkman is, in a sense, as valid a symbol of individualism as his son. He has lived his own life at enormous cost to himself and to those around him and he clings stubbornly, until the very moment of his death, to his dream of power. Valency, on the other hand, seems to miss the rather important point that it is not his own career that Erhart sacrifices but rather one which others wish to impose upon him. Indeed, Erhart has no "career," no freely chosen goal, except that of happiness. Moreover, all three seem to suggest that Ibsen recommends Erhart's choice as superior or preferable to that of Borkman.[19] A closer examination of the play casts some doubt even on this conclusion.

Raphael bases a good deal of his argument on the alleged similarity between Erhart and Borgheim. They are alike in the fact that they are both young and that they both seek to find joy in life, but the crucial difference lies in the nature of that joy. Borgheim's joy of life does not seem to involve sensual pleasure, at least not primarily. He talks, to be sure, of pleasure, but that pleasure is to be found in his work, because it provides him with an opportunity to meet challenges and overcome obstacles. He is, of course, in love with Asta, but he seems in that love less to seek self-gratification than to look for an opportunity to share the enormous joy that he finds in life and in road building. Indeed, if there is a weakness in *Little Eyolf* and in Borgheim as a symbol of the new man, it is that the road builder is such a boy scout as to be very nearly incredible. One wonders how long he can continue in real life without having his bumptious joy dashed or dimmed. Erhart's life, on the contrary, is to be devoted to sheer self-indulgence. He seeks bright lights, music, and "young happy faces." Work is one of the things he specifically rejects in favor of traveling to the south with Fanny

Wilton. There is a qualitative difference between the two kinds of joy, and Ibsen was hardly unaware of that difference.

The relationship with Fanny Wilton has an important bearing upon the quality of the way of life that Erhart selects and her character must, therefore, be examined in some detail. Beginning with externals, it must be noted that she is an outsider. Whether she is English or American is not clear, but her name is not Norwegian. She is, moreover, a divorcée, which at the time would have set her sharply apart from society. An examination of her physical appearance is also instructive. She is "a strikingly handsome, well-developed woman, in her thirties. Broad, red smiling lips. Playful eyes. Rich dark hair." The immediate impression is one of vitality and undeniable sexual attractiveness. This obvious sexuality, in fact, makes Fanny Wilton a rare case in Ibsen's later plays. This is not to say that his "realistic" dramas do not contain vital and strong-minded women but, except for Fanny Wilton and Rita Allmers, their sexuality tends to be muted. Indeed, to find such women one must go all the way back to the cowherd girls of *Peer Gynt*.

There are two details about Mrs. Wilton that may be significant. The first is her age in contrast to Erhart's. He is described as a young man with bright, cheerful eyes and the beginnings of a mustache. The suggestion is that he must be no older than his early twenties, whereas Fanny is in her thirties. She admits to seven years difference in their ages, but if one allows for feminine vanity, one can legitimately conclude that the difference is greater than that. The second detail is the matter of hair. Luxuriant hair is commonly associated by Ibsen with vitality, especially in *Hedda Gabler*, but Professor Höst points out that *dark* hair, in that play, is clearly associated with the evil character, Judge Brack, and with the brilliant libertine, Eilert Lövborg.[20] When all of these details are put together, the picture that emerges is of a woman who is a great deal wiser and more experienced in the ways of the world than is Erhart. She understands the habits and needs of men and may be adept at "luring" them.

Regardless of what Erhart says about his personal independence and his free choice of Fanny Wilton, the audience never sees him except under her power. When he first appears he has just looked in, on his way to a party at the Hinkels'. Fanny Wilton is lurking in the background. The discovery that his Aunt Ella has come places Erhart in a conflict situation. Significantly, he turns to Mrs. Wilton for its resolution. Only when she insists that he stay at home with his aunt does he agree to do so. It could, of course, be argued that Erhart simply owed a debt of courtesy to Fanny, but Ibsen does not stop there; in the lines which follow he refers explicitly to her control over Erhart:

> MRS. WILTON. . . . But now beware, Mr. Borkman — I warn you!
>
> ERHART. Why should I beware?
>
> MRS. WILTON. Why, as I go down the road — alone and deserted as I said — I shall try to cast a spell over you.
>
> ERHART. (Laughing) Oh, are you going to try that again now?
>
> MRS. WILTON. (Half seriously) Yes, be careful now. As I go down the road I will say to myself, right out of my innermost will — I will say: Mr. Erhart Borkman, take your hat at once.
>
> MRS. BORKMAN. And will he take it, then, do you think?
>
> MRS. WILTON. (Laughing) You can be sure of it; he will grab his hat right away. And then I will say: put on your overcoat, Erhart Borkman! And your galoshes! Don't forget your galoshes! And follow after me! Obediently, obediently, obediently!

All this is spoken at least half in jest, but only a few minutes later Erhart becomes very restless and ultimately does leave for the Hinkels' party, almost as if in response to the "spell" with which she threatened him. It is true that in the third act she insists that Erhart formed an alliance with her of his own free will, but that is only what she might be expected to say under the circumstances. It would seem, then, that Fanny Wilton is a siren figure exercising a spell over Erhart Borkman. All that the audience sees of the relationship belies the supposition that he is acting of his own free will.

Thus, Erhart too follows a guide. Whereas his father's guides were the spirits of the metal, Erhart's is assuredly of the flesh. His father's guides called upon him to work and to create a financial empire; Erhart's calls upon him only to seek happiness in self-indulgence. Mrs. Wilton even takes Frida Foldal along so that when Erhart tires of her (or she of him?) he may have another readily available companion. Ibsen does not, to be sure, explicitly suggest that Erhart's way of life is as destructive as that of Borkman, but the issue is, at best, ambiguous. It is difficult to accept Erhart Borkman and Fanny Wilton as symbols of the way life ought to be lived. Youth drives hell-bent over age in its search for happiness, as symbolized by the fact that Fanny Wilton's sleigh, containing Foldal's own daughter, knocks down Old Foldal as it rushes to the south. Youth may, however, be literally hell-bent — rushing to its own destruction.

John Gabriel Borkman must be regarded as one of the most pessimistic of Ibsen's plays. All alternatives for human happiness seem closed, or at least highly doubtful. The heights of idealism are an illusion, for man's ideals are sullied by his own self-interest. The underground world may have creative potential but in this play it holds man in a completely destructive grip. The lowlands, where human beings dwell, are frozen and dead, and whatever happiness there may be in another climate is called into question by the way that happiness is defined and by the fact that Erhart, no less than Borkman himself, seems to be in the grip of temptation, though of a quite different sort.

This play, like the others since *Hedda Gabler*, almost totally excludes the outside world of social and political affairs. It is complete in itself; those characters, outside of the Borkman family, who intrude are directly related to the Borkman fate. One critic has commented that the play has the grandeur and concentration of a Greek tragedy.[21] This may be an overstatement, but certainly Ibsen has achieved a concentration here that is unmatched in any of his other plays, with the possible exception of *The Master Builder*. He has once more created a microcosm, a total universe that completely embodies his view of life.

As in the two previous plays, the myth/ritual nature of *John Gabriel Borkman* is heightened by the language, which begins on the level of everyday speech but breaks the bounds of realism and soars at times to poetic heights. The most obvious instances of this are the occasions when Borkman talks about his kingdom, a number of which have been quoted. The language becomes most poetic just before his death, when he seems almost literally to see the kingdom of which he had dreamed, and addresses to it his rhapsodic message of love. At other times the language tends to become incantatory. The most striking instance of this is at the very end of the play, as the two sisters stand over Borkman's dead body. The passage is nearly stychomythic and the repetition of key words and phrases lend it a distinctly unreal quality:

MRS. BORKMAN. The night air has killed him, then —

ELLA. So it appears.

MRS. BORKMAN. — he, the strong man.

ELLA. Will you not look at him, Gunnhild?

MRS. BORKMAN. No, no, no. He was a miner's son — he, the bank director. He could not stand the fresh air.

ELLA. It was rather the cold that killed him.

MRS. BORKMAN. The cold you say? The cold had killed him long ago.

ELLA. And turned us into shadows.

MRS. BORKMAN. You are right in that.

ELLA. One dead man and two shadows — that is what the cold has done.

MRS. BORKMAN. Yes, the coldness of the heart. — And so we two can reach out our hands to one another, Ella.

ELLA. I think we can now.

MRS. BORKMAN. We two twin sisters — over him we both have loved.

ELLA. We two shadows — over the dead man.

The director who senses and invokes the ritualistic quality of this scene may be well on the way to solving the problem of what otherwise might seem to be a difficult and anticlimactic conclusion.

In *John Gabriel Borkman* Ibsen has presented the winter and death phase of the myth in terms applicable to his own day and to ours. The dead king is a financier, a prototype of the nineteenth-century industrialist. Strong-willed and self-reliant, to outward appearances, he has actually been following the siren call of the underground powers, tempters who provided him with a dream of personal glory and power that overshadowed all other considerations. He had thought, in following them, to bring happiness to many, but he has brought only misery and unhappiness to his wife and family, and death to himself. The world of the play is one in which only desolation rules. The cosmos presented is either dead or ultimately death-dealing. If there is any hope at all for happiness, it must be realized by another generation — yet that generation, too, seems to be off on what is, at best, an ambiguous and, at worst, a fundamentally wrong track. Neither the heights nor the lowlands seem to be livable in this play. Ibsen was not, however, finished with the problems with which he had been dealing at least since *The Wild Duck*. His next and final play also deals with death, but beyond the mist that shrouds the mountaintop there is sun and a faint, glimmering hope of resurrection.

When We Dead Awaken · The Myth of Resurrection

With *When We Dead Awaken* Ibsen, for the second time in his career as a prose dramatist, violated his usual policy of coming out with a new play every two years. The first such instance was *An Enemy of the People*, which seems to have been written in only a year when Ibsen was indignant over the reception of *Ghosts*. His final play took three years, from the publication of *John Gabriel Borkman* in 1896 to the release of *When We Dead Awaken* in November of 1899. There are at least two conflicting descriptions of the circumstances under which it was written. Archer quotes Julius Elias to the effect that Ibsen labored feverishly on this last play, sensing all the while that death was near and that he must finish the work in time. His relatives, said Elias, were convinced that Ibsen knew this to be his last play and that after it was finished he would write no more.[22] Exactly contradictory testimony, however, comes from his daughter-in-law, Bergliot: "While Henrik Ibsen was writing *When We Dead Awaken* he had not felt very well but he got better again and none of us had any idea that this would be his last play. He resumed his daily walks and the habit he had formed in the south of daily visits to one particular cafe."[23]

Ibsen had subtitled his play *A Dramatic Epilog*, but this does not necessarily seem to have meant that he was giving up any future plans of producing another work. In March of 1900 he wrote to Moritz Prozor: "I cannot say yet whether or not I shall write another drama; but if I continue to retain the vigor of body and mind which I at present enjoy I do not imagine that I shall be able to keep permanently away from the old battlefields. However if I were to make my appearance again it would be with new weapons and in new armor." [24] In the same letter he confirmed Count Prozor's conjecture that the series of plays which began with *The Master Builder* was now concluded with *When We Dead Awaken*.[25] Koht reports that on another occasion Ibsen remarked that the play was the last of a series that began with *A Doll's House*.[26]

Much of the objection to the final play is based on the assumption that, since he called it an epilog, Ibsen knew it to be his last drama. A corollary assumption is that the play was written hastily by an old man who felt his powers failing and that the weaknesses in the play are reflections of the playwright's faltering imagination. Bergliot's testimony, Ibsen's letter to Count Prozor, and the time factor would all seem to contradict those assumptions. Not only did no one in the dramatist's immediate family, according to the testimony of his daughter-in-law, suspect that his dramatic career was coming to a conclusion, but the fact that the play took three years to write hardly coincides with the picture of a man working in feverish haste to complete his lifework. The letter to Prozor indicates that Ibsen had not firmly decided to write no more dramas. Indeed, the specific reference to "the vigor of body and mind which I now enjoy" seems also to contradict the picture of an old man with failing mental and physical powers. A perhaps more reasonable view is that Ibsen labored carefully over this final work, fully cognizant of the fact that it was a departure from his other work and being extremely concerned with getting it exactly right.

There are, then, three, not necessarily mutually exclusive, possibilities as to what he meant by the subtitle. First of all, the play obviously deals with the same problems and elements that had preoccupied the dramatist at least since *The Master Builder* and perhaps a good deal longer. Second, he may have meant *When We Dead Awaken* to conclude the series of prose dramas that were, at least to outward appearances, presentations of everyday life. This supposition is lent strength by the remark about new weapons and new armor contained in the letter to Prozor. Ibsen may have been contemplating a complete and radical departure from the methods that had served him so well during his long career. The third possibility is that he may have meant the play to be an end to the series in which he more or less directly drew upon material from his own life and engaged in a considerable amount of self-examination. As Koht points out, Rubek can be taken as a self-portrait, and the attitudes and ideas he expresses may very well be those of his creator.[27] I should like, however, to offer a fourth possibility. If Ibsen has been working at least since *The Wild Duck* to develop a mythical world picture contained within the framework of ostensibly realistic drama, *When We Dead Awaken* may mark its termination, not only in terms of theme but also of technique. Ibsen's comment to Prozor may indicate that he was aware that if he were to continue to explore both the depths and heights of human experience, he would have to sever his remaining ties with realism and forge off into entirely new paths, perhaps those marked out by Strindberg in his post-Inferno drama.[28]

In order to discover what the play is, it is first advisable to consider some of the reactions to it, many of which were negative in the extreme. Archer, for example, calls the play "melancholy" and "purely pathological," and complains that Ibsen had "sacrificed the surface reality to the underlying meaning." [29] Weigand also criticizes the play's lack of "realism" and goes into considerable detail to demonstrate the factual contradictions in the various accounts of Rubek's life as they are revealed in his two principal scenes with Maja and in those with Irene.[30] Storm Jameson calls the play "a technical as well as an artistic failure." To her, the characters are "merely symbolic puppets, whom he arranges to present a truth." [31]

All of these objections are valid if we accept the assumption on which they rest. The play is full of factual contradictions. The chronology of events in the protagonist's life are inconsistent. The statue which Rubek has supposedly carved is a patent impossibility. Yet all of these criticisms rest upon the assumption that Ibsen was trying to write a realistic play. If he was not, they must be rejected. Archer was quite correct in saying that Ibsen sacrificed surface reality for a deeper meaning. That, after all, is one of the characteristics of myth. Factual details are less important than the overall shape and/or theme of the story.

There is one theme which unites the entire play and one principal symbol in which that theme is embodied. The theme is resurrection and Rubek's statue is its symbolic embodiment. The play was originally given the same title which Rubek gave to his statue, *Oppstandelsens Dag* (*Resurrection Day*). As in *Rosmersholm* and *The Lady from the Sea*, Ibsen seems to have selected a title that suggested the theme, though not so obviously as the original one. As in *John Gabriel Borkman*, the major characters of this play are, for all practical purposes, dead, but the emphasis is slightly shifted from death to the other half of the mythic cycle, resurrection.

The sculptor, Rubek, has much in common with Borkman and Solness. Like them he is a creator (if we can consider Borkman's visionary financial empire a kind of creation). He has won worldwide fame through his sculptural group, "Resurrection Day." Like his predecessors, however, he has fallen on evil days. Beset by doubts and the gnawings of guilt, he has lost his creative drive and has even begun to question the value of the artistic vocation itself. Since he has finished his masterpiece he has produced no other major work, but contents himself with carving portrait busts on commission. Maliciously he conceals behind the portraits of the self-satisfied burghers who hire him, animal visages: ". . . respectable pompous horse-faces and self opinionated donkey muzzles, and lop-eared, low-browed dog skulls, and fatted swine snouts — and sometimes brutal bull fronts as well." Although this amuses him, it is hardly a substitute for the great masterpieces that he is apparently capable of creating. He has also built for himself a mansion in the city and a villa on Lake Taunitz, and married a young wife. With her he has apparently tried to live a life of idleness and pleasure, interrupted only occasionally by the carving of a portrait bust.

Thus, he seems to have experimented with many of the alternative modes of life suggested by Rita and Allmers in *Little Eyolf* and pursued by Erhart in the preceding play — travel, friends, and sensual self-indulgence. By the time the play opens all this has palled on him. He says he is happy, but clearly he is bored with his life and with his young wife, Maja. They have returned, at the beginning of the play, to a health resort in the mountains of Norway, but this has not helped to relieve Rubek's boredom nor that of his wife, who seems as weary of their life as he. Rubek is, like Borkman and Solness, at an impasse in his existence. In contrast to Solness, however, he is specifically described as elderly, and in contrast to Borkman, he has no dream of glory to sustain him. His creative energies are dead, and the life he leads gives him no real satisfaction.

Like Borkman, and to a lesser degree like Solness, he also is guilty of a crime. Years before (how many years is ambiguous, one of the troubling inconsistencies in the play) he had a model who posed for the central figure in his "Resurrection Day" group. She loved Rubek and, in a way, he loved her, but he used her only as a model; when the modeling of her figure was complete he thanked her for "a priceless episode." At that point she left him and he had not seen her again until they meet at the spa. Then she, like Ella Rentheim in the previous play, accuses him of having "killed" her, of having murdered the love life in a human being.

The story of the Irene-Rubek relationship is told in the two interviews between them in the first and second acts of the play. A great many things have happened to both of them since their work on "Resurrection Day," but the experiences related are principally those of Irene. She has "posed on a turntable in variety shows. Posed as a naked statue in living pictures," and the implication is that she has been a prostitute. She has been married twice, first to a South American who killed himself and second to a Russian whom she says she killed. She has also spent some time in a madhouse, wrapped in a straitjacket and confined to a padded cell. She is now accompanied by a Sister of Mercy, who keeps a constant and close watch on her. All this, she says, has resulted from Rubek's rejecting her.

Irene's story is a highly melodramatic one and is unrealistic in a way that even Weigand and Archer do not question. It is unlikely that anyone but a very disturbed young woman would react so violently to a mere word (*episode*), especially since the dismissal does not seem to have been clear-cut. There is, after all, no reason why a love relationship could not have arisen between them after her work on the statue was finished and the "distance" that Rubek insists had to be maintained between artist and model was no longer necessary. The significance of the relationship, then, and of what subsequently happened to Irene, must lie in its symbolism. On the obvious level, of course, it simply illustrates the nature of Rubek's "crime," the rejection of love. On a deeper level, however, the symbolic significance of Irene's career is to be found in the fact that it consists of a passage from innocence to experience. That passage is paralleled also by Rubek's career and by the development of the statue, which Irene refers to as their "child."

The progress through which the statue has passed since its original conception is the symbolic embodiment of the course of Rubek's life and his understanding of the world. The progress is recounted in a rather long passage that is worth quoting almost in its entirety:

> RUBEK. I was young then — with no knowledge of life. The Resurrection, I thought, would be most beautifully and exquisitely figured as a young unsullied woman — with none of our earth-life's experience — awakening to light and glory without having to put away from her anything ugly and impure.
>
> . . . .
>
> RUBEK. I learned worldly wisdom in the years that followed, Irene. "The Resurrection Day" became in my mind's eye something more and something — something more complex. The little round plinth on which your figure stood erect and solitary — it no longer afforded room for all the imagery I now wanted to add.
>
> IRENE. What imagery did you add then? Tell me!
>
> RUBEK. I imaged that which I saw with my eyes around me in the world. I had to include it — I could not help it, Irene! I

expanded the plinth — made it wide and spacious. And on it I placed a segment of the curving, bursting earth. And up from the fissures of the soil there now swarm men and women with dimly suggested animal faces. Women and men — as I knew them in real life.

IRENE. But in the middle of the rout there stands that young woman radiant with the joy of light? — Do I not Arnold?

RUBEK. Not quite in the middle. I had, unfortunately to move that statue back a little, for the sake of the whole work, you understand. Otherwise it would have dominated too much.

IRENE. But the joy in the light still transfigures my face?

RUBEK. Yes, it does Irene — in a way at least. A little subdued perhaps — as my altered view demanded.

For Rubek, too, then, the passage has been from innocence to experience, to "worldly wisdom." The statue had needed to be altered to make room for what is basically a vision of evil, the submerged evil animalistic nature of man that breaks through the surface of being.[32] In the light of that vision the transfiguring beauty of the Resurrection Day has had to be somewhat subdued. This, however, does not complete the alterations which have been made in the statue:

Yes, but listen now how I have placed myself in the group. In front of the fountain, like here, sits a guilt-laden man who cannot quite free himself from the earth's crust. I call him remorse for a forfeited life. He sits there and dips his fingers in the purling stream — to wash them clean — and he is gnawed and tortured by the thought that never never will he succeed. Never in all eternity can he freely attain the life of the resurrection. He will remain forever sitting in his own hell.

Rubek's vision, then, has been more profound than that of Irene. Despite all that has happened to her she has retained a mental image of herself in the middle of the statuary group, transfigured by the light of innocence. Rubek, on the contrary, has discovered that the evil exists not only in the world but in the sculptor too. He who has had a vision of the resurrection and eternal life is also earthbound, and that discovery has led him to lose faith in the beauty or even the possibility of resurrection.

Some have said that the three stages of Rubek's statue, like the three phases of Solness' building career, parallel the three stages of Ibsen's work: the idealism of *Brand* and the other early plays, the portrayal of social evil in his domestic dramas, and the autobiographical, self-analytical work of his later years.[33] This is undoubtedly true, but the critic must not allow himself to be so blinded by autobiographical details that he fails to see that those stages parallel the life of every man. The innocence of youth necessarily gives way to the recognition of evil, to the knowledge that all is not what it should be and that life is not full of infinite possibilities. That, in turn, gives way to, if not loss of faith and deep despair, at least a period of reckoning up and self-examination. Earth-life's experience, as Rubek puts it, is exactly what cannot be avoided. It is a necessary prelude to any resurrection.[34]

In a sense, the entire Ur-myth is subsumed within the play and within Rubek's statue. The progress of both Rubek and Irene has been from the innocence of youth, to the disillusionment of maturity, to defeat, and at last, to death. They have arrived at this last stage by the time the play begins. Irene constantly refers to herself as dead, insisting that she has been killed by Rubek and perhaps, in a larger sense, by life. From a realistic point of view this constant harping on her own death is simply the deluded raving of a madwoman, but from the symbolic standpoint it is true. As far as her life's possibilities are concerned Irene is dead, and this is visually communicated in her whole appearance and bearing. The stage directions describing her first entrance make this unmistakable:

A slender lady, dressed in fine cream-white cashmere and followed by a Sister of Mercy in black with a silver cross hanging by a chain on her breast, comes forward from behind the hotel and crosses the park toward the pavilion in the foreground on the left. Her face is pale and its lines appear to have stiffened; the eyelids are drooped and the eyes seem without the power to see. Her dress comes down to her feet and clings in perpendicular folds to her body. Over her head, neck, breast, shoulders and arms she has a large shawl of white crepe. She holds her arms crossed on her breast. She carries her body immovably. Her steps are stiff and measured.

Visually at least, Rubek exhibits more vitality than Irene, but in terms of his life's possibilities he too is dead. Realistically, he is an elderly man and, thus, on the point of death. Symbolically, his whole life has been wrapped up in art, as was Borkman's in finance, but his creative urge has vanished. He has sought life through an alliance with a much younger wife, but that too has proved unsatisfactory. Without the ability to create and without the ability to discover joy in life, Rubek, like Borkman, can be regarded as only technically alive. Again, as in the previous play, the point is specifically made in dialogue:

> IRENE. — And when I heard you saying with such deathly, icy coldness — that I was nothing but an episode in your life —
> RUBEK. It was you that said that, Irene, not I.
> IRENE. (Continuing) — Then I had my knife out. I wanted to stab you in the back with it.
> RUBEK. And why did you not stab me, then?
> IRENE. Because it occurred to me with horror that you were already dead — long ago.
> RUBEK. Dead?
> IRENE. Dead. Dead, you as well as I. We sat there by the Lake of Taunitz, we two clammy bodies — and played with each other.[35]

Rubek protests that he is not dead, that his passionate love for Irene is still alive; however, that passion, like Borkman's dream of a visiting deputation, is not something that can be realized in life, a fact of which both Rubek and Irene are instinctively aware.

Yet the emphasis of the play is not on death but on resurrection. This is indicated not only in the title, but also in the fact that the dialogue abounds in images of and references to resurrection. Indeed, the temporal and physical setting of the play holds, implicitly at least, the potential of a re-awakening of life.

Temporally the death-resurrection cycle is contained in the play in two ways. *John Gabriel Borkman* was a play of winter in which the surrounding landscape was frozen, snow covered, and dead. The action of *When We Dead Awaken* occurs in the summer, when nature is alive and vegetation is abundant. The stage directions for the first act read, "An open park-like place with a fountain, groups of fine old trees, and shrubbery. To the left there is a little pavilion almost covered with ivy and Virginia creeper." More significant, however, is the temporal cycle through which the three acts of the play pass. Act One begins on "a calm, warm and sunny summer morning." The second act occurs on "a summer afternoon, toward sunset." In the third act, "It is nearly morning. Dawn is breaking. The sun has not yet risen." The temporal symbolism of the play is dual. As Frye has pointed out, the spring and summer phase of the myth coincide with the beginning and the fullness of life. The seasons of the year and their relation to the phases of human life are, moreover, paralleled by the four segments of the day, morning, noon, evening, and night.[36] Thus, morning suggests the beginning of life and its unrealized potential, late afternoon suggests the waning years of life, the immediate prelude to sunset, and night is, of course, death itself. The hour before dawn is, therefore, the prelude to the rebirth of life. The action of the play coincides with these stages. In the morning of the first act, Rubek has the reunion with Irene that sets him to symbolically reliving his life. In the second act he reveals the alteration of the statue, the passage from innocence to experience and from hope to despair, and he admits that both his life and Irene's have been forfeit. In the third act Irene specifically pronounces him dead and, a few minutes later, they make their climb to the top of the mountain where the newly risen sun can witness their "marriage feast." [37]

Physically, the symbolism is perhaps less apparent, but again the stages of life are suggested. The action takes place at a spa where people come, presumably, to take mineral baths for their health. Thus, it is a place of the sick and the glimpse we get of the other guests, though admittedly brief, bears this out. The stage directions in the first act read, "Visitors to the baths, most of them women, begin to pass, singly and in groups, through the park from the right and out to the left." There is little suggestion here of life or vitality. The guests are anonymous and inactive figures, Rubek is elderly, and Irene, as has been indicated, visually suggests one already dead. Nevertheless, there are within the play two authentic and unmistakable symbols of life. The most obvious of these is the bear hunter, Ulfheim, who will be discussed later.[38] The appearance of the second at the beginning of the second act is especially significant. The time of that act is the hours just before sunset (symbolically, death). A portion of the stage directions read as follows: "At some distance over the upland, on the other side of the brook, a troop of children are singing, dancing and playing. Some are dressed in peasant costumes, others in town-made clothes. Their happy laughter is heard, softened by distance, during the following." Children are, like morning and springtime, suggestive of the potential of life and their juxtaposition here, at sunset, against Rubek and his musings over his misspent life, can hardly be regarded as accidental. Indeed, the children are brought directly into the action twice, in ways that reinforce the significance of that juxtaposition. Maja, who is herself young and alive, finds them annoying:

> MAJA. Oh, Rubek — how can you manage to sit there and listen to those children scream! And watch all the crazy antics they are doing too!
>
> RUBEK. There is something harmonious — almost like music — in their movements — once in a while. In the middle of all the clumsiness. And it's amusing to sit and watch those individual moments when they come.

Maja scornfully accuses him of remaining always an artist, and Rubek admits to the charge. More significant than his aesthetic appreciation of their movements, however, is the fact that this old man, on the point of death, admires the beauty of innocent and uncorrupted life. Maja, who does not share Rubek's proximity to death nor his disillusionment with life, finds the children annoying, not graceful or charming or beautiful. The second instance, when Irene is brought into the action, is even more interesting: "Irene advances from the right over the upland. The children at their play have already caught sight of her and run to meet her. She is now surrounded by them; some appear confident and at ease, others uneasy and timid. She talks low to them and indicates that they are to go down to the hotel; she herself will rest a little beside the brook. The children run down the slope to the left." Irene is, as I have indicated, symbolically dead, perhaps a symbolic embodiment of death itself. Thus the children are drawn to her and approach her as people are drawn to death, "some . . . confident and at ease, others uneasy and timid." Yet at the same time Irene is the figure of "Resurrection Day" — she, in her youthful innocence and beauty, was the model for the figure and though time has changed her it may be that some of that original beauty can be perceived by the children, whose own eyes are unclouded by "earth-life's experience." Irene, however, dismisses the children; she has business not with them but with the elderly sculptor.

The entire life of man, then, is symbolically contained within the play. There is childhood, youth as represented by Maja and perhaps Ulfheim, middle age as represented by the guests at the hotel, and old age and death, as represented by Irene and Rubek. Life in its various stages and degrees of vitality is juxtaposed against death, and the representation of all these stages of life suggests, as do the seasons of the year and the time of the day, the cyclical movement of existence.

Rubek, however, seeks a more personal kind of resurrection than that contained in the cyclical rebirth of nature. It is this more personal form which he has attempted to embody in his statue and in which he has now apparently lost faith. The theme is treated in various ways in the dialogue; the action and the characters go from faith and hope to despair and back to hope again. As Rubek's model Irene had first sought the resurrection of her childhood. Similarly, Rubek had sought to embody in her the pure woman, awakening on Resurrection Day, having left the earth and come into a "higher, freer, happier region." In this both have failed. Irene's attempted resurrection led her to degradation and ultimately death, at least the death of the soul. In the long empty years after Irene's departure Rubek learned worldly wisdom and came to doubt the ability of the earth creature ever to free himself from the earth's crust. He deduced that man could never ascend to that brighter, happier re-

gion that he had once envisioned, at least not in the happy innocence he had sought to embody in his statue. It was, of course, life,
not death, that both of them sought to escape in their search for
radical innocence and beauty, and life, which necessarily involves
corruption and decay, has taken revenge on both of them. With
the return of Irene, however, whatever small sparks of faith remain
are rekindled in Rubek. He looks to her for resurrection of the inspiration he once had. Yet that is not Irene's mission in his present
life, nor the kind of resurrection destined for either of them. This
point is gradually developed in a series of exchanges throughout
the play. The first of these is somewhat ambiguous — Rubek takes
Irene's words, as, I suspect, does the audience, to mean something
other than what they do mean. The passage occurs near the end of
their first interview in the first act:

> IRENE. Where are you thinking of going with her?
> RUBEK. Oh, on a tedious coasting voyage to the North, I sup-
> pose.
> IRENE. (Looks at him, smiles almost imperceptibly, and whis-
> pers) You should rather go high up into the mountains. As
> high as you can. Higher, higher, — always higher, Arnold.
> RUBEK. (With eager expectation) Are you going up there?
> IRENE. Have you the courage to meet me once again?
> RUBEK. (Struggling with himself, uncertainly) If we could —
> oh, if only we could — !
> IRENE. Why can we not do what we will? (Looks at him and
> whispers beseechingly with folded hands) Come, come, Ar-
> nold! Oh, come up to me — !

The dialogue is here interrupted and, except for Rubek's an-
nouncement to Maja that he is going to the mountains, the subject
is not mentioned again in the first act. Rubek, it seems, interprets
Irene's invitation as a veiled promise that she will aid in the renewal
of his creative drive. He still sees his resurrection as embodied in
her, as is indicated when she reappears in the second act. Maja describes her as coming across the plain "like a marble statue," but
Rubek replies that she looks like the resurrection incarnate. Yet the
dialogue that follows indicates that he is looking to Irene for the

wrong kind of resurrection. Three times this point is made in the dialogue of the second act:

RUBEK. You shall see that the day will dawn and lighten for us both.
IRENE. Do not believe that.
RUBEK. (Urgently) I do believe it! And I know it! Now that I have found you again —
IRENE. Risen from the grave.
RUBEK. Transfigured.
IRENE. Only risen, Arnold, not transfigured.

A few minutes later Rubek renews his plea for her to inspire him once again:

RUBEK. . . . You could open all that is locked up in me. Can you not find it in your heart, Irene?
IRENE. I no longer have the key to you, Arnold.
RUBEK. You have the key! You and you alone possess it! Help me — that I may be able to live my life over again!
IRENE. Empty dreams! Idle — dead dreams. For the life that you and I led there is no resurrection.

There is in this passage an explicit denial of Irene's intention or capability of renewing Rubek's creative potential and an implicit denial of the possibility of renewing the love relationship that he had previously ignored. The nature of Rubek's request here is significant. He does not ask for a new life, for a new beginning or for new creative opportunities; he asks for the chance to live his life over again. But one cannot live one's life *over again* or live it any differently than it has already been lived. In Rubek's life he has made choices and taken actions, and those choices cannot now be repealed nor those actions expunged. Reliving one's life and correcting past errors is as impossible as escaping the corrupting influence of "earth-life's experience" altogether. Rubek's dream of reinspiration and rebirth of his creative energies is the equivalent of Borkman's dream of a visiting delegation to invite him back into the financial world. Both men must learn to live with the choices they have already made.

Gradually this awareness begins to dawn on Rubek. He begins

to see that his dream of being reinspired is no longer achievable and to understand how his life has gone wrong. A life with Irene, he says, might have been "a summer night on the uplands." Irene, however, is still discouraging:

IRENE. We see the irretrievable only when —
RUBEK. When — ?
IRENE. When we dead awaken.
RUBEK. (Shakes his head mournfully) What do we really see then?
IRENE. We see that we have never lived.

In the third act Irene's mission in the play becomes clear. She has come to kill Rubek, or at least to convince him that he is already dead. At last she succeeds. Rubek looks at her no longer as merely an object and a source of inspiration, but admits that he has wronged her in placing "the dead clay image above the happiness of life — of love." It is now his turn to inspire her. He convinces her that there is, after all, a hope of resurrection for them above the mists where the blasts of the wind sound, as he tells Ulfheim, like the "prelude to Resurrection Day." She is infected by his passion and they go up the mountain to celebrate their marriage feast where all the powers of light and darkness can look upon them. If one were to interpret this literally and conclude that these two old people were going up to the mountaintop to lose themselves in sexual ecstasy, the effect would be merely grotesque. Rather, what they seek on the mountaintop is what they find; like Brand they are buried in an avalanche. He too had climbed a mountain in search of a God who could tell him where his life had gone wrong, and was buried under an avalanche while a voice boomed out, "He is the God of love." In a similar fashion Solness climbed his tower and was struck down while Hilda heard "harps in the air." In both instances death is accompanied by a kind of epiphany which occurs in a high place. Rubek and Irene climb "through all the mists, and then right up to the tower that shines in the sunrise." They climb in search of life at its most intense and find death in the avalanche while a benediction is pronounced on them — not, as in *Brand*, from above, but from below by the Sister of Mercy. If there is a resurrection in this, as the entire emphasis of the play suggests, the resurrection is not the traditional Christian one. The reader or auditor is left with a mystery rather like that at the end of *Oedipus at Colonnus*. Indeed, the parallel with the Oedipus plays is an interesting one if not pushed too far. Not only Rubek but also Borkman and Solness have, like the ancient Greek, committed crimes (not, admittedly, such horrendous ones). Each seems to have murdered the love potential in another human being in search of his own goals and objectives. Though they are, to a greater or lesser degree, tormented by guilt, they do not repent in Christian fashion. Rather, the crucial action of each play is the hero's reassertion of himself. Prompted by a figure from the past, each of them embraces his fate and accepts his identity, even Borkman, whose past crime Ibsen seems to have judged most harshly. Certainly two of the three seem, at the moment of defeat and death, to have triumphed in some mysterious way over the power that destroys them. At the conclusion of this play and the conclusion of Ibsen's work Rubek and Irene appear to have attained to something beyond mortality, though the nature of that something the playwright does not presume to tell us.

It is not possible yet, however, to leave the Rubek-Irene relationship. The full significance of Ibsen's last treatment of the life-problem can only be revealed through a closer examination of the nature of Rubek's "crime" against Irene. There is no doubt that he has wronged both her and Maja in much the same way that Borkman wronged the two Rentheim sisters. He has awakened the love potential in both of them by promising to take them up on the mountains and show them "all the glories of the world." [39] In reality he has used them both, Irene as a source of inspiration for his art and Maja as a means to fill the emptiness of his life after the springs of his creativity have dried up. Furthermore, as Weigand points out, he still wishes to use Irene as a source of renewed inspiration when he finds her again.[40] Thus, Rubek, like Borkman, clings to his old dream and persists in the habit of using people as the means to a personal end. Yet Rubek does progress beyond Borkman's position. At very nearly the last minute he sees that he has been wrong and he recognizes the nature of his crime. Once he has come to this realization he is able to lead Irene up the mountainside in search of a genuine resurrection for both of them. Like his predecessor in the earlier play, Rubek has been an incomplete human being, but he comes to recognize his incompleteness and this moves the play beyond the death stage of the myth to the hope of resurrection. But Ibsen is aware that the problem is not quite that simple. He is not offering the moralistic platitude "don't be selfish" or "don't use other people." Rubek is guilty of ignoring life and love but he is, after all, an artist and that fact places upon him special responsibilities and burdens him with special problems. Rubek explains this to Maja, though he does not at this point seem to be completely aware of its full significance for his life. "I live at such high speed, Maja. We live so, we artists. I, for my part, have lived through a whole lifetime in the few years we have known each other. I have come to see that it is not for me to seek happiness in indolent enjoyment. Life does not arrange itself in that way for me and my kind, I must continue to work — to create work after work — right up to my last day . . ." Rubek has here grasped an important fact about himself; he belongs to that company of exceptional men that also includes Solness and Borkman. He cannot seek happiness in ordinary ways. Yet he still thinks about the possibility of renewing his inspiration through Irene, through a renewal of their love. His clinging to this hope is evidence that he has still not understood the complete significance of his role as artist.

The sculptor is faced with the old set of alternatives, problems posed for so many of Ibsen's characters since *Emperor and Galilean* — idealism versus happiness, the heights versus the lowlands, freedom versus necessity. Rubek first chose the heights of idealism and art; in so doing he wronged one woman and found no satisfaction. He then turned to Maja and the life of the lowlands, but he found no happiness there either. Of course one could argue that he could have combined life's happiness and the artistic vocation had he just chosen correctly in the beginning, had he not rejected Irene. A close examination of their relationship, however, calls that conclusion into question. Rubek used Irene as a model and kept a "distance" between them, fearing that if he touched her he would in some way profane the object of his inspiration. It is with this that Irene reproaches him:

> IRENE. . . . You did wrong to my innermost nature —
> RUBEK. I — !
> IRENE. Yes, you! I exposed myself completely and unreservedly to your gaze — . . . And never once did you touch me.
> RUBEK. Irene, didn't you understand that many times I was driven almost insane by your loveliness?
> IRENE. And yet — if you had touched me I think I would have killed you on the spot. For I had a sharp needle with me always, concealed in my hair . . .

Rubek has wronged Irene by not touching her. He has chosen art over life. But if he had touched her she would have killed him. His position, then, is, from the standpoint of ordinary happiness, completely untenable. The reconciliation between art and love, which he seeks through "a summer night on the uplands," leads to the top of the mountain and the avalanche. The Rubeks, Borkmans, and Solnesses of this world are doomed to forfeit earthly happiness; the only kind of joy which is to be theirs is that terrible joy found at the top of the mountain, beyond the avalanche, or at the top of the tower at the moment of falling. Rubek comes to realize this painful fact whereas Borkman does not, and that too allows the final play to move beyond death to resurrection. One critic asserts that even Irene's powerless longing for resurrection earns them redemption and that this is the significance of the "Pax Vobiscum" spoken over them by the Sister of Mercy.[41] The happiness of the earth is out of the question for Irene and Rubek but, as in *John Gabriel Borkman*, an alternative is proposed for those who are differently constituted.

The possibility of happiness in the life of the earth is embodied in the Maja-Ulfheim relationship. The marriage between Maja and Rubek is clearly an unsuitable one, though the reasons for this are not so clear-cut as they initially appear to be. At first glance Maja seems much too simple a creature, perhaps too much of a child, to be a suitable wife for a man as complex as Rubek. This she frankly admits on several occasions, saying that it is "too hard" for her to complete Rubek and supply what is lacking in his nature. Far from understanding the inner workings of an artist's psyche, she admits that she has only an imperfect understanding of her own. The psychological subtleties required of an artist's wife are too much for her and she is immediately attracted to the straightforward bear hunter.

Yet Maja's failure as Rubek's wife does not necessarily result from an inadequacy in her. Though at times she displays an almost motherly solicitude for her husband, he seems to have consistently shut her out of his inner life. As he had Irene, Rubek had once promised Maja to take her up on the mountain and show her all the glories of the world. When Maja reproaches him with his failure to do so, he first tries to pass the promise off as a game or a figure of speech and later argues that Maja is not really meant to be a mountain climber. To this she replies, "Yet at one time you seemed to think I was."

There seems to be a clear parallel here between the Maja-Rubek relationship and that between Borkman and Gunnhild. Rubek may be correct in asserting that his young wife is not suited to be a mountain climber — that is, not fit to be a wife for a man who dwells on the creative heights. Certainly there does seem to be an air of childishness, of impatience with complexities, about Maja. She, on the other hand, may be quite justified in her implications that he has taken her only as a plaything and has never attempted to discover whether or not she has the potential to fulfill his needs. Like Borkman, he has never come to his wife for understanding.

There is little complexity and little need for Rubek's kind of understanding in Ulfheim. If Rubek and Irene are, in a sense, personifications of death, there can be no doubt that Ulfheim is the very embodiment of life at its most vital, vigorous, and primitive. This is indicated by the way he lives, by his speech, by his companions, and by his diet. He is, apparently by profession, a bear hunter, though he pursues all kinds of game, including, he says, women. He struggles with living, resisting flesh rather than with cold marble. His speech is not soft, indirect, and civilized, but loud, direct, profane, and vigorous. He lives in the open with his hunting dogs and dines, like them, on large chunks of meat. He is proud of his strength and scorns all those who are sick or weak. In Freudian terms, Ulfheim is pure Id; he takes what he wants, whether food, women, or wild beasts, through sheer strength and has little use for the trappings of civilization. There is, furthermore, a consistent association with the animal. He hunts bears, he lives with dogs, the first syllable of his name means wolf, and Maja, in the climactic seduction scene, calls him a faun or forest devil with goat's legs, a beard, and horns. Earlier, in discussing Rubek's statue, I indicated that there was a vision of evil contained in the image of men and women with animal faces breaking through the crust of the earth. Is Ulfheim, then, pure evil? The answer is, not entirely, for, when faced with Maja's clear vision, he seems to come to an understanding of himself and to be willing at last to establish a relationship with another person. After he and Maja have exchanged their stories of betrayal he says:

ULFHEIM. Now listen to me, my good companion of the chase —
MAJA. Well, what is it now?
ULFHEIM. Shouldn't we two tack our poor shreds of life together?
MAJA. Has his honor the desire to be a patching tailor?
ULFHEIM. Yes, he has. Couldn't we two try to draw the rags together here and there — so as to make some kind of human life out of them?
MAJA. And when the poor rags are completely worn-out — what then?
ULFHEIM. Then we shall stand there free and happy — as that which we really are.

There is, then, a kind of resurrection for Maja and Ulfheim also. Both lives have been flawed. Maja has been leading a captive existence with a man whom she does not understand and who does not understand her. Ulfheim has suffered a betrayal in love and as a result has romanticized himself and led a purely self-centered existence. Maja's clear vision — her ability to perceive his goat's legs and to see that his "hunting lodge" is little more than a pigsty — forces him to see himself for what he is, while his vigor and appetite for life convinces her that all her possibilities are not gone. They are, as Valency points out, the precise opposites of Irene and Rubek and counterbalance them. They go down the mountain to life, while Rubek and Irene ascend to death and the hope of an ambiguous resurrection. "The symbols are clear. Life, with its happiness, is for those who are suited for it. Art, with its torments, is for those who can endure it." [42] Valency's comment is succinct and accurate except that for "art" one should perhaps read any kind of idealism or devotion to abstractions.

Ibsen's understanding of the possibilities held forth by the life of the lowlands seems more sophisticated and more ambiguous in this play than in the two preceding plays. One is forced to wonder, in considering the character of Borgheim, how long his boyish enthusiasm can endure in the precarious world inhabited by the other characters. He is simply too good to be true. If Borgheim represents the extreme of optimism, however, Erhart Borkman may represent the extreme of pessimism. A slave to Fanny Wilton, he rejects all possibilities of a constructive life to go off and lose himself, under her tutelage, in a life of sensual self-indulgence. It is difficult to imagine Ibsen recommending Erhart's way of life except in despair. *When We Dead Awaken*, however, represents a compromise. Neither Maja nor Ulfheim is a youthful innocent; both have been damaged by life. Each is incomplete by himself; together they complement each other. The prospect of a world given over to Ulfheim as he first appears is a frightening one—in that world, perhaps the prototype of a Nazi world, the strong would survive by destroying the weak. Originally, Ulfheim is totally dedicated to the troll principle. Maja, when associated with Rubek, is listless, helpless, and petty, of little use to herself or anyone else. Ulfheim's vitality arouses in her a desire for life: she forces him to take a critical look at himself and to modify his selfishness. By combining the traits that each represents, a synthesis may be achieved.

If, however, the play is guardedly optimistic about the possibility of a life of happiness in the lowlands, it is pessimistic about the idealist's ability to realize his dream in life. If there is to be another world and another mode of life, the Rubeks will apparently not create it. The best they and their like — Borkman, Solness, Rosmer, and even, perhaps, Hedda Gabler and Gregers Werle — can do is to follow their fate though it leads inevitably to death. The demands they make on life go beyond what life is capable of providing. In this sense they are perhaps true tragic characters, so constituted that they can never make the accommodation to life that is possible for smaller and simpler people. If Ibsen's dream of a third empire is to be realized in life, by the Ulfheims and Majas, the empire is a much smaller thing than he had originally envisioned. Any larger empire must be realized only in the soul, on the mystical heights at the moment of death.

Traditional mythic materials have not so far been discussed, for the entire drama is so constructed that these elements do not obtrude. For the first time the play is itself myth, completely self-contained, rather than depending on external correspondences for effect. Ibsen has no need here for mysterious figures hovering between the real and the supernatural, nor for a pattern based on traditional legend: the whole play exists on the plane of the unreal or the surreal. In this sense, it constitutes an epilog to the movement toward myth that has been developing since *The Wild Duck;* the play moves completely into myth and severs almost all remaining ties with realism. This, perhaps, is what frustrated and annoyed those critics who were devoted to the tradition of psychological and social realism. Of those roughly contemporary with Ibsen only James Joyce seems to have been attuned to what the playwright was here attempting. Joyce commented: "On the whole *When We Dead Awaken* may rank with the greatest of the author's works — if, indeed, it be not the greatest." [43]

Joyce may well overstate the case, but later critics, who have been acquainted with Freud and Jung and who have become accustomed to looking at the world through the eyes of Maeterlinck, Strindberg, and Pirandello, react much more favorably to the play than did Ibsen's contemporaries. Valency, for example, argues that Ibsen was attempting, for the first time, to achieve a Maeterlinckian quality and that the vagueness and contradictions of the play which so bothered Weigand are necessary to that effect.[44] Brustein indicates that Archer's objections can readily be dismissed if we remember that Archer criticized Elizabethan drama because of its "unrealistic" asides and soliloquies. He comments:

> When we cease regarding Ibsen purely as a prose realist, we will be able to see that *When We Dead Awaken* is not so much a new departure as a continuation and intensification of all his old themes, in which his mysticism, no longer concealed under an authenticated surface, has become rampant and overt. . . . Like *The Winter's Tale*, for example, the play is full of minor flaws, and often inconsistent in plot and character. But it shows no falling off at all in dramatic power. Quite the contrary, it is one of the most valuable testaments we have to Ibsen's extraordinary mind and vision.[45]

When We Dead Awaken is not a perfect play, but its faults do not lie in its failure to be realistic. Rather, its occasional melodramatic touches[46] and sometimes diffuse symbolism result, as Brustein suggests, from the fact that Ibsen is no longer concerned with surface realism but with the overriding theme or idea. *When We Dead Awaken* marks the culmination of the movement toward myth. Ibsen's letter to Prozor would seem to indicate that he knew this and that he realized that if he were to write more plays he would have to forsake his old techniques and break entirely new ground. Be that as it may, the "Dramatic Epilog" completes the world picture that he has been developing through his last eight plays and represents his final comment on the life-problem.

CONCLUSION · IBSEN IN PERSPECTIVE

❦ IN THE twentieth century the sense of rootlessness, meaninglessness and absurdity has become a common experience, first among artists and intellectuals and later among the ordinary men in the street. *Alienated man* and *fragmented man* have become popular terms to describe the modern individual as he struggles to find a place in an indifferent cosmos. In the following passage William Barrett summarizes man's progress into the modern world, a journey that had its beginnings in the Renaissance and was greatly accelerated during the nineteenth century.

> Thus, with the modern period, man . . . has entered upon a secular phase of his history. He entered it with exuberance over the prospect of increased power he would have over the world around him. But in this world, in which his dreams of power were often more than fulfilled, he found himself for the first time *homeless*. Science stripped nature of its human forms and presented man with a universe that was neutral, alien in its vastness and force, to his human purposes. Religion, before this phase set in, had been a structure that encompassed man's life, providing him with a system of images and aspirations toward psychic wholeness. With the loss of this containing framework man became not only a dispossessed but a fragmentary being.[1]

Conclusion

What Barrett is describing here is, in effect, a loss of mythology. The ancient Greeks had ready access to a body of myth which, if not literally believed in by the writers themselves, at least provided a matrix of belief and attitude within which the individual member of the *polis* could locate himself in relation to the events of the play.[2] Dante and Milton had, in Christianity, a similarly viable body of myth, still widely believed, to serve as the basis for their art. Shakespeare, too, had an ordered cosmos in which every man knew his place in reference to God, the Crown, and all the levels of human society, a cosmos in which the fall of a prince could still disturb the universe. Even the Enlightenment, though skeptical in matters of religion, had a kind of secular myth in the sense that thinkers of the period shared the firm belief that the world was subject to human control through the exercise of reason. If God assumed a lesser place in this age, man assumed a greater, for science endowed him with unprecedented power. Within such comparatively unified societies playwright and audience could meet on common ground, could share a common point of reference. They could communicate with one another in the same artistic language.

By the end of the nineteenth century, the period in which Ibsen's last plays were written, this common basis of communication no longer existed. The advance of science which had placed in the hands of man the kind of power over his environment that he had never before enjoyed, had other, less encouraging, effects. Theoretically man was the master of his universe, but he was also left alone in it. The effect of the Copernican-Newtonian revolution was, as W. T. Stace points out, to push God further and further into the background, if not to banish Him from the universe altogether.[3] Whereas the religious view sees the universe as being a moral order, as having purpose, and as being governed by a supreme intelligence or spiritual force, the scientific sees it as morally indifferent, purposeless, and governed by blind natural forces.[4] By the mid-nineteenth century the advance of science had led to the conclusion that in the entire universe man had no friend, no God, no principle to guarantee him success. He was in fact, "alone, absolutely alone, in a universe in which his very appearance is a kind of cosmic accident." [5] Indeed, the theory of evolution developed during the nineteenth century went even further. Not only did it isolate man in the universe, it even questioned the assumption that he was ultimately in control of his environment. Though the reactions to Darwin's theory and the ideas of his colleagues and followers were varied, Barzun is probably correct in asserting that the net effect of Darwin's stress on natural selection from accidental variations was to thoroughly demolish the idea of purpose either in the universe or in the individual human life. [6]

The reactions to rationalism, positivism, and scientism during the nineteenth century were many and complex. They ranged from total pessimism, to Promethean defiance of nature, to a reaffirmation of faith in history itself — including the notions of creative evolution and the inevitable progress of the human race. [7] Movements such as Romanticism, Hegelian idealism, and political liberalism could all be described as attempts to restore a sense of meaning and order to the universe and to re-endow man with a sense of belonging. [8] Artists, particularly, keenly felt the absence of God and many attempted, through their art, to rediscover Him or re-establish Him in the universe. This, in the eyes of one critic, gave rise to a new kind of tragedy, the tragedy of the artist who tries and fails to bridge the gap between man and the remote Deity. [9]

The Romantic drama of Goethe and Schiller was one such reaction, but little of quality was produced outside of Germany and even in its homeland the Romantic drama gave way rather quickly to the sentimental melodrama of Kotzebue on the one hand and, on the other, to the strangely prophetic but largely ignored drama of chaos as exemplified in Georg Büchner. The next movement in the theater that produced significant drama seemed not to be a reaction against scientism but an avowal of it, the movement known as realism-naturalism. Rather than portraying man as in control, even precarious control of his world, it tended to portray him as a victim of the blind forces of heredity and environment. It was a theater, as Fergusson asserts, of vastly shrunken dimensions in comparison with that of the Greeks and Shakespeare.[10]

Ibsen's career as a dramatist, starting in the middle of the century and continuing to the end, spanned and reflected many of these movements and reactions. It had its beginnings in the national Romanticism of Scandinavia, was influenced by Hegelian idealism, turned to realism and naturalism, and, in the later years broke away again and moved in a different direction. In the previous chapters I have attempted to demonstrate that Ibsen never completely accepted the mechanistic view of the universe but was always searching for some principle, some more unified and satisfying explanation of human destiny and the course of history. In his early plays he portrayed heroic idealists such as Catiline, Falk, Haakon, Brand, struggling to transcend the limitations of life and bring a salvation to their fellow men. In *Emperor and Galilean* he proposed a third empire which would arise out of the clash of paganism and Christianity and transcend them both, an empire in which the spirit of man would come into its own at last. In the plays which follow *An Enemy of the People*, however, the faith in progress which he had affirmed in his world-historical drama, following Hegelian ideas, seemed to diminish. Ibsen was not ready to give up heroic idealism nor to completely relinquish his faith in the third empire, but in his last eight plays he goes through an existential struggle in which he portrays the world as a highly precarious place in which to live, takes a variety of positions toward the idealist and the question of how to live in such a world, and alternates between hope and despair. In *The Wild Duck* he excoriates the idealist in the person of Gregers Werle, seeing him as a destroyer of the few human comforts that make it possible for man to live at all. He is little kinder to Johannes Rosmer and Rebecca West. In *The Lady from the Sea* and *Little Eyolf*, separated by two plays and four years, he seems to recommend an accommodation, on a modest level, with life, and to question the value of striving after transcendent ideals. In *Hedda Gabler* he portrays a character who longs for a finer and more beautiful life but who is aborted or warped in such a way that she can bring only destruction to herself and many of those around her; the world is left in the hands of the unscrupulous Judge Bracks and the unimaginative Tesmans and Thea Elvsteds. In *The Master Builder, John Gabriel Borkman,* and *When We Dead Awaken,* however, Ibsen seems once again to have some sympathy for his tragic idealists. They are still destructive to themselves and others, but in two of the three plays they attain a mysterious triumph even through their destructiveness. Even Borkman, who seems not to triumph in the same sense as Solness and Rubek, continues to possess a kind of grandeur. They are all men who are doomed or ordained to follow their paths, even though those paths lead them to defeat and death. Lesser creatures can adjust to life; the Borkmans, Solnesses, and Rubeks must seek their high places and die there. But Ibsen's optimism, in these plays, is at the very best guarded. One cannot be completely convinced that there is a great future for the world in the hands of the Ulfheims, Majas, and Erharts, nor can one readily understand the kind of triumph purchased on the heights by the idealists. If the third empire is to be established, it seems, by the end of Ibsen's career, that it is a spiritual empire which must be established in men's souls at the moment of their deaths rather than a physical one which will be established in life on the earth.

Ibsen's universe is not, in these later plays, an indifferent one, though it is by no means beneficent. The mysterious world of nature and the supernatural intervenes in human conduct but, usually, in a destructive way, frequently to bring punishment for past crimes or mistakes. His universe consists of three parts, the heights, the lowlands, and the sea, with each part acting as a power and on each of which man moves precariously, never certain that a misstep will not lead him to destruction. Ibsen's characters confront this universe not as an impersonal it, but as a personal entity; there seems to be a spirit at work in the universe but not necessarily a spirit that is working things out for the good of man. Though perhaps Ibsen, to the end of his career, would have liked to have believed in the possibility of human ennoblement and in a universe in which man could ultimately find a home, he did not hold that faith so firmly as he had in the days of *Emperor and Galilean*. In this connection it is interesting to note that in only two of his last plays did Ibsen attempt a positive conclusion, and those two plays are aesthetically the least convincing and satisfying of the lot.

Ibsen's "new mythology" consists, then, of this pattern, this heroic striving to escape, ennoble, or transcend the human condition: Man can follow the path of idealism that leads him to the mountaintops or he can go down the mountain and dwell in the lowlands, but in neither can he be secure. Some men are fitted for one, some for the other. A form of destiny works in each and man cannot, in the final analysis, avoid the role he is destined to play. This picture of existence, this answer to the question of how to live in the world is of more ultimate significance than the fact that Ibsen incorporated into his later plays mythic materials and built them on mythic frameworks. It is his answer rather than his method that makes him a pivotal figure in the history of modern drama.

Many playwrights have since attempted in various ways to *employ* myth; few have been successful in *creating* a myth. Artists such as Claudel and Eliot have attempted to re-establish the Christian myth as a viable explanation of human destiny, but they have been fighting a rear guard action. Others, such as Cocteau, Giraudoux, Anouilh, Sartre, even Eugene O'Neill, have returned to the content and form of classic myths, attempting to re-endow them with meaning and substance for modern man. Perhaps, until very recently, only Yeats and Strindberg really attempted the creation of a myth. Yeats put his together out of bits and pieces of Celtic and Eastern myths and legends, yet it remains essentially personal—instead of employing and modifying the conventions of Western theater, he tried to impose upon it a form borrowed from the Japanese Noh drama and frankly admitted that he did not intend his work for general consumption.[11] Strindberg, too, pieced together out of Christianity, Judaism, Buddhism, and Hinduism a syncretistic religion or mythology that has much relevance for modern man. Unlike Yeats he remained within the allowable conventions of Western theater and in terms of form exerted an enormous influence upon that theater. And yet Strindberg placed himself constantly at the very center of his dramas; as a result he has suffered from a misunderstanding that is in many ways similar to that suffered by Ibsen — those critics who have not dismissed him as a madman have tended to occupy themselves with searching out the autobiographical elements in a body of work that was never meant solely to be the record of an individual life. Only in recent years has a thorough reassessment of both great Scandinavians been undertaken.

Perhaps the closest thing to a mythology that the modern theater has produced (defining *mythology* as a unified picture of the nature of existence and human destiny) is the drama of existentialism and the absurd. It is a drama that depicts man as alone in an incomprehensible universe, responsible only to himself for his actions and uncertain of his fate or the meaning of his existence. In the bleak landscape of Beckett and the cluttered rooms of Ionesco and Pinter modern man recognizes himself and his existence. There is but a short step, it seems to me, from the barren mountaintops of Ibsen's last plays to the bleak landscapes of Beckett. Wylie Sypher points out, in one of the most stimulating works of literary and art criticism to be written in recent years, that the modern age has been one in which the concept of self held so strongly by the Romanticists has declined and degenerated.[12] In a sense, Ibsen may be said to have presided over that decline of the Romantic self. We go in his plays from the gigantic character of Brand to the somewhat querulous and pathetic characters of Solness and Rubek; the dignity of being answered by God from the avalanche, which is the lot of Brand, does not occur to Solness or Rubek. Hope and faith in idealism diminish, though the tragic necessity for them in the heart of man seems to remain. In play after play Ibsen shows the bedrock of certainty on which his characters think their life is based being blasted away. In play after play he shows them discovering the corruption and guilt that is present not only at the center of their own lives but, in his later plays, at the center of the universe. Man, in Ibsen's drama, is left, as it were, walking a tightrope over an abyss, cast into an uncertain world with only his own freedom to sustain him — and even that freedom turns out to be destructive. It would not be too bold to say that Ibsen, like many another artist of his day, anticipated the cataclysms that were, in the twentieth century, to strip away the last vestiges of certainty from Western man. His characters are not only archetypes of the moral dilemma, they are archetypes of modern man — preachers, builders, bankers, artists, all faced with the basic question, How does one live in this insecure world? and answered, it seems, with a question mark.

Notes and Bibliography

NOTES

Introduction · An Approach to Ibsen

1. Eric Bentley, *The Playwright as Thinker* (New York, 1957), p. 92.
2. George Steiner, *The Death of Tragedy* (New York, 1963), pp. 291–92.
3. Rolf Fjelde, "Introduction," *Ibsen: A Collection of Critical Essays* (Englewood Cliffs, N.J., 1965), pp. 4–10.
4. In an article in *Drama Review* (Winter, 1969), Brian Johnston contends that in his last twelve plays Ibsen developed a history (or mythology) of the evolution of mankind, deliberately paralleling Hegel's *Phenomenology of Mind*. Here and in other writing Johnston includes much valuable comment on mythic materials in Ibsen, though I am not in agreement with him on the interpretation of individual plays nor, I suspect, on the development of the total world view.

Myth and Literature · A Definition and a Relationship

1. Bronislaw Malinowski, *Sex, Culture and Myth* (New York, 1962), pp. 304–5.
2. *Ibid.*, p. 249.
3. Mircea Eliade, *The Sacred and the Profane*, trans. Willard R. Trask (New York, 1961), pp. 99–113.
4. Malinowski, p. 309.
5. This discussion of the contrast between the mythic and scientific world views is largely dependent upon Ernst Cassirer's admirable *The Philosophy of Symbolic Forms*, trans. Ralph Mannheim (New Haven, 1955), II, *Mythical Thought*, pp. 35–58.
6. *Ibid.*, p. 69.
7. Ernst Cassirer, *An Essay on Man* (New Haven, 1944), p. 82.

8. Cassirer, *The Philosophy of Symbolic Forms*, p. 175.

9. Eliade, p. 117.

10. Cassirer, *An Essay on Man*, pp. 76–77.

11. *The Philosophy of Symbolic Forms*, p. 218.

12. Cassirer advances this argument in one way or another in all of his writings on myth. For a discussion of this specific point see *The Myth of the State* (New Haven, 1946), p. 279.

13. *Ibid.*, p. 280. In fairness to Cassirer, I must point out that he is in this book concerned with the political myths fostered by totalitarian systems such as Nazism, which can indeed be regarded as demonic in substance and effect.

14. C. Kerenyi, "Prolegomena," in Jung and Kerenyi, *Essays on a Science of Mythology*, trans. R. F. C. Hull (New York, 1963), pp. 3–4.

15. Carl G. Jung, "The Psychology of the Child Archetype," in *Essays on a Science of Mythology*, pp. 73–74.

16. Carl G. Jung, *Symbols of Transformation*, trans. R. F. C. Hull (New York, 1956), pp. 11–16.

17. *Ibid.*, p. 25.

18. Joseph Campbell, *The Hero with a Thousand Faces* (New York, 1961), p. 11.

19. Steiner, pp. 196–98.

20. *An Essay on Man*, p. 75.

21. *Ibid.* Cassirer insists on emotion or feeling as the source of myth in this essay and all of his other writings on the subject. In his chapter on art in the same work he seems clearly to regard emotion also as the ultimate source of art. For a further discussion of the sources of both myth and art as well as the fundamental distinction between them, see the works of Susanne Langer, Cassirer's student – especially "The Symbol of Feeling" in *Feeling and Form* (New York, 1953).

22. Richard Chase, *The Quest for Myth* (Baton Rouge, La., 1949), p. 97.

23. Richmond Y. Hathorne, *Tragedy, Myth and Mystery* (Bloomington, Ind., 1962), p. 27.

24. Harold H. Watts, "Myth and Drama," in James C. Calderwood and Harold E. Toliver, eds., *Perspectives on Drama* (New York, 1968), pp. 113–18.

25. Northrop Frye, *Fables of Identity* (New York, 1963), pp. 30–33.

26. Northrop Frye, *Anatomy of Criticism* (Princeton, N.J., 1957), pp. 136–40.

27. *Ibid.*, pp. 141–50.

28. Frye, *Fables of Identity*, pp. 15–18.

29. *Ibid.*, p. 16. Frye discusses the stages of the myth in much more detail in *Anatomy of Criticism*, pp. 151–239.

30. Campbell, p. 30.

Ibsen's Earlier Career · From Myth to Social Realism

1. Halvdan Koht and Julius Elias, eds. *Breve fra Henrik Ibsen* (Copenhagen & Christiania, 1904), I, p. 160; hereafter cited *Breve*. Throughout, all translations from the Norwegian are, unless otherwise noted, my own.

2. This is the point of view taken by his daughter-in-law, Bergliot Ibsen, in *The Three Ibsens*, trans. Gerik Schjelderup (New York, 1952), pp. 34–35.

3. Rolf Fjelde, "Foreword," *Ibsen: Four Major Plays* (New York, 1965), p. ix.

4. *Ibid.*, p. ix–xxiv.

5. *Ibid.*, p. xxi.

6. See, for example, Hermann J. Weigand, *The Modern Ibsen* (New York, 1960), p. 301, and Theodore Jorgenson, *Henrik Ibsen: A Study in Art and Personality* (Northfield, Minn., 1945), p. 465.

7. Brian W. Downs, *Ibsen: The Intellectual Background* (Cambridge, 1946), p. 36.

8. Halvdan Koht, *Henrik Ibsen: Eit Diktarliv* (Oslo, 1954), I, p. 69.

9. That play was *Sancthansnatten*, usually translated as *St. John's Eve*. His purpose in this play, according to Koht, was to show that only the guiltless and simple-hearted could come into communion with the natural powers that reveal themselves in folklore and are the deepest truths of life. *Ibid.*, p. 94.

10. Henrik Ibsen, *Samlede Verker: Hundreaarsutgave*, eds. Francis Bull, Halvdan Koht, and Didrik Arup Seip (Oslo, 1928–57), I, p. 8.

11. *Ibid.*, "Forord til Anden Udgave," p. 123.

12. Arnulf Stromme, "Ibsens Mystikk," *Ibsen Aarbok, 1955–56* (Skien, 1956), *passim.*

13. Frye, *Anatomy of Criticism*, pp. 195–96.

14. Here would seem to be the first evidence that Ibsen's drama was strongly influenced by Hegel's philosophy, except for the fact that Ibsen had said in a letter to Hoffory in 1888 that *Emperor and Galilean* was the first play he wrote under the influence of German thought. *Hundreaarsutgave*, XVIII, p. 154. Professor McFarlane argues in the introduction to *Emperor and Galilean* that it is unlikely that Ibsen made any intensive study of Hegel but that he may have picked up bits of Hegelian philosophy through reading the newspapers or through conversation. The playwright, he says, "was greatly receptive to any ideas that were in the air." James Walter McFarlane, ed. *The Oxford Ibsen* (London, 1960–), IV, p. 10.

15. G. Wilson Knight, *Henrik Ibsen* (New York, 1962), p. 7.

16. *Hundreaarsutgave*, III, pp. 32–33.

17. Henrik Ibsen, "Vorwort zur Ersten Deutschen Ausgabe, 1876," *Sämtliche Werke*, eds. Julius Elias and Paul Schlenther (Berlin, 1907), I, p. 368. My translation.

18. McFarlane, *The Oxford Ibsen*, II, pp. 1–6.

19. For a detailed discussion of the *fylgje* see E. O. G. Turville-Petre, *Myth and Religion of the North* (New York, 1964), pp. 221–29.

20. Actually, according to Koht, Ibsen drew on a number of other sagas as well for his material — specifically, the *Laxdölasaga, Egil's Saga*, and *Njaal's Saga*. "Inledning," *Hundreaarsutgave*, IV, pp. 17–20. Whether the bear may have appeared in one of the "family sagas" to which Ibsen referred I do not know, but Margaret Schlauch, in the introduction to her translation of the *Volsunga Saga* indicates that Ibsen made the change in the story and made no use of the supernatural episodes. With the latter point, of course, I should certainly disagree. *The Saga of the Volsungs* (New York, 1930), p. xxvii.

21. McFarlane, *The Oxford Ibsen*, II, pp. 7–8.

22. Campbell, p. 58.

23. The rendering here is literal rather than poetic. In the original the passage reads:

Nej, i dybet maa jeg ned;
der er fred fra evighed.
Bryd mig vejen, tunge hammer
til det dulgtes hjertekammer! —

24. The original reads:

Nu er jeg staalsat, jeg fölger det bud,
det byder i höjden at vandre!
mit lavlands liv har jeg levet ud;
heroppe paa vidden er frihed og gud,
dernede famler de andre.

25. Koht, *Henrik Ibsen: Eit Diktarliv*, I, pp. 172–77.

26. See Maurice Valency's discussion of *Peer Gynt* in *The Flower and the Castle* (New York, 1963), p. 138.

27. Irving Deer, "Ibsen's *Brand*: Paradox and the Symbolic Hero," in Fjelde, *Ibsen: A Collection of Critical Essays*, p. 57.

28. Aside from being the mysterious mentor and guide to which Campbell refers, Gerd has specific suggestive potential for those acquainted with Norse myth. Her namesake was the daughter of the giant Gymir. A violent love for her was inflicted on the god Frey because he had once ventured to sit in Odin's seat. Thus, the name suggests, first, a giantess and an enemy of the gods; second, a figure who could arouse great love and longing in one of the gods; and third, a penalty for presumption or hybris. Brand's Gerd is certainly a paradoxical figure, calling him forward to his duty, a duty which results in the death of his son, his wife, and ultimately, himself. For a discussion of the original Gerd see Peter Andreas Munch, *Norse Mythology*, trans. Sigurd B. Hustvedt (New York, 1926), pp. 15–16.

29. The fish are an obvious symbol of material prosperity and as such have clear biblical overtones.

30. Deer, pp. 58–59.

31. The English rendering of this phrase does not seem capable of carrying the connotations of indifference to other men and selfishness that are suggested by the Norwegian, "Troll, vaer dig selv — nok!"

32. George Groddeck, "*Peer Gynt*," in Fjelde, *Ibsen: A Collection of Critical Essays*, pp. 63–67. Valency makes the same point in *The Flower and the Castle*.

33. "Inledning," *Hundreaarsutgave*, VI, pp. 21–22. Both Fjelde, in the notes to his translation, and Archer, in the introduction to his version, trace many of the mythic and folkloristic references to their sources.

34. *Breve*, I, p. 266.

35. *Ibid.*, p. 275. (Both of the cited letters are translated in Evert Sprinchorn, ed., *Ibsen: Letters and Speeches* (New York, 1964).)

36. Valency, pp. 155, 162–63.

37. *Breve*, I, p. 270.

38. Translation taken from Sprinchorn, p. 114. The Norwegian reads, "som et eneste stort skibbrud"—"as simply a great shipwreck." *Breve*, I, p. 234.

39. In a letter to his publisher, Hegel, July 12, 1871. *Hundreaarsutgave*, XVI, p. 371.

40. Paulus Svendsen, "*Emperor and Galilean*," trans. Allen Simpson, in Fjelde, *Ibsen: A Collection of Critical Essays*, pp. 80–90.

41. In an article in *Scandinavian Studies* (August, 1962) John C. Pearce

notes Hegelian influence also in *Catiline* and *The Pretenders*. The problem of determining influence with Ibsen is complicated by his tendency to deny vigorously the influence of any other thinker or writer on his work. See, for example, his well-known comments on Kierkegaard's possible influence on *Brand*. See also my earlier note on Hegelian influence.

42. Daniel Haakonsen makes a good case for equating the past concealed action which serves as a motivating force in many of the later plays with the operation of fate in classical tragedy. Thus it would constitute a suprahuman force that impels characters to action. Three out of the four plays with which Haakonsen deals, however, are from the group that I am treating as myth (*The Wild Duck, Rosmersholm*, and *John Gabriel Borkman*; the exception is *A Doll's House*). Haakonsen, *Henrik Ibsens Realisme* (Oslo, 1957), pp. 27-34.

The Wild Duck and *Rosmersholm* · The Re-entry of the Mythic

1. After *Rosmersholm* Ibsen wrote to a friend that he would write no more "polemical plays," but I agree with Lucas that he had already departed from the polemical after finishing *An Enemy of the People*. F. L. Lucas, *Ibsen and Strindberg* (London, 1962), p. 188.

2. *Breve*, II, p. 122.

3. *Ibid.*, p. 136.

4. *Breve*, I, p. 89.

5. "This work does not deal with political or social or with any public concerns at all. It develops entirely within the boundaries of family life. It could quite likely stir up discussion; but it will not be capable of giving offense to anyone." *Hundreaarsutgave*, XVIII, p. 25.

6. *Breve*, II, p. 137.

7. See, for example, Robert Brustein, *The Theatre of Revolt* (Boston, 1964), pp. 73-74.

8. Koht, *Henrik Ibsen: Eit Diktarliv*, II, p. 213.

9. Arne Duve, *Symbolikken i Henrik Ibsens Skuespill* (Oslo, 1945), p. 287.

10. Jorgenson, p. 377.

11. John Northam, *Ibsen's Dramatic Method* (London, 1953), pp. 105-6.

12. Else Höst, *Vildanden av Henrik Ibsen* (Oslo, 1967), *passim*.

13. The phrase "en svaer buk" is here translated literally, but in contemporary American idiom it would have more of the flavor of the original if rendered as "a real stud" or something similar.

14. Northam, pp. 86-90.

15. From the standpoint of myth it is interesting to note that both Hjalmar and Gregers try at various times to deny their fathers, Hjalmar in the party scene and Gregers several times later.

16. Knight, p. 56.

17. Northam, pp. 94-102. Gina Ekdal seems, in spite of her intellectual shortcomings, a remarkably level-headed woman. It seems doubtful to me that she believes in the life-lies which sustain the other characters, but as a dutiful wife she "plays along" with Hjalmar's dream-invention. She is well aware, as she points out in the fourth act, that she has kept the family going and that Hjalmar would not have got on very well in life without a wife like her.

18. One critic has suggested that the loft and its contents perform the

same functions for the Ekdals as does the church for believers. See Robert Raphael, "Illusion and the Self in *The Wild Duck, Rosmersholm* and *The Lady from the Sea*," in Fjelde, *Ibsen: A Collection of Critical Essays*, p. 121.

19. Frye, *Anatomy of Criticism*, p. 149.

20. Eliade, p. 29.

21. This is evident not only in the myths collected by Munch but also in many of the folk and fairy tales collected by Asbjörnson and Moe.

22. Frye, p. 146.

23. *Ibid.*, p. 150.

24. Eliade, p. 130.

25. *Ibid.*, p. 135.

26. H. R. Ellis-Davidson, *Gods and Myths of Northern Europe* (Baltimore, 1964), pp. 138–39.

27. Haakonsen, pp. 48–50.

28. A comparison of the draft material with the final version of the play reveals some interesting changes. Both versions suggest that Old Ekdal didn't know what he was doing, though that suggestion is subtler in the final version. The first draft clearly suggests that Werle paid off or recompensed Old Ekdal for the time he spent in prison; that suggestion is less clearly made in the final version. The reference to Ekdal's having played a "dirty trick" on Werle doesn't appear until the final version. The net effect of all these changes seems to me to be to put Werle's complicity in the crime more in doubt and to suggest that Ekdal was a little less innocent. *Hundreaarsutgave*, X, pp. 176–77, 183–88. See also McFarlane, *The Oxford Ibsen*, VI.

29. Professor Höst seems to accept this as proof that Hedvig is in fact Werle's child (p. 119). In support she quotes one Dr. Knud H. Krabbe to the effect that the blindness is the result of inherited syphilis, which, however, can be transmitted only through the mother; he adds that one cannot expect Ibsen to be clear about such subtle medical questions (p. 257). However reliable Krabbe's medical testimony may be, it seems to me that he is here indulging in a rather tenuous bit of mind reading or second-guessing about Ibsen's knowledge and intentions.

30. A number of critics have noted this resemblance and have also compared Hjalmar with Peer Gynt. See Brustein, pp. 73–74, and Brian W. Downs, *A Study of Six Plays by Ibsen* (Cambridge, 1950), pp. 156–57.

31. Gregers' resentment seems to grow largely out of sympathy for his deceased mother, whom he felt his father "mistreated." (It is interesting that Höst again seems to accept Gregers' version of the relationship between his parents at face value, p. 90.) Berta Sörby's version of the story, however, suggests that Mrs. Werle may have resembled the young Helen Alving – that is, so steeped in puritanism that she was unable to share her husband's "joy of life."

32. Haakonsen, pp. 60–61.

33. Haakonsen sees the possibility of ennoblement in Hjalmar's one sympathetic line to Gina as they carry off Hedvig's body. It seems to me, however, that there is little in Hjalmar's character to warrant such an optimistic reading. Haakonsen, p. 58.

34. Brian Johnston, "The Metaphoric Structure of *The Wild Duck*," in Daniel Haakonsen, ed., *Contemporary Approaches to Ibsen* (Oslo, 1965), pp. 86–91. This interpretation is, I think, a little strained. First of all, it is difficult to see Gregers in such a positive light. As for Old Werle, the god

metaphor is probably justified but Raphael's interpretation of him as a beneficent providence seems far more logical in the light of the role he plays in the action. It seems clear that Gregers, whatever his intentions, brings destruction to a family that was doing fairly well under his father's care. See Raphael, p. 121.

35. Johnston, p. 83.

36. Robert Means Lawrence, *The Magic of the Horse-Shoe* (New York, 1899), pp. 331–32.

37. Koht, *Henrik Ibsen: Eit Diktarliv*, II, p. 162.

38. *Ibid.*, pp. 166–67.

39. *Breve*, II, p. 164.

40. *Ibid.*, p. 159.

41. Henrik Jaeger, *Henrik Ibsen: A Critical Biography*, trans. W. Morton Payne (Chicago, 1901), p. 260.

42. *Breve*, II, p. 168.

43. P. 18 above.

44. William A. Craigie, *Scandinavian Folklore* (London, 1896), pp. 329–30.

45. *Ibid.*, p. 402. The ghost horse, of various colors, sometimes complete and sometimes headless, is a common motif in folklore. A fascinating though not very scholarly book by M. Oldfield Howey entitled *The Horse in Magic and Myth* (New York, 1958) recounts literally hundreds of such instances from all parts of Europe. The connection of the white horse with the mill run suggests also the sea or river horse referred to in Old Norse as *nennir* or *nikkur*. See Jacob Grimm, *Teutonic Mythology*, trans. James Steven Stallybrass (New York, 1966), II, pp. 487–99 (a reprinting of a work originally published in English in 1883–88).

46. Turville-Petre, p. 229.

47. Pavel Fraenkl, "*Fruen fra Havet* og Nordisk Folketro," in *Ibsen Aarbok, 1954* (Skien, 1955), p. 8.

48. Campbell, pp. 98–100 and 100n.

49. I will grant that this may be pushing symbol hunting a bit far, yet Ibsen did take pains to establish clearly that Rebecca came from Finmark and that her mother's name was Gamvik.

50. *Henrik Ibsen: Eit Diktarliv*, II, pp. 178–79.

51. Sprinchorn, p. 249.

52. Haakonsen, p. 69.

53. Eliade, pp. 61–62.

54. Valency, p. 178.

The Lady from the Sea and *Hedda Gabler* · Myth and Psychological Study

1. Koht, *Henrik Ibsen: Eit Diktarliv*, II, pp. 184–86.

2. *Ibid.*, p. 186.

3. Henrik Ibsen, *Efterladte Skrifter*, eds. Halvdan Koht and Julius Elias (Christiania, 1909), III, pp. 142–43.

4. *Ibid.*, p. 143.

5. *Ibid.*, p. 148–49.

6. *Henrik Ibsen: Eit Diktarliv*, II, pp. 193–94.

7. *Ibid.*, p. 190.

8. The time factor between Ellida's acquaintance with the Stranger and her marriage with Wangel precludes the possibility that the child could have been the seaman's.

9. Munch, pp. 258–59.

10. *Hundreaarsutgave*, XVIII, p. 201.

11. Knight, p. 72.

12. Arild Haaland, *Seks Studier i Ibsen* (Oslo, 1965), p. 63.

13. Valency, p. 191.

14. Haaland, pp. 65–66.

15. See, for example, Richard Schechner, "The Unexpected Visitor in Ibsen's Late Plays," *Educational Theatre Journal*, XIV (May, 1962), 121–27. This article also appears in Fjelde, *Ibsen: A Collection of Critical Essays*.

16. Archer, "Introduction" to *The Lady from the Sea, Works of Henrik Ibsen*, III, pp. 209–10.

17. Fraenkl, pp. 10–11.

18. The song is entitled "The House Carpenter" in the American version and many variations of it are to be found in the Kentucky and West Virginia mountains.

19. Fraenkl, pp. 15–16.

20. Valency, pp. 190–91.

21. Quoted in Duve, p. 310.

22. Henry James, "Henrik Ibsen," *Essays in London* (London, 1893), p. 249.

23. Edmund Gosse, *Henrik Ibsen* (New York, 1908), p. 176.

24. *Breve*, II, pp. 193–94. The difficulty with accepting any of Ibsen's statements about his work at face value lies in his tendency to deny the presence of "symbolism," influence, or hidden meanings in his plays. Other statements about the play do seem to suggest the presence in it of mythical material. See p. 85, nn. 34&35.

25. Fjelde, "Introduction," in *Ibsen: A Collection of Critical Essays*, p. 9.

26. Maude Bodkin, *Archetypal Patterns in Poetry* (New York, 1958), pp. 116–67.

27. See J. O. Wisdom, "The Lust for Power in *Hedda Gabler*," *Psychoanalytic Review*, XXXI (1944), 419–37.

28. Bodkin, pp. 152–58.

29. Frye, *Anatomy of Criticism*, pp. 195–96.

30. Indeed, the presence of that pagan principle is made quite clear in the name that Ibsen elects to give to the partner of Eilert's revels, Diana. Lest anyone should miss the connection, Judge Brack refers to her as a "mighty huntress of men." Brian Johnston also comments upon this dialectical pattern operating throughout the play and refers to Mlle Diana as Hedda's "alterego." "The Corpse in the Cargo," *Drama Review*, XIII (Winter, 1969), 57.

31. James E. Kerans, "Kindermord and the Will in *Little Eyolf*," in Travis Bogard and William Oliver, eds., *Modern Drama: Essays in Criticism* (New York, 1965), pp. 192–93. Kerans may stretch the point, but there is no denying that the motif appears in the later plays with great frequency.

32. Jung, "The Psychology of the Child Archetype" and "The Special Phenomenology of the Child Archetype," in *Essays on a Science of Mythology*, pp. 83, 89.

33. Archer, "Introduction" to *Hedda Gabler, Works of Henrik Ibsen*, V, p. 12.

34. *Efterladte Skrifter*, III, p. 191.

35. *Hundreaarsutgave*, XVIII, p. 270.

36. James, p. 254.

37. Ibsen's notes indicate that the general fell from fortune and died without leaving anything, though this detail is not mentioned in the text itself. *Efterladte Skrifter*, III, p. 189.

38. She tells Brack that the men in her circle did not display an overwhelming desire to marry her and implies that Tesman was, in fact, the only one who ever asked her.

39. This, at least, is what she tells Brack, and it is with him that she seems to be most honest.

40. Else Höst, *Hedda Gabler: En Monografi* (Oslo, 1958), p. 125.

41. Professor Höst has counted eighty-five *what*'s in the text and there are almost as many *think of that*'s. P. 139.

42. *Ibid.*, p. 126.

43. *Efterladte Skrifter*, III, p. 190.

44. In examining the character of Tesman one cannot help being reminded of the many jokes in which the young bridegroom calls mother to ask what he should do on his wedding night.

45. Höst, pp. 159–62.

46. She had used the pistol earlier to repel the advances of Eilert Lövborg, and she uses it in the play symbolically to hold off Judge Brack.

47. *Hundreaarsutgave*, XVIII, p. 280.

48. Höst, p. 120.

49. Professor Höst indicates that in an earlier draft Hedda had put the pistol away herself. *Ibid.*, pp. 165–68.

50. And yet, further ambiguities remain. Despite his reputation for dissipation Lövborg has written two books, whereas Tesman has, so far as we know, done nothing.

51. Höst, p. 187.

52. When Jörgen tells Hedda that Eilert had made a long speech in honor of the woman who inspired him, they both assume he means Thea. That fact, however, is not nearly so clear for the audience.

The Master Builder · Prometheus and the Dying King

1. This is the approach taken by Archer, by Jorgenson, by Koht, and most recently by Arild Haaland.

2. Examples of this approach can be found in Weigand, in Arne Duve, and, in its Freudian extreme, in Michael Meyer's introduction to his translation of the play.

3. Höst, pp. 192–94.

4. Certainly the audiences of Ibsen's day did not bring with them such acquaintance with Freud. It can be argued that our own psychologically oriented era tends to impose such interpretations on literature, interpretations which never occurred to either the author or his contemporary audience.

5. Maurice Maeterlinck, "The Tragical in Daily Life," *The Treasury of the Humble*, trans. Alfred Sutro (New York, 1905), p. 115.

6. Both Fjelde, in his foreword to his translation of the play, and Brian Johnston, in an essay published by the Minnesota Theatre Company and distributed at the Tyrone Guthrie Theatre, have favored the mythic interpreta-

tion of the play. The latter's interpretation resembles mine in many respects, though his is less detailed and we differ somewhat on specifics.

7. Weigand, p. 289.

8. Downs, *A Study of Six Plays by Ibsen*, p. 180n.

9. *Ibid., passim*. Downs clearly wishes to dispose of all the symbolism in the play as something that Ibsen did not intend, but the only way he can do so is to assume pathological conditions on the part of both main characters. Even there he runs into difficulty with the tower on Solness' new house, which is real and not imagined by either character.

10. Valency, p. 208.

11. Munch, pp. 30–33 and 301–2.

12. *Ibid.*, pp. 32–33. The Valkyries most commonly named were Gondul, Skogul, Lokk, Rist, Mist, and *Hild*. In some legends the Valkyries and the Norns are treated as synonymous, whereas in others they are considered to be separate groups of female deities.

13. In the course of his quest the hero frequently encounters a guide or helper who may be either male or female. See above, pp. 13 and 24, and Campbell, pp. 69, 72–73.

14. Valency, p. 208.

15. *Ibid.*, p. 212.

16. Northam, p. 174.

17. *Ibid.*, p. 175.

18. *Ibid.*

19. James G. Frazer, *The New Golden Bough*, ed. Theodore Gaster (New York, 1959), pp. 31–32.

20. *Ibid.*, pp. 274–90.

21. Brian Johnston makes this point also in the previously cited essay (n. 6 above).

22. Frye, *The Anatomy of Criticism*, p. 207.

23. *Ibid.*, pp. 208–9.

24. *Ibid.*, p. 217.

25. The Norwegian here reads "fem öre." The *öre* is a coin of very small denomination, so "five cents" seems to be the appropriate English rendering.

26. Such "points of epiphany" are points of contact between the divine or "apocalyptic" world and the world of nature. They find such frequent use in literature and mythology that they have become archetypal. According to Frye the most common settings for such confrontations are the mountaintop, the island, the tower, the lighthouse, and the ladder or staircase. *The Anatomy of Criticism*, p. 203.

27. Brustein, p. 77.

28. It is interesting to note in this connection that in three out of the last four plays the leading characters are creators of some sort and that they all return, in one way or another, to the heights of *Brand*.

29. Inga-Stina Ewbank, "Ibsen's Dramatic Language as a Link between His 'Realism' and His 'Symbolism,'" in Haakonsen, *Contemporary Approaches to Ibsen*, pp. 104–5.

30. Campbell's comments on the "refusal of the call" are interesting, especially in connection with *The Master Builder*. To refuse to accept the call to adventure and heroism has drastic results for him who fails to answer. "His flowering world becomes a wasteland of dry stones and his life feels mean-

ingless. . . . *Whatever house he builds it will be a house of death.* . . . All he can do is create new problems for himself and await the gradual approach of his disintegration." *The Hero with a Thousand Faces,* p. 59 (emphasis mine).

31. Northam, p. 184.

32. James, p. 263.

33. Johnston comments that the presence of the helpless doctor is an ironic counterpoint on the sickness that pervades Solness' home. Certainly, Ibsen has made use of a doctor in such a way before, the most notable instance being *The Wild Duck,* but I think the importance of the sickness theme can be overstressed here. Solness' sickness is ultimately a metaphysical condition, and that is why the doctor is helpless. Hilda is the only one who can bring him a "cure," which causes his death.

34. Chester Clayton Long, "Cocteau's *Orphee*: From Myth to Drama and Film," *Quarterly Journal of Speech,* LI (October, 1965), 314.

35. Even an early and traditional critic was aware of this aspect of the play — in his introduction Archer refers to it as "the soul-history of Halvard Solness." *Works of Henrik Ibsen,* V, p. 236.

36. Northam, pp. 183–84.

37. The importance of an accurate rendering of the rhythms and connotations of their talk is stressed in an article by Allen Simpson in *Drama Survey,* VII (Winter, 1968–69), 154–57.

38. Except perhaps for *Little Eyolf.*

39. *Breve,* II, pp. 214–15.

Little Eyolf · The Myth of Sacrifice and Redemption

1. I must admit that this is a neat and oversimplified schematization. There is another sense in which the play could be called a combination of mythic *form* and realistic *content.*

2. Weigand, pp. 311–55.

3. Frye, *Anatomy of Criticism,* p. 220.

4. There is a clear suggestion here of the traditional Pied Piper story, but Koht indicates that Ibsen based the character on an old woman whom he remembered from his childhood in Skien. II, p. 266.

5. It is this situation, of course, that Allmers proposes to remedy after his sojourn in the mountains.

6. Further analysis, however, will suggest that there is reason to doubt the permanence of Eyolf's effect on his parents.

7. Mark I:7, King James version.

8. In this sense too the play resembles *The Wild Duck,* where the duck plays a vital part in the action but is never seen.

9. Koht, II, p. 266.

10. W. Morton Payne in his addenda to the Jaeger biography, p. 296.

11. Kerans' previously cited analysis of the play in terms of the *Kindermord* theme is a great deal more rewarding, though I cannot agree completely with his psychosexual interpretation.

12. Valency, p. 214.

13. And then he reproaches himself about *that.* Weigand remarks that it is natural for Allmers to get hungry, but to wonder in the midst of his grief *what* he is having for dinner makes him kin to Hjalmar Ekdal (p. 332).

14. Koht, p. 266.

15. Weigand, pp. 314–19.

16. In view of the sacrifice-redemption theme, however, this may be another reference to Christ, who was also referred to as the "complete man" or the "true man," especially since it occurs immediately after Eyolf has slipped out to follow the Rat-Wife.

17. Duve sees this as an indication, also, that Allmers has suppressed aggressive tendencies (pp. 339–40).

18. Borgheim is a road builder (*veibygger*), and the literal translation of the Norwegian is most appropriate in this context. The word *vei* however, can be rendered *way*, with all of the mystical or religious connotations that the word carries in English — cf. "Strait is the gate and narrow the *way*" or "I am the *way*, the truth and the life."

19. This contrast between doing one's work out of joy and out of duty is given direct expression in *The Master Builder* when Hilda objects to the use of the word *duty* by Aline and says that she prefers to have things done warmly from the heart.

20. Allmers, of course, is a freethinker. Nevertheless his idealism and asceticism are equally as opposed to the "joy of life."

21. Solness' high place is a tower rather than a mountain but it functions symbolically in essentially the same way.

22. Schechner, p. 122.

23. See, for example, the entire second half of the previously cited article by Kerans.

24. Frye, *The Anatomy of Criticism*, p. 161.

25. Ellis-Davidson, pp. 27–28.

26. Frye, *The Anatomy of Criticism*, p. 145.

27. *Ibid.*, p. 203.

28. *Ibid.*, pp. 146–50.

29. Valency, p. 217.

30. Knight, p. 82.

31. The Norwegian word here is *Söndagstemming* — literally, "Sunday mood."

32. Koht, p. 268.

John Gabriel Borkman and *When We Dead Awaken* · Myths of Death and Resurrection

1. Ibsen does not stress the combat portion of the myth; thus, I have followed Frye's lead and placed more emphasis on the death-rebirth cycle. A fascinating study of the ancient variants of the combat myth, however, may be found in Fontenrose's *Python: A Study of the Delphic Myth and its Origins* (Berkeley, 1959).

2. Frye, *Fables of Identity*, p. 18.

3. *Ibid.*, p. 16.

4. Koht, II, pp. 270–71.

5. Archer, "Introduction" to *John Gabriel Borkman, Works of Henrik Ibsen*, VI, p. 173. He recognizes, of course, that *Borkman* is the much superior play.

6. Valency, p. 221.

7. Knight, p. 90. Knight provides no evidence that Ibsen consciously and

deliberately reached this conclusion, but it should have been clear to the playwright, as to his nineteenth-century contemporaries, that the financier can and does exercise kingly power.

8. Steiner, p. 296.

9. Hinkel seems to have been the man responsible for the detection of Borkman's crime (and hence, for his fall) and the inheritor of his glory. His home is ablaze with light while Borkman's is in darkness.

10. Russell H. Conwell, *Acres of Diamonds* (New York, 1966), pp. 23–24. This speech, delivered with great success throughout the United States, is almost a classic of the folklore of capitalism.

11. Haakonsen, p. 130.

12. Reidar Th. Christiansen, ed. *Folktales of Norway* (London, 1964), p. xxxvii.

13. "Mattias Skytters Historie" in Asbjörnson and Moe's *Norske Folke og Huldre-eventyr.*

14. Ellis-Davidson, p. 28.

15. Frye feels that such a recognition, together with an implicit comparison with the potential life forsaken by the hero, is essential to tragedy. This play, therefore, probably belongs to that phase of the myth he designates "ironic." *Anatomy of Criticism*, p. 212.

16. Payne, pp. 306–7.

17. Valency, pp. 219–21.

18. Robert Raphael, "From *Hedda Gabler* to *When We Dead Awaken*: The Quest for Self-Realization," *Scandinavian Studies*, XXXVI (1964), 43–44.

19. Valency, however, is aware of the genuine ambiguity between the two ways of life.

20. Höst, *Hedda Gabler: Et Monografi*, pp. 157–58.

21. Herbert J. Muller, *The Spirit of Tragedy* (New York, 1956), p. 272.

22. Archer, "Introduction," *Works of Henrik Ibsen*, VI, pp. 353–54.

23. Bergliot Ibsen, p. 135.

24. *Breve*, II, pp. 214–15.

25. *Ibid.*

26. Koht, II, p. 289.

27. *Ibid.*, pp. 288–92.

28. Valency indicates that Strindberg had sent Ibsen a copy of *To Damascus II* for his seventieth birthday and that Ibsen, contrary to his usual practice, had read it carefully (p. 218).

29. Archer, VI, p. 357.

30. Weigand, pp. 379–92.

31. Storm Jameson, *Modern Drama in Europe* (New York, 1920), p. 88.

32. These figures which break out through the crust of the earth suggest the *underjordiske* of Norse myth, but they also suggest the theories of Jung insofar as they call to mind the imperfectly repressed evil and animalistic aspects of the human character.

33. See, for example, Weigand, p. 401.

34. Jung points out that in the middle years, after one has largely accomplished one's lifework, one is faced with a psychological crisis that requires one to come to terms with oneself. It is this process of coming to terms with and accepting one's nature that Jung calls individuation. See *Modern Man in*

Search of a Soul, trans. W. S. Dell and Carey F. Baynes (New York, 1933), especially pp. 104–14.

35. The conversation to which Irene refers took place the previous afternoon, but it coalesces in her mind with others that occurred years before.

36. Frye, *Anatomy of Criticism*, p. 160.

37. The symbolic marriage is a common part of ancient ritual and ended most ancient comedies. It is in itself a symbol of the renewal of life. See, for example, the description of the Anthesteria in Sir Arthur W. Pickard-Cambridge, *The Dramatic Festivals of Athens* (Oxford, 1968).

38. Maja might also be considered a life symbol, but it seems to me that she stands between the dead sculptor and the living bear hunter and derives her life largely from the latter.

39. There is a clear echo here of Satan's words to Christ (Luke 4:5–7).

40. Weigand, p. 406.

41. Stromme, pp. 136–37.

42. Valency, p. 225.

43. James Joyce, "Ibsen's New Drama," *The Critical Writings*, eds. Ellsworth Mason & Richard Ellman (New York, 1964), p. 67.

44. Valency, pp. 227–28.

45. Brustein, p. 79.

46. Particularly annoying is Irene's constant playing with her knife as indicated in Ibsen's stage directions. In production, however, a wise director can excise much of that business.

Conclusion · Ibsen in Perspective

1. William Barrett, *Irrational Man: A Study in Existential Philosophy* (New York, 1962), p. 35.

2. One critic, however, has asserted that the Greek tragedians did indeed believe in the myths which they presented as literally true. Leo Aylen, *Greek Tragedy and the Modern World* (London, 1964), pp. 31–32.

3. W. T. Stace, *Religion and the Modern Mind* (New York, 1952), p. 86.

4. *Ibid.*, p. 143.

5. John Herman Randall, Jr., *The Making of the Modern Mind* (Cambridge, Mass., 1954), pp. 583–84.

6. Jacques Barzun, *Darwin, Marx, Wagner: Critique of a Heritage* (New York, 1958), pp. 8–13.

7. Randall, pp. 583–87.

8. The best single treatment that I know of the complicated intellectual developments of the nineteenth century is Randall's, in the chapter entitled "The Growing World — Thought and Aspiration in the Last Hundred Years."

9. J. Hillis Miller, *The Disappearance of God* (Cambridge, Mass., 1963), pp. 13–14.

10. Francis Fergusson, *The Idea of a Theatre* (Garden City, N.Y., 1953), pp. 159–60.

11. W. B. Yeats, "The Theatre," *Essays and Introductions* (New York, 1961), p. 166.

12. Wylie Sypher, *The Loss of the Self in Modern Literature and Art* (New York, 1964), *passim*.

BIBLIOGRAPHY

Primary Sources

Ibsen, Henrik. *Efterladte Skrifter*, ed. Halvdan Koht & Julius Elias. Christiania: Gyldendalske Boghandel, Nordisk Forlag, 1909. 3 vols.
———. *Samlede Verker: Hundreaarsutgave*, ed. Francis Bull, Halvdan Koht, & Didrik Arup Seip. Oslo: Gyldendal Norsk Forlag, 1928–57. 21 vols.
Koht, Halvdan, & Julius Elias, eds. *Breve fra Henrik Ibsen*. Copenhagen & Christiania: Gyldendalske Boghandel, Nordisk Forlag, 1904. 2 vols.

Secondary Sources

Archer, William, ed. *The Works of Henrik Ibsen*. Boston & New York: Jefferson Press, 1911. 6 vols.
Aylen, Leo. *Greek Tragedy in the Modern World*. London: Methuen, 1964.
Barrett, William. *Irrational Man: A Study in Existential Philosophy*. Garden City, N.Y.: Doubleday, 1962.
Barzun, Jacques. *Darwin, Marx, Wagner: Critique of a Heritage*. Garden City, N.Y.: Doubleday, 1958.
Bentley, Eric. *The Playwright as Thinker*. New York: Meridian Books, 1957.
Bodkin, Maude. *Archetypal Patterns in Poetry*. New York: Vintage Books, 1958. Paperback.
Brustein, Robert. "Henrik Ibsen," in *The Theatre of Revolt*. Boston: Little Brown, 1964.
Campbell, Joseph. *The Hero with a Thousand Faces*. New York: Pantheon Books, 1961.
Cassirer, Ernst. *An Essay on Man: An Introduction to a Philosophy of Human Culture*. New Haven, Conn.: Yale University Press, 1944.
———. *The Myth of the State*. New Haven, Conn.: Yale University Press, 1946.

———. *The Philosophy of Symbolic Forms. Vol. II, Mythical Thought*, trans. Ralph Mannheim. New Haven, Conn.: Yale University Press, 1955.

Chase, Richard. *The Quest for Myth*. Baton Rouge: Louisiana State University Press, 1949.

Christiansen, Reidar Th., ed. *Folktales of Norway*. London: Routledge, 1964.

Conwell, Russell H. *Acres of Diamonds*. New York: Little Inspirational Classics, 1966.

Craigie, William A. *Scandinavian Folklore*. London: Alexander Gardner, 1896.

Deer, Irving. "Ibsen's *Brand*: Paradox and the Symbolic Hero," in Rolf Fjelde, ed., *Ibsen: A Collection of Critical Essays*. Englewood Cliffs, N.J.: Prentice-Hall, 1965.

Downs, Brian W. *Ibsen: The Intellectual Background*. Cambridge: Cambridge University Press, 1946.

———. *A Study of Six Plays by Ibsen*. Cambridge: Cambridge University Press, 1950.

Duve, Arne. *Symbolikken i Henrik Ibsens Skuespill*. Oslo: Nasjonalforlaget, 1945.

Eliade, Mircea. *The Sacred and the Profane*, trans. Willard R. Trask. New York: Harper, 1961.

Elias, Julius, & Paul Schlenther, eds. *Henrik Ibsen: Sämtliche Werke*. Berlin: S. Fischer Verlag, n.d. 5 vols.

Ellis-Davidson, H. R. *Gods and Myths of Northern Europe*. Baltimore: Penguin Books, 1964. Paperback.

Ewbank, Inga-Stina. "Ibsen's Dramatic Language as a Link between His 'Realism' and His 'Symbolism,'" in Daniel Haakonsen, ed. *Contemporary Approaches to Ibsen*. Oslo: Universitatsforlaget, 1966.

Fergusson, Francis. *The Idea of a Theatre*. Garden City, N.Y.: Doubleday, 1953. Paperback.

Fjelde, Rolf, trans. "Foreword," in *Henrik Ibsen: Four Major Plays*. New York: New American Library, 1965. Paperback.

———, ed. *Ibsen: A Collection of Critical Essays*. Englewood Cliffs, N.J.: Prentice-Hall, 1965. Paperback.

———, trans. *Peer Gynt*. New York: New American Library, 1964. Paperback.

Fontenrose, Joseph Eddy. *Python: A Study of the Delphic Myth and Its Origins*. Berkeley: University of California Press, 1959.

Fraenkl, Pavel. "*Fruen fra Havet* og Nordisk Folketro," in *Ibsen Aarbok, 1954*. Skien: Oluf Rasmussens Boktrykkeri, 1955.

Frazer, James George. *The New Golden Bough*, ed. Theodore Gaster. New York: Mentor, 1959. Paperback.

Frye, Northrop. *Anatomy of Criticism: Four Essays*. Princeton, N.J.: Princeton University Press, 1957.

———. *Fables of Identity: Studies in Poetic Mythology*. New York: Harcourt, 1963. Paperback.

Gosse, Edmund. *Henrik Ibsen*. New York: Scribner, 1908.

Grimm, Jacob. *Teutonic Mythology*, trans. James Steven Stallybrass. New York: Dover, 1966. 4 vols.

Groddeck, George. "*Peer Gynt*," in Rolf Fjelde, ed., *Ibsen: A Collection of Critical Essays*. Englewood Cliffs, N.J.: Prentice-Hall, 1965.

Haakonsen, Daniel. *Henrik Ibsens Realisme*. Oslo: H. Aschehoug, 1957.

Haaland, Arild. *Seks Studier i Ibsen.* Oslo: Gyldendal Norsk Forlag, 1965.

Hathorne, Richmond Y. *Tragedy, Myth and Mystery.* Bloomington: Indiana University Press, 1962.

Höst, Else. *Hedda Gabler: En Monografi.* Oslo: H. Aschehoug, 1958.

———. *Vildanden av Henrik Ibsen.* Oslo: H. Aschehoug (W. Nygaard), 1967.

Howey, M. Oldfield. *The Horse in Magic and Myth.* New York: Castle Books, 1958.

Ibsen, Bergliot. *The Three Ibsens,* trans. Gerik Schjelderup. New York: American-Scandinavian Foundation, 1952.

Jaeger, Henrik. *Henrik Ibsen: A Critical Biography,* trans. W. Morton Payne. Chicago: A. C. McClurg, 1901.

James, Henry. "Henrik Ibsen," in *Essays in London.* London: James R. Osgood, McIlvaine & Co., 1893.

Jameson, Storm. *Modern Drama in Europe.* New York: Harcourt, 1920.

Johnston, Brian. "The Corpse in the Cargo," *Drama Review,* XIII (Winter, 1969), 47–66.

———. *The Master Builder.* Minneapolis: Minnesota Theatre Company, 1968.

———. "The Metaphoric Structure of *The Wild Duck,*" in Daniel Haakonsen, ed., *Contemporary Approaches to Ibsen.* Oslo: Universitets Forlaget, 1966.

Jorgenson, Theodore. *Henrik Ibsen: A Study in Art and Personality.* Northfield, Minn.: St. Olaf College Press, 1945.

Joyce, James. "Ibsen's New Drama," in *The Critical Writings,* ed. Ellsworth Mason & Richard Ellman. New York: The Viking Press, 1964. Paperback.

Jung, Carl Gustav. *Modern Man in Search of a Soul,* trans. W. S. Dell & Carey F. Baynes. New York: Harcourt, 1933.

———. *Symbols of Transformation,* trans. R. F. C. Hull. New York: Harper, 1956.

——— & C. Kerenyi. *Essays on a Science of Mythology: Myths of the Divine Child and the Divine Maiden,* trans. R. F. C. Hull. New York: Harper, 1963.

Kerans, James E. "Kindermord and the Will in *Little Eyolf,*" in Travis Bogard & William Oliver, eds., *Modern Drama: Essays in Criticism.* New York: Oxford University Press, 1965.

Knight, G. Wilson. *Henrik Ibsen.* New York: Grove Press, 1962.

Koht, Halvdan. *Henrik Ibsen: Eit Diktarliv.* Oslo: H. Aschehoug, 1954. 2 vols.

Langer, Susanne K. *Feeling and Form.* New York: Scribner, 1953.

Lavrin, Janko. *Ibsen: An Approach.* London: Methuen, 1950.

Lawrence, Robert Means. *The Magic of the Horse-Shoe.* Boston & New York: Houghton Mifflin, 1898.

Long, Chester Clayton. "Cocteau's *Orphee*: From Myth to Drama and Film," *Quarterly Journal of Speech,* LI (October, 1965), 311–25.

Lucas, F. L. *Ibsen and Strindberg.* London: Cassell, 1962.

McFarlane, James Walter, ed. *The Oxford Ibsen.* London: Oxford University Press, 1960– . 8 vols. to date.

Maeterlinck, Maurice. "The Tragical in Daily Life," in *The Treasury of the Humble,* trans. Alfred Sutro. New York: Dodd, Mead, 1905.

Malinowski, Bronislaw. *Sex, Culture and Myth.* New York: Harcourt, 1962.

Miller, J. Hillis. *The Disappearance of God.* Cambridge, Mass.: Harvard University Press, 1963.

Muller, Herbert J. *The Spirit of Tragedy*. New York: Knopf, 1956.

Munch, Peter Andreas. *Norse Mythology: Legends of Gods and Heroes*, trans. Sigurd B. Hustvedt. New York: American Scandinavian Foundation, 1926.

Northam, John. *Ibsen's Dramatic Method*. London: Faber & Faber, 1953.

Pearce, John C. "Hegelian Ideas in Three Tragedies by Ibsen," *Scandinavian Studies*, XXXIV (August, 1962), 255-57.

Pickard-Cambridge, Sir Arthur W. *The Dramatic Festivals of Athens*. Oxford: Clarendon Press, 1968.

Randall, John Herman, Jr. *The Making of the Modern Mind*. Cambridge, Mass.: Houghton, Mifflin, 1954.

Raphael, Robert. "From *Hedda Gabler* to *When We Dead Awaken*: The Quest for Self-Realization," *Scandinavian Studies*, XXXVI (1964), 36-47.
———. "Illusion and the Self in *The Wild Duck*, *Rosmersholm* and *The Lady from the Sea*," *Scandinavian Studies*, XXXV (February, 1963), 37-50. (Also in Fjelde, *Ibsen: A Collection of Critical Essays*.)

Schechner, Richard. "The Unexpected Visitor in Ibsen's Late Plays," *Educational Theatre Journal*, XIV (May, 1962), 120-27. (Also in Fjelde, *Ibsen: A Collection of Critical Essays*.)

Schlauch, Margaret, trans. *The Saga of the Volsungs*. New York: American Scandinavian Foundation, 1930.

Simpson, Allen. "Ibsen's First Non-Appearance at the Guthrie," *Drama Survey*, VII (Winter, 1968-69), 154-57.

Sprinchorn, Evert, ed. *Ibsen: Letters and Speeches*. New York: Hill & Wang, 1964. Paperback.

Stace, W. T. *Religion and the Modern Mind*. New York: Lippincott, 1952. Paperback.

Steiner, George. *The Death of Tragedy*. New York: Hill & Wang, 1963.

Stromme, Arnulf. "Ibsens Mystikk," *Ibsen Aarbok, 1955-56*. Skien: Oluf Rasmussens Boktrykkeri, 1956.

Svendsen, Paulus. "*Emperor and Galilean*," trans. Allen Simpson, in Rolf Fjelde, ed., *Ibsen: A Collection of Critical Essays*. Englewood Cliffs, N.J.: Prentice-Hall, 1965.

Sypher, Wylie. *The Loss of the Self in Modern Literature and Art*. New York: Vintage Books, 1964. Paperback.

Turville-Petre, E. O. G. *Myth and Religion of the North: The Religion of Ancient Scandinavia*. New York: Holt, 1964.

Valency, Maurice. *The Flower and the Castle*. New York: Macmillan, 1963.

Watts, Harold H. "Myth and Drama," in James C. Calderwood & Harold E. Toliver, eds., *Perspectives on Drama*. New York: Oxford University Press, 1968. Paperback.

Weigand, Hermann J. *The Modern Ibsen*. New York: Dutton, 1960. Paperback.

Wisdom, J. O. "The Lust for Power in *Hedda Gabler*," *Psychoanalytic Review*, XXXI (1944), 419-37.

Yeats, William Butler. "The Theatre," in *Essays and Introductions*. New York: Macmillan, 1961.

Index

INDEX